Codeswitching
English-Mediui

NEW PERSPECTIVES ON LANGUAGE AND EDUCATION

Series Editor: Professor Viv Edwards, *University of Reading, Reading, Great Britain*
Series Advisor: Professor Allan Luke, *Queensland University of Technology, Brisbane, Australia*

Two decades of research and development in language and literacy education have yielded a broad, multidisciplinary focus. Yet education systems face constant economic and technological change, with attendant issues of identity and power, community and culture. This series will feature critical and interpretive, disciplinary and multidisciplinary perspectives on teaching and learning, language and literacy in new times.

Full details of all the books in this series and of all our other publications can be found on http://www.multilingual-matters.com, or by writing to Multilingual Matters, St Nicholas House, 31–34 High Street, Bristol BS1 2AW, UK.

Codeswitching in University English-Medium Classes

Asian Perspectives

Edited by
Roger Barnard and James McLellan

MULTILINGUAL MATTERS
Bristol • Buffalo • Toronto

Library of Congress Cataloging in Publication Data
A catalog record for this book is available from the Library of Congress.
Codeswitching in University English-Medium Classes: Asian Perspectives/Edited by
Roger Barnard and James McLellan.
New Perspectives on Language and Education: 36
Includes bibliographical references and index.
Summary: In the multilingual societies of the 21st century, codeswitching is an everyday
occurrence, and yet the use of students' first language in the EFL classroom has been
consistently discouraged. This volume begins by examining current theoretical work on
codeswitching and then proceeds to examine the convergence and divergence between
university language teachers' beliefs about codeswitching and their classroom practice.
1. Code switching (Linguistics) 2. Code switching (Linguistics) – Case studies. 3. College
students – Asia – Language. 4. English language – Study and teaching (Higher) – Foreign
speakers. I. Barnard, Roger, 1946– editor of compilation. II. McLellan, James, editor of
compilation. III. Series: New Perspectives on Language and Education: 36.
P115.3.C644 2013
306.44–dc23 2013032424

British Library Cataloguing in Publication Data
A catalogue entry for this book is available from the British Library.

ISBN-13: 978-1-78309-090-7 (hbk)
ISBN-13: 978-1-78309-089-1 (pbk)

Multilingual Matters
UK: St Nicholas House, 31–34 High Street, Bristol BS1 2AW, UK.
USA: UTP, 2250 Military Road, Tonawanda, NY 14150, USA.
Canada: UTP, 5201 Dufferin Street, North York, Ontario M3H 5T8, Canada.

The policy of Multilingual Matters/Channel View Publications is to use papers that
are natural, renewable and recyclable products, made from wood grown in sustainable
forests. In the manufacturing process of our books, and to further support our policy,
preference is given to printers that have FSC and PEFC Chain of Custody certification.
The FSC and/or PEFC logos will appear on those books where full certification has been
granted to the printer concerned.

Typeset by R. J. Footring Ltd, Derby
Printed and bound in Great Britain by TJ International Ltd

Contents

Contributors

Ain Nadzimah Abdullah (BA, MA, PhD) is associate professor in the Department of English Language, Universiti Putra Malaysia. Her areas of specialisation include sociolinguistics, language planning and policy, and bilingualism and multilingualism; she teaches graduate and undergraduate courses in these and many other areas. She has been a principal investigator in many funded research projects at both national and university level, including (with Chan Swee Heng) 'Defining parameters of multilingualism in terms of economic values', and a co-investigator in others. She has co-authored many articles in national and international journals and academic books, and co-edited *The Pulse of a Malaysia University: Ethno- and Socio-linguistic Issues and the TESOL Dimension*, published by Peter Lang in 2008.

Roger Barnard is an associate professor in applied linguistics at the University of Waikato. Before taking up his present post in New Zealand in 1995, he worked in England, Europe and the Middle East as teacher, teacher educator, manager and adviser to ministries of education. He has recently accepted visiting professorships in Japan, Korea and Vietnam, where he has taught undergraduate and postgraduate courses and undertaken joint research projects. His most recent book is *Language Teacher Cognition and Practice: International Case Studies*, which he co-edited with Anne Burns, published by Multilingual Matters in 2012.

Chan Swee Heng (DipEd, BA (Hons), MEd, PhD) is a faculty member of the Department of English at Universiti Putra Malaysia, where she teaches a wide range of undergraduate and postgraduate courses in linguistics and applied linguistics. Her research interests focus on discourse and identity, and language testing and evaluation. Among her current collaborative research projects are 'The development of a socio-psychological framework to map language choice and use in the legal workplace' (with Ain Nadzimah Abdullah) and 'Innovating automatic essay scoring (AES) in Malaysia public examinations'. She co-authors numerous articles in national and international journals, and has recently contributed chapters to several academic books.

Ching-Yi Tien received her PhD in applied linguistics and teaching English to speakers of other languages (TESOL) from the University of Leicester, UK. She is currently teaching in the Department of Applied English at I-Shou University, Taiwan. Her research interests include codeswitching, language and culture, classroom observation, ESP (English for specific purposes) and teaching methodology. She was a contributor to Barnard and Torres-Guzman (eds) *Creating Classroom Communities of Learning: International Case Studies and Perspectives*, published by Multilingual Matters in 2009.

Moyra Sweetnam Evans has MA and D Litt et Phil degrees in applied linguistics (teaching English to speakers of other languages, TESOL) from the University of Johannesburg, South Africa, and an education diploma and BA degree majoring in English, linguistics, Afrikaans and Dutch from Rhodes University, South Africa. She is a senior lecturer in applied linguistics in the Department of English and Linguistics at the University of Otago, Dunedin, New Zealand, where she coordinates undergraduate courses training ESOL teachers and supervises postgraduate research in TESOL, reading, discourse and bilingualism. She is active on TESOL committees in Otago and has served on the national TESOLANZ executive. She is fluent in English and Afrikaans, speaks Zulu and can understand French, Dutch and Flemish. She spent many years lecturing in English language and literature at three South African universities, mainly to non-native speakers of English. Before relocating to New Zealand, she was senior lecturer in linguistics at the Rand Afrikaans University (now the University of Johannesburg) for seven years. She was principal of an English language school for international students in Christchurch and has been active in professional development for New Zealand, Chinese and Korean ESOL teachers.

Liyana Ghani is an English language lecturer at the Language Centre of Universiti Brunei Darussalam. She holds a masters degree in applied linguistics (teaching English to speakers of other languages, TESOL)) from the University of Melbourne, Australia, in addition to a BA (in teaching English as a second language, TESL) from Universiti Brunei Darussalam. Her interests include vocabulary knowledge and development as well as motivational factors that affect learners of English as a second language.

Fuad Abdul Hamied is professor of English education at Indonesia University of Education, Bandung, Indonesia. He obtained his first degree from IKIP Bandung, Indonesia, and his MA in English as a foreign language as well as his PhD from Southern Illinois University, USA. Currently he is TEFLIN President and an EC member of Asia TEFL. Recent conference presentations include: 'English at schools in the Indonesian context', at the 20th MELTA Conference in Trengganu, Malaysia; 'English as a lingua franca: An Indonesian perspective', at the 4th ELF International Conference in Hongkong; and 'Southeast Asian English teacher associations: Advocacy and concerns', a colloquium at the 45th Annual TESOL Convention at New Orleans, USA, 2011. 'EFL assessment in Indonesia' is a chapter in Moon & Spolsky (eds) (2010) *Language Assessment in Asia*, and 'English in multicultural and multilingual Indonesian education' is a chapter in Kirkpatrick & Sussex (eds) (2012) *English as an international language in Asia*.

Saidai Haji Hitam is Director of the Language Centre at Universiti Brunei Darussalam. He holds a masters degree in Arabic studies (Universiti Kebangsaan Malaysia, 2001) and underwent training at the American University in Cairo (1997) specialising in the Arabic language. In terms of research, Saidai is particularly interested in teaching Arabic as a second language, Arabic language morpohology as well as in codeswitching practices among Bruneian Arabic learners.

Simon Humphries is an assistant professor at Doshisha University in Kyoto. He received his PhD in linguistics from Macquarie University in 2012 and his MSc in teaching English to speakers of other languages (TESOL) from Aston University in 2005. In addition to codeswitching and classroom interaction, his recent and forthcoming publications focus on action research, the analysis of English teaching textbooks, issues in implementing communicative approaches and issues in classroom observation.

Hyun-Ju Kim is an associate professor of English at Dankook University in Korea, where she teaches undergraduate and graduate courses in teaching English as a second language (ESL), language testing and applied linguistics. She has recently accepted visiting scholarships in the USA where she has worked on several research projects on second language acquisition and language testing. She received her PhD in the programme of Foreign Language and ESL Education at the University of Iowa. Her research interests are in world Englishes, L2 assessment and the integration of world Englishes perspectives into non-native speakers' English language proficiency tests.

Andy Kirkpatrick is Professor in the School of Languages and Linguistics at Griffith University, Brisbane. Directly prior to this appointment, Professor Kirkpatrick was Director of the Research Centre into Language Education and Acquisition in Multilingual Societies at the Hong Kong Institute of Education. He is the author of *English as a Lingua Franca in ASEAN: A Multilingual Model* (Hong Kong University Press, 2010) and editor of the *Routledge Handbook of World Englishes* (2010). He is also editor of the journal *Multilingual Education* and of the book series of the same name (both with Springer). His most recent book is *English as an International Language in Asia: Implications for Language Education*, co-edited with Roland Sussex (Springer, 2012).

Claudia Kunschak holds an MA in translation and interpreting from the University of Vienna, Austria, and a PhD in education from the University of Arizona, USA. Over the years, she variously taught English, German and Spanish in Austria, China, Japan, Scotland, Spain, Ukraine and the USA. During 2008–11, she served as the executive director of the English Language Centre at Shantou University, China. At that time, she was able to study in depth the English language curriculum and classroom in China and conducted research on English as a lingua franca, multilingual communities and language, culture and identity. Since 2011 she has been based in Japan, teaching at Ritsumeikan University and Kyoto Sangyo University as well as at the local Goethe Institute. Her research interests include multilingualism, intercultural communicative competence, and language awareness and attitudes.

Le Van Canh (MA TESOL from Saint Michael's College, USA; PhD from University of Waikato, New Zealand) is a senior lecturer in applied linguistics at the VNU University of Languages and International Studies, Hanoi, Vietnam, where he teaches graduate courses in the methodology of teaching English to speakers of other languages (TESOL), materials development and evaluation, and research methodology in applied linguistics. He has published in the areas of context-based pedagogy, language policy and planning, and teacher cognition. His most recent publications include several book chapters and refereed journal articles. He is also a book reviewer, TESOL convention reviewer and an executive member of Asia TEFL Association. He was a plenary speaker at the 9th Asia TEFL Association International Conference in Seoul (2011). His research interests include second language acquisition, second language teacher education, teacher cognition, teacher methodology in action, and language policy and planning.

Ha Rim Lee is currently a PhD student at the Department of Applied Language Studies and Linguistics at the University of Auckland, New Zealand. She majored in linguistics at the University of Otago and completed her MA in English language education at Seoul National University. Herself a bilingual, Ha Rim Lee has a keen interest in the area of learning and teaching English as a second language. Her major areas of research include L2 acquisition, spoken L2 production, L2 syntax, construction grammar and child L2 acquisition.

David C.S. Li obtained his BA in English in Hong Kong (1982), MA in applied linguistics in Besançon, France (1984) and PhD in linguistics in Cologne, Germany (1991). Trained in general linguistics and applied linguistics, he has since developed a keen interest in social aspects of language learning and use in multilingual settings. In addition to contrastive aspectology, he has published in world Englishes and 'Hongkong English', bilingual interaction and codeswitching in Hong Kong and Taiwan, and EFL learners' difficulties and error-correction strategies. He spent 16 fruitful years at City University of Hong Kong before joining the Hong Kong Institute of Education in 2008. His research was supported by various grants, including two Competitive Earmarked Research Grants (CERGs). He speaks Cantonese, English and Putonghua/Mandarin fluently, and is conversant in German and French.

Ernesto Macaro is Professor of Applied Linguistics and currently Director of the Department of Education at the University of Oxford. After obtaining a first degree in French and English from the University of Kent, he went on to teach languages in UK secondary schools for 16 years before becoming a teacher educator and applied linguist at university level. There are two major strands to Ernesto's research activity: oral discourse and interaction between second language teachers and learners, and second language learning strategies. A developing interest is interaction in classrooms where English is the medium of instruction for academic subjects. He has published many books and journal articles and in 2009 he edited *Continuum Companion to Second Language Acquisition*, published by Continuum.

Isabel Pefianco Martin is associate professor at the Department of English, Ateneo de Manila University. She is also chair of the Board of Trustees of the Philippine Social Science Council (PSSC). Prior to these posts, she served as president of the Linguistic Society of the Philippines, chair of the Ateneo English Department and research coordinator of the Ateneo School of Humanities. Her research interests include sociolinguistics, descriptions of English, world Englishes, Philippine English and languages in education.

James McLellan is a senior lecturer in English language and linguistics at Universiti Brunei Darussalam. He taught at secondary and tertiary levels in Brunei from 1985 to 2002, and has also taught in the UK, France, Malaysia, Australia and Aotearoa (New Zealand). He obtained his PhD from Curtin University of Technology, Australia, in 2005. His research interests include language alternation (codeswitching), southeast Asian Englishes, Borneo indigenous languages, and language policy and planning in education.

Kenneth Keng Wee Ong is a lecturer at the Language and Communication Centre of Nanyang Technological University, Singapore, where he teaches courses in English for academic purposes (EAP) and English for specific purposes (ESP). His research interests are in bilingual semantic and conceptual representation, bilingual language processing, cognitive second language vocabulary acquisition, computer-mediated discourse analysis and language and the internet. He is an associate editor of the *Asian EFL Journal* and his recent publications include an article in *Discourse Studies* (April 2011) and a paper co-authored with Lawrence Jun Zhang in the *Journal of Psycholinguistic Research* (June 2010).

Noor Azam Haji-Othman is Associate Professor and the Dean of the Faculty of Arts and Social Sciences at Universiti Brunei Darussalam. He teaches on the English language and linguistics programme, as well as media and communication studies. He has been active in the teaching of indigenous languages of Brunei at the Language Centre as part of Universiti Brunei Darussalam's minor programme in Borneo languages. He is interested in the interplay between the various languages used in Brunei, including Malay and English, in terms of, or as a result of, state policy on language and education.

Matthew G. Robinson is currently based in Bhutan, where he is a lecturer at the Institute of Language and Culture Studies. Passionate about teaching, he has 10 years of experience teaching a range of subjects to students of all ages and levels, for various educational institutions in the USA, Bhutan, East Timor, Kiribati and Thailand. He obtained his MA in teaching English to speakers of other languages (TESOL) from the Monterey Institute of International Studies, where he completed the Peace Corps Master's International Program. Before coming to Bhutan in 2010, he was an English Language Fellow for the US State Department. His current research interests lie at the intersection of education, linguistics and anthropology, and his current projects concern curriculum development, community research, and the preservation and promotion of culture and identity in Bhutan.

Richmond Stroupe has worked with university and professional language learners from Asia since 1989. He is currently the chair of the Masters Program in International Language Education, teaching English to speakers of other languages (TESOL) at Soka University, Japan. He is professionally active both in Japan, with the Japan Association for Language Teaching as the former chair of the Association's International Affairs Committee, and internationally, with the TESOL International Association in the USA, as the former chair of the Standing Committee on Standards, and as a member of the advisory board of the online publication *Language Education in Asia*. His professional and academic interests include curriculum design, teacher training in the development context, and international comparative education.

Hajah Suciyati Haji Sulaiman graduated in 2005 from the University of South Australia with a bachelor of education and in 2006 with a masters of education, specialising in teaching English to speakers of other languages (TESOL). Suciyati joined the Language Centre of Universiti Brunei Darussalam in 2007 and has been teaching English language modules, in particular academic writing, communication skills, as well as intensive English programmes for diplomatic officers from southeast Asia. Her research interests are in the areas of second language acquisition and the methodology of English language teaching for speakers of other languages.

Chamaipak Tayjasanant is an assistant professor in the Department of Linguistics at Kasetsart University, Thailand. She obtained a PhD in education (teaching English as a foreign language) from the University of Exeter. She is currently teaching both undergraduate and postgraduate courses and has interests in teacher cognition, language, culture, nature and communication. Her recent articles include 'Language teachers' beliefs and practices regarding the appropriateness of communicative methodology: A case study from Thailand', published in the *Journal of Asia TEFL* in 2010, and 'Thai university students' understanding and perception of English metaphors in news articles', in the *International Journal of the Humanities*, volume 9.

Lili Tian is an associate professor in English at the School of Foreign Languages, Renmin University of China. She has over eight years' teaching experience at university level in China. She holds a PhD in applied linguistics from the University of Oxford (2009) on the effect of teacher codeswitching on vocabulary acquisition during classroom interaction. Her research interests mainly lie in codeswitching, vocabulary learning and learning strategies.

Lawrence Jun Zhang obtained a BA and two MA degrees from Chinese universities and was a postdoctoral fellow at the University of Oxford, where he worked with Ernesto Macaro, among others. He is currently associate professor and associate dean at the Faculty of Education of the University of Auckland, New Zealand, having previously been associate professor at Nanyang Technological University from 1999 to 2012. His research and publications cover a wide range of interests, such as cognitive, linguistic, sociocultural and developmental factors in reading/biliteracy development, critical reading awareness in language education, metacognition, self-regulated learning (SRL) and reading development in L1 and L2 contexts. For many years, he has served as an editorial board member for several international journals, including *TESOL Quarterly*, *Applied Linguistics Review*, *Metacognition and Learning* and *RELC Journal*.

Hajah Zurinah Haji Ya'akub joined the Language Centre of the Universiti Brunei Darussalam in 2008 and is currently a lecturer there. She has been involved in teaching Malay language and communication skills, as well as in some English language proficiency classes at lower levels. She obtained her masters in applied linguistics from the University of New South Wales in 2010. She has also been a member of the Brunei Darussalam Linguistics Organisation since 2010.

Transcription Conventions in Data Extracts

1, 2	number of extract
1b, 1c	interaction which follows immediately after previous extract
01, 02	speaker turn
T	teacher
S1, S2	unknown students
Ss	more than one student speaking
[ ]	overlapping speech
/, //, ///	pause (length in seconds)
bold	emphasis given by speaker
(xxx)	unintelligible speech
(hello)	guessed speech
{ }	activity associated with the speech
< >	interpretive comment
italics	translation of original speech in vernacular

NB. All names of teachers and students are pseudonyms (except where specifically stated to the contrary)

Introduction

Roger Barnard and James McLellan

Setting the Scene

In many parts of the complex multicultural world of the 21st century, people switch between languages on a regular, even everyday basis. In this book we refer to this phenomenon as *codeswitching*, although other terms are used in the relevant literature, such as code mixing, code/language selection/ alternation, or simply translation. In fact, there are now very few entirely monolingual societies. For example, the Republic of Korea – until recently regarded as firmly mono-ethnic and mono-cultural – now has thousands of immigrant residents, mostly women and children, for whom Korean is an additional language and who have to adjust to an unfamiliar social and educational culture. Similarly, New Zealand, once a bastion of colonial English language and culture, became officially bilingual in 1987, when the Maori Language Act was passed. Since then, it has opened its doors to im- migrants and refugees from many countries. Today, New Zealand citizens of European, mainly British, descent account for about two-thirds of the population, while Maori constitute about 15% and residents of Pacific Island or Asian or African descent account for over 7% each. The proportion of children of non-European descent in the nation's schools is even greater than that in the nation's overall population.

The worldwide influx of learners from different language backgrounds presents challenges to educational systems in all nations, from preschools to universities. The present volume focuses on specific university contexts in a number of Asian countries where the perceived importance of English as *the* global language of communication, technology and business has led univer- sity authorities to promote the use of English as the medium of instruction. The pressure of such policies is felt by learners and teachers both within the universities and in subordinate educational institutions where English is taught a foreign language as well as used as the medium of instruction in an increasing number of other subjects in the curriculum.

The use of students' first languages in classrooms where English as a Foreign Language (EFL) is taught has tended to be disparaged by textbook writers, methodologists and educational policymakers in many countries. Consequently, the exclusive use of the target language has dominated English language teaching methodology for over a century, since the rejection in theory (but not usually in practice) of the Grammar-Translation approach, and its suggested replacement, successively, by the Direct Method, Audiolingualism, the Natural Approach and Communicative Language Teaching. Increasingly over the past two decades, however, there has been a resurgence of publications arguing that codeswitching in English language instruction can be socially, pedagogically and educationally valuable (Anton & DiCamilla, 1998; Cook, 2001; Dailey-O'Cain & Liebscher, 2009; Macaro, 2001, 2005, 2009; Swain & Lapkin, 2000). Recently, Guy Cook has argued that 'translation can help and motivate students in a variety of pedagogical contexts ... [and] is suited to different types of teachers, and different ages and stages of students' (Cook, 2010: xvii). Some 20 years ago, Widdowson (1994) argued that monolingual methods of teaching English excessively privileged the status of teachers who are first language users of English, a matter which has given rise to organisations and networks which have sought to redress this professional imbalance, such as the Nonnative Speaker Movement (Braine, 2010). Thus, there are convincing reasons to explore the use of codeswitching in university classrooms where English is either the subject or the medium of instruction.

This volume of international case studies and perspectives discusses these issues in depth. The book begins with Ernesto Macaro's consideration of the directions that research into classroom codeswitching (CS) might take, and this is followed by eight chapters focusing on specific university classrooms in a range of Asian contexts. Each of these chapters presents a case study concerned with investigating the extent of, and motivations for, CS in one particular situation, and the interactive and pedagogical functions for which alternative languages are used. The first part of each case study begins with a brief introduction to the linguistic, sociocultural and institutional context in which the data were collected. This is followed by extracts from classroom data, and a quantitative and qualitative analysis of the extent of CS that occurred in that particular context. In most cases, comments from interviews with the teachers in that institution are reported and interpreted. Each of these case studies is followed by a commentary by a researcher in a relatable context, providing an alternative (or similar) point of view, usually with additional empirical data from the commentator's own context. The book concludes with an Afterword by Andy Kirkpatrick. We believe that this book will have direct relevance to all practising or potential teachers interested in exploring language use in English language classrooms. In particular, the book will reflect the extent of convergence and divergence between university language teachers' beliefs and practices relating to CS in a range of contexts. This book is also likely to appeal to other readers: classroom researchers for whom language use in foreign language education is a matter of current concern; teacher educators involved in the professional development of language teachers in universities and elsewhere; and those involved in policymaking and management in bi- and multi-lingual institutions. While the focus of this book is on language alternation in English classes in Asian universities, there are important implications for those teaching learners of all ages in other contexts. With very few excep-tions, the university teachers presented in these chapters believe that CS serves valuable functions in their classes, and they use it for various reasons, and provide arguments for their beliefs and practices. If such arguments are academically and professionally convincing, they might encourage teachers in primary and secondary schools to evaluate their own beliefs and practices as to the value of the principled use of the learners' – and their own – first language in their own professional contexts.

Summarising the Chapters

Ernesto Macaro's overview of research issues in classroom CS provides readers with valid and valuable pointers towards a theoretical framework for ongoing and future research in this developing field. He poses a key question about whether interaction in language classrooms should resemble 'naturalistic' interaction in other settings, before discussing the nature of CS in L2 classrooms. His second key question, 'what is the pedagogical orienta-tion of the classrooms that we are considering or observing in which this phenomenon occurs?', is closely aligned to the co-editors' principal research interest in this field: the investigation of language teachers' beliefs. The attempt to uncover aspects of teacher beliefs and to investigate these in relation to their actual classroom practices is a key driver in our conceptu-alisation and planning of this volume.

The sequence of case studies in this book reflects the complexity of CS in university classrooms. The case study in Chapter 1 reports Ching-yi Tien's exercise in reflective practice on her use of CS in a Taiwanese university. She chooses to explore the issue in three consecutive lessons in an *Introduc-tion to Linguistics* course, noting that 'it is a requirement that all the courses offered by the Department of Applied English should be taught exclusively in English'. Despite this policy, her use of Taiwanese ranges from about 6% of her total talking time to over 30%, and after presenting transcript data illustrating the barrier function served by CS, she explains her reasons for doing so. In her final comments, Tien notes that reflecting on her practice in this way has helped her to gain insights about her current and future CS practice. In his commentary, David C.S. Li discusses her findings from the perspective of Conversation Analysis, and relates them to his own experience of CS, and that of others, in Hong Kong. He argues that the supportive role of learners' first language in English-medium classes is insufficiently recognised by language policymakers at national and institutional levels, and concludes that 'codeswitching is pedagogically conducive to teaching and learning in many ways'.

This is followed by two chapters with parallel case studies. In Chapter 2, Lili Tian explores the use of CS by two EFL teachers in a university in Beijing. As was the case in the Taiwanese English-medium class, the teachers used the first language of their students – and themselves – for about 10% of their total talking time – for explaining grammar or vocabulary, giving further information, or making personal comments. However, CS served different purposes in the two lessons analysed, which Tian ascribed to the different lesson types: one of the lessons focused on intensive reading, where the EFL teachers' role might be seen as a lexical and grammatical resource, and the second was an advanced course specialising in Journalism English, where the teacher was more of a cultural informant. Claudia Kunschak's commentary compares Tian's findings with those from elsewhere in China, and in particular with two surveys, one published in 2010 and the other more recently conducted by Kunschak herself among EFL lecturers working in a university's English language centre. She reports that both these surveys revealed commonalities with Tian's data in terms of Chinese university teachers' beliefs about CS – primarily that teachers may not consider CS desirable but nevertheless see it as a useful tool for improving the effectiveness and efficiency of English language teaching.

Chapter 3 considers codeswitching in two Japanese institutions. Simon Humphries's case study considers lessons by two Japanese EFL lecturers, both highly proficient users of English, in a *Kosen* (community college), and analyses their CS in terms of four interactional modes: managerial, materials, skills, and classroom context. He found a very heavy reliance by both teachers on Japanese (72% and 90%), and in his interviews with them they explained that this was very largely due to the very low motivation of their students. His commentator, Richmond Stroupe, considers the extent to which Humphries's findings would apply to his own teaching context in an English language learning context elsewhere in Japan. Therefore, he surveyed 18 university language instructors, the majority of whom, both native speakers of English and Japanese, reported a high proficiency in the two languages. His questionnaire elicited the respondents' perceptions of the purposes for which they might codeswitch, the pedagogical or institutional factors which influenced L1 use, and how the choice of language was related to their personal and professional identities. Stroupe concludes that his results mirror those of Humphries, in that the exclusive use of L2 is not relevant to the practical experience of even highly competent bilingual EFL teachers, and that CS can be an efficient method for classroom management and knowledge transmission.

The next two chapters compare and contrast the use of CS in four very different national contexts. Chamaipak Tayjasanant's examination of EFL lessons taught by two teachers in Thailand reveals that although both frequently switched between English and Thai, their reasons for doing so differed. The more frequent user, who had no teacher training background, switched to Thai in order to enhance her learners' understanding of grammar rules. On the other hand, her colleague, a firm believer in the Communicative Approach, used Thai primarily to improve the classroom atmosphere. Matthew Robinson begins his commentary with an overview of the language and education situation in Bhutan, where there is an urgent need to standardise and promote the use of Dzongkha as a national language, as well as to develop English competence among the people. Comparing Tayjasanant's findings with data from his recent interviews with two Bhutanese teachers, he points out that the students in both contexts were non-English majors. Like the Thai teachers, his two Bhutanese participants differed in their attitudes towards CS in their classrooms – but in this case this divergence reflects the fact that one of the teachers taught English literature at an institution training candidates in traditional culture and language, where 80% of the courses are taught in Dzongkha, whereas the other taught academic English skills at an institution preparing health workers through the medium of English.

In Chapter 5, Le Van Canh reports a Vietnamese university teacher's use of the first language in four 45-minute EFL lessons. Her CS ranged from about 15% to over 30%, the major functions of which included classroom management, enhancing motivation, explaining grammar, pronunciation and lexis, and checking students' comprehension. She explained that students would not understand if she did not translate key information into Vietnamese. Canh argues that, instead of promoting a deficit view of CS, teacher education programmes should introduce effective and codified CS practices among both prospective and practising language teachers.

Both Canh and his commentator, Fuad Abdul Hamied, from an Indonesian perspective, point to the scarcity of research into the issue of CS in their respective countries – especially in university contexts. Hamied compares Canh's findings to an observational and interview study with one of his own teaching colleagues, and his findings are very similar to those in the Vietnamese context. He follows up this study with a survey of the attitudes of students in that teacher's class. Interestingly, one of his findings is that over 70% of the students thought that their teacher's CS was due to his inadeqacy in English – although Hamied considers that his actual English proficiency was far above that required to teach his subject entirely in English.

The case study in Chapter 6 firstly looks at the attitudes towards CS of three Bruneian English–Malay bilingual tutors in a university language centre: two were teaching English, and one was teaching both English and an indigenous language, Tutong. Although the first two accepted that there could be some benefits to CS, only the latter reported that he actually switched languages in his Tutong classes: approximately 50% Tutong, 20% Malay and 30% English. However, all three reported that their students frequently switched between languages in class, and Noor Azam Haji-Othman and his colleagues provide transcript data to illustrate typical examples. Despite their general reluctance to switch to Malay themselves, all three teachers recognised that some students needed to codeswitch to fully understand what was being taught, especially in lower-level classes. Commenting on this case study, Ain Nadzimah Abdullah and Chan Swee Heng firstly consider the extent to which the language-in-education situation in Malaysia is similar to that in Brunei. They then report a study they undertook with 14 language teachers in their own university to see if there were parallels to the Brunei situation. All the Malaysian teachers said that they codeswitched to some extent: 43% responded 'seldom', 36% said 'often' and 21% said 'always', explaining that they switched codes mainly to facilitate understanding, especially of vocabulary. The commentators conclude that studies focusing on the socio-psychological implications of CS, such as those so far reported in this book, usefully complement other studies more oriented towards linguistic descriptions and explanations of CS.

It is precisely such a linguistic analysis that Kenneth Keng Wee Ong and Lawrence Jun Zhang conducted on samples of CS by 22 undergraduate students in a Singapore university, all of whom reported their frequent use of CS in and outside class, described in Chapter 7. Building on an earlier study they carried out, the authors focus on the students' use of determiner phrases in English and Mandarin. Their results challenge a number of widely espoused CS models and hypotheses, and refine or expand others. The main pedagogical implication of their study is that, rather than perceiving students who switch between languages as being lazy or incompetent English users, teachers should recognise that CS is an economic way of mapping thought onto language. They also recommend that EFL teachers reinforce the teaching of English determiners to their students. Isabel Pefianco Martin begins her commentary by pointing out the dominance of English in Philippine society, and that CS is commonplace, particularly among the educated classes. While Filipino teachers are expected to use only English in teaching content courses, a number of studies into classrooms have indicated CS is widespread. Martin illustrates such use with several examples of transcript data from university-level science courses. These show that CS was used as a pedagogical tool for motivating student response and action, ensuring rapport and solidarity, promoting shared meaning, checking student understanding, and maintaining the teaching narrative. She points out that both teachers and students are not imperfect bilinguals and therefore the CS used by both is a smooth, grammatical and natural form of communication.

In the eighth and final case study, the focus is on Korean students at a New Zealand university. Unlike all the preceding case studies and commentaries, which discuss spoken classroom data, Moyra Sweetnam Evans and Ha Rim Lee analyse written extracts from a reading comprehension task in which the students were asked to recall and to comment on texts of five diverse genres. Written classroom CS is generally less researched than is spoken CS, although it is becoming something of a growth area, with researchers (e.g. Callahan, 2004; Sebba, 2012) approaching the topic from linguistic, psycholinguistic and especially sociolinguistic perspectives. The co-authors of this case study make the pertinent point that the Korean student participants were under no restrictions or constraints as to their language choice for accomplishing the reading recall and comment task. Normally CS is considered to be less likely to occur in the written mode, but the nature of the task allowed the students room to negotiate between their shared L1 and their L2. As noted in the commentary by Hyun-Ju Kim, patterns of CS are crucially determined by contextual factors as well as by the bilingual competences of the participants. She begins her commentary by outlining the intense pressure in all sectors of Korean education to learn English, and the recent moves towards English-medium instruction in universities. Kim then provides data from a small-scale survey she conducted which indicated that the majority of her participating university lecturers perceived that CS might assist the students to understand the content of the classes, and might raise motivation, but would not be beneficial for the students' linguistic development, apart from reading skills.

The Afterword by Andy Kirkpatrick picks up and recycles some of the major issues addressed by Macaro and by the other contributors. The tensions between policymakers and teachers who may feel guilty about their CS use is brought into sharp relief by the discussion of the situation in Hong Kong. Kirkpatrick usefully refers to the practical guidelines which he co-authored with Merrill Swain and Jim Cummins which aim to help teachers overcome their feelings of guilt about their use of their L1, Cantonese, in English language classes.

Looking Forward

The case study and commentary contributions were independently compiled. The Overview by Ernesto Macaro, 'Where should we be going with classroom codeswitching research?', and Andy Kirkpatrick's Afterword, by contrast, make references to the data and the analyses of some of the eight central chapters. Thus Macaro and Kirkpatrick are able to stand back and reflect on the global significance of these Asian university case studies and commentaries, linking data examples and analysis and providing pointers towards a theory of classroom CS as well as a rationale for it.

Many of the contributors make a case for a more tolerant and nuanced view of the use of the L1 in L2 classrooms, thus attempting to redress the previous dominance of the zero-tolerance position of approaches such as the Direct Method and the Natural Approach of Krashen and Terrell (1983). As noted throughout this volume, this zero-tolerance policy is still the norm in many Asian education systems, imposed by ministries of education and by key stakeholders in academic institutions. Of course, it should not be dismissed out of hand. For instance, one justification for imposing such an embargo on L1 use is that when learners know that whatever is said in the L2 will be repeated in the L1, they will soon cease to pay any attention to the L2 input.

It is our hope that readers will be challenged by the different stances adopted by the contributors to this volume on CS, and by the divergent opinions which they report. Some readers, we also hope, will feel inspired to take up the challenge to conduct further research studies of their own in different learning and teaching contexts, thereby further advancing our knowledge and moving towards better theoretical and practical understanding of the complexities of interaction in language classrooms. The chapters in this collection almost all deal with contexts where learners form homogeneous groups, sharing the same L1 as their instructors. In many university language classrooms elsewhere, the learners bring with them a multiplicity of L1s, and thus CS is not an option, as the instructor is unlikely to be able to switch into every learner's L1. Perhaps a further set of case studies from such multilingual contexts could be collected in a follow-up volume to this one.

References

Anton, M. and DiCamilla, F.J. (1998) Socio-cognitive functions of L1 collaborative interaction in the L2 classroom. *Modern Language Journal* 83 (2), 233–247.

Braine, G. (2010) *Nonnative Speaker English Teachers: Research, Pedagogy, and Professional Growth*. New York: Routledge.

Callahan, L. (2004) *Spanish–English Codeswitching in a Written Corpus*. Amsterdam: John Benjamins.

Cook, G. (2010) *Translation in Language Teaching: An Argument for Reassessment*. Oxford: Oxford University Press.

Cook, V.J. (2001) Using the first language in the classroom. *Canadian Modern Language Review/La revue canadienne des langues vivants* 57 (3), 402–423.

Dailey-O'Cain, J. and Liebscher, G. (2009) Teacher and student use of the first language in foreign language classroom interactions: Functions and applications. In M. Turnbull and J. Dailey-O'Cain (eds) *First Language Use in Second and Foreign Language Learning* (pp. 131–144). Bristol: Multilingual Matters.

Krashen, S. and Terrell, T. (1983) *The Natural Approach*. Hayward, CA: Alemany Press.

Macaro, E. (2001) Analyzing students teachers' code-switching in foreign language classrooms: Theories and decision-making. *Modern Language Journal* 85 (4), 531–548.

Macaro, E. (2005) Codeswitching in the L2 classroom: A communication and learning strategy. In E. Llurda (ed.) *Non-native Language Teachers: Perceptions, Challenges and Contributions to the Profession* (pp. 63–84). New York: Springer.

Macaro, E. (2009) Teacher use of codeswitching in the L2 classroom: Exploring 'optimal' use. In M. Turnbull and J. Dailey-O'Cain (eds) *First Language Use in Second and Foreign Language Learning* (pp. 35–49). Bristol: Multilingual Matters.

Sebba, M. (2012) Researching and theorising mixed-language texts. In M. Sebba, S. Mahootian and C. Jonsson (eds) *Language Mixing and Code-Switching in Writing: Approaches to Mixed-Language Written Discourse* (pp. 1–26). London: Routledge.

Swain, M. and Lapkin, S. (2000) Task-based second language learning: The uses of the first language. *Language Teaching Research* 4 (3), 251–274.

Widdowson, H.G. (1994) The ownership of English. *TESOL Quarterly* 28 (2), 377–398.

Overview: Where Should We Be Going With Classroom Codeswitching Research?

Ernesto Macaro

Introduction

Classroom codeswitching (CS) is in desperate need of some theorising. The vast majority of studies that I have come across appear to ask empirical questions without first establishing a set of logical propositions which either relate to an existing theory or purport to be offering a new one. Yet, I would argue, the question of whether the first language (L1) should be used in the oral interaction or the written materials of second or foreign language (L2) classrooms is probably the most fundamental question facing second language acquisition (SLA) researchers, language teachers and policymakers in this second decade of the 21st century. Because it is so important, it is not surprising that the topic has figured prominently in numerous SLA and bilingualism journals and it is for this reason that so many doctoral dissertations continue to appear on the topic of CS. It is not just more important than other SLA questions, it subsumes virtually all of them. It is hard to envisage a discussion about, say, implicit and explicit learning without referring to the role of the L1 in those processes. Such an important question needs a solid foundation on which to build a concerted empirical enquiry.

I am therefore hugely grateful to the editors of this volume for giving me the opportunity to attempt a theoretical framework for CS research, one which I hope will lead to a more focused research agenda in the coming years.

Two Fundamental Problems

In order to answer the question in the chapter title I believe we have to begin by considering two fundamental problems. Firstly, what do we mean by CS in L2 classrooms? In other words what is the construct that we are considering or the phenomenon that we are observing? Why is it, moreover, that some observers call it 'codeswitching' (Raschka *et al.*, 2009), some call it 'use of mother tongue' (Kharma & Hajjaj, 1989) and some call it 'code choice' (Levine, 2011)? Secondly, what is the pedagogical orientation of the classrooms that we are considering or observing in which this phenomenon occurs? In other words, what is in the mind of teachers when they enter the classroom? What outcomes are they trying to achieve both in the short term (the lesson or part of that lesson) or in the long term (the rate of progress and ultimate attainment of the students in their charge)? Just as importantly, what is in the minds of the learners as they walk into the classroom? Do they have the same pedagogical orientation as the teacher? Do they even know what the teacher's intended short- and long-term outcomes are? These two problems are inter-related, as I hope to demonstrate.

What is 'Codeswitching' in L2 Classrooms?

A term that is often used in the relevant literature is 'naturalistic codeswitching'. This refers to the presence of CS in interaction that occurs in everyday situations. The term immediately poses a problem for the researcher of classroom CS. If naturalistic CS refers to everyday situations, does that make it incompatible with CS that occurs in classrooms? The answer might well be 'no' if we take a sensible and broad view of 'everyday situations'. For example, I would imagine that no linguist would object to studying the CS which occurs in a business meeting or among academics engaged in a discussion about their area of interest. If we take this broad view of 'everyday situations' then classroom CS is an everyday phenomenon like the rest, because it happens frequently and ubiquitously. However, there is potentially one fundamental difference between 'naturalistic CS' and L2 classroom CS – and that is that, in the latter, the purpose of the interaction between the participants in the conversation/discourse is both to communicate with each other and (for one set of interlocutors at least) to learn or improve or in some way advance their L2. In naturalistic CS, the overarching purpose is communication. There may be some fairly rare occasions in naturalistic CS when one of the participants 'teaches' the interlocutor some aspect of one of the languages through a switch (for example interactions between bilingual parents and their children or among bilingual siblings) but, generally, it is argued that naturalistic CS occurs for the purposes of furthering communication' (Myers-Scotton, 2001) or results from managing communication through preference marking and repair (Li Wei *et al.*, 2000).

What is the Pedagogical Orientation of the Classroom Codeswitching?

So, are naturalistic and classroom CS irreconcilable? If switching in L2 classrooms occurs with the intention of advancing the L2, does it change the very nature of that form of CS? In order to try to answer that question we have to consider who it is that gives a particular discourse its legitimacy: is it the general context (the perspective of 'the outsider' or 'the bird's eye view') or is it the actual participants in the discourse? If we can agree that it is the latter, then it follows that CS for the purpose of learning as well as for communication becomes legitimised if and only if the participants in the discourse agree that the interaction containing the CS is fit for the purpose for which it is intended. In other words, it becomes authenticated – as Van Lier (1996) would say – by the participants in the discourse.

Now, that sounds pretty straightforward, but it isn't, because, in order for CS discourse to be authenticated, it has to be accepted by all participants in that classroom (both teachers and learners) and we know that, like language teachers, language learners have different beliefs with regard to how languages should be learned. In a recent study (Macaro et al., 2012) Japanese university students of English, on an intensive short course in the UK, had very different conceptions of how best to learn an L2. The design of the study was as follows: in one class, CS was encouraged through the presence of a bilingual assistant and a monolingual teacher; in another class, it was strongly discouraged, operationalised by both the teacher and the assistant being monolingual. (By the term 'monolingual teacher' I mean a teacher who, in a particular educational context, can teach through the medium of only one language – the L2 that the students are learning. A bilingual teacher would therefore be one who can teach by using not only the language that is being learned but also the first language of the students. Clearly, then, this does not prevent a 'monolingual teacher' from being a bilingual or even a multilingual human being.) We found in fact that students' perceptions and attitudes echoed an earlier proposal of mine (Macaro, 1997, 2001) regarding the three positions that teachers take with regard to L2-only or CS:

(1) They adopted the 'virtual position'. They considered that the classroom had to be like the world outside, where they would not be able to use Japanese to communicate. In which case, CS had no value whatsoever; the best way to learn English was through English.
(2) They adopted the 'maximal position'. They also thought that the classroom should be like the world outside. However, they claimed

that either they or their classmates did not have the proficiency level to exclude Japanese completely. In other words, they adopted a somewhat unhealthy deficit model.

(3) A few adopted the 'optimal position'. They saw both the value of CS in terms of facilitating communication and learning as well as the dangers that CS could bring if its use was unprincipled and ad hoc.

To return to the argument, then: in order for classroom CS to be reconcilable with naturalistic CS, it has to be agreed by the participants in the classroom discourse that it is fit for purpose, in the same way that (presumably) participants in naturalistic CS accept switching as being fit for their purpose. In order for this state of affairs to pertain in classrooms, all participants need to have the same conceptualisation of the intended educational outcomes. That this state of affairs is so difficult to achieve creates the very tensions with regard to CS that have been documented between teachers and learners, teachers and other teachers, teachers and institutions, and teachers and policymakers (Ferguson, 2003; Raschka *et al.*, 2009). Put simply, the tension exists because of the lack of consensus regarding the outcomes of language education. One lack of consensus is centred on the eternal debate between language use and knowledge about language, or implicit versus explicit learning. As has been well documented in the literature (and is further documented in this volume, for example in Chapter 6), despite government agencies and policymakers stating that the curriculum and teaching practices should have communicative competence as their central outcome, many classrooms are characterised by a focus on extensive explanations of syntax and morphology.

Thus, unless we first establish what the teachers' (and if possible the learners') intended educational outcomes are, the debate on CS is nothing short of meaningless. There is no point in observing, recording and analysing a lesson for its CS content if that lesson's main pedagogical orientation is the comparison of the two languages (the L2 and the L1) and the explicit teaching of the vocabulary and structures of the L2 through frequent recourse to the L1. This type of lesson is what Guy Cook (2010) termed the inter-lingual approach, one characterised by frequent translations in both directions. To observe, record and then conclude that a lesson such as this contained, say, 50% L1 use is, in my view, a pointless exercise. Yet in many studies on CS that I have read we find these sorts of percentages. In many studies we read that the functions of CS include 'translation', 'grammar ex-planations' and 'metalinguistic commentary'. As far as can be ascertained, therefore, the amount of CS and the functions to which it is being put merely tell us that these lessons (or at least large chunks of these lessons) are likely to be non-communicative – they focus not on language use but on knowledge about language.

Now, I am not making some sort of value judgement about one teaching method over another. I am merely positing a point of view (and I am sure it will be a highly contentious one) that the only L2 lessons worth analysing for CS content are those where the proportion of CS by the teacher is below 15% (Macaro, 2001) and where the majority of functions for which it is used are not for language comparison or explanation of structures but for some kind of communicative function. Examples of communicative functions would be to signal a topic switch, brief socialising moves and expressions of emotions. They might also be for brief L1 information on L2 lexical items (for the purpose of maintaining L2 communication – for example when giving instructions for a task) or when L2 paraphrase of that lexical item is proving counterproductive or indeed impossible (I return to this point below). In other words, these are lessons which adopt an intra-lingual approach (again using Guy Cook's terminology) but ones where communication is facilitated by brief switches and where CS is used for 'focus on form' (Long, 1991) in communicative activities. Note the last emphasis on focus on form. An intra-lingual approach does not exclude a focus on form with regard to morphology and syntax, but it does so through communication in the L2 and without constant language comparison.

The Nature of Codeswitching

This brings us to an examination of the nature of the CS itself, and we return therefore to the presence in the literature of the multiple ways of labelling the phenomenon: codeswitching; L1 use; language alternation; code choice. Why so many labels? One possible reason is that authors who do not use the term 'codeswitching' are simply not familiar with the literature on naturalistic CS. That's fair enough – there is no reason why someone cannot talk about 'L1 use' in the classroom without a background in linguistics. However, I would argue that in the adoption or the avoidance of the term 'codeswitching' lies the distinction between research on communicatively oriented classrooms and those where language comparison and analysis prevail. To support this point of view it is necessary to return to the phenomenon of naturalistic CS.

When two bilinguals talk to each other, more than one language might occur in their conversation. However, there are many variables both in the characteristics of the bilinguals and in the resulting CS that takes place. Firstly, it is not the case that both participants in the conversation have to be fluent in both languages. It may be, for example, that one participant is highly fluent in two languages but the interlocutor is fluent in only one (his or her L1) and has only a smattering of the second language. The fluent bilingual may therefore use the interlocutor's L1 most of the time and switch occasionally to the interlocutor's L2 for a few words that she or he knows the interlocutor uses, for example some technical terms or often used phrases. The L2 in this case is likely to be a 'global' language such as English or Spanish.

Secondly, if the participants in the conversation are both fluent in the two languages they share, then, once again, it is highly likely that one language predominates and the other language (sometimes referred to as the 'marked language') is introduced at the lexical level or at the clause level. It is somewhat rare for bilinguals to speak one language on one occasion and on another occasion opt for the other language unless they are trying to make some sort of sociolinguistic statement (for example, they use one language in a particular social context and the other language in another social context). This is sometimes described as 'code choice', whereas CS seems to suggest brief insertions of one language into another. Now, it seems to me that, for the researcher of classroom CS, and the language teacher, it is these brief insertions that are of interest, not the long stretches of one language alternating with long stretches of another. If, as I have argued above, CS is worth exploring only in communicative classrooms (where an intra-lingual approach is being adopted) then it is in the nature and the reasons for the brief switches that the pedagogical interest and debate lie.

Readers will no doubt be familiar with the distinction (in the naturalistic literature) between inter-sentential switching, intra-sentential switching and tag switching. These are useful distinctions even though they have associated problems. The most obvious problem is that we do not often speak in full sentences, so what is really meant is 'switching between clauses, or within clauses'. Even though this latter definition may prove problematic (we sometimes utter fragments which can be retrieved as clauses only by knowing the context) we can at least work with it for the purposes of a discussion on classroom CS.

Readers will also be familiar with the naturalistic literature which describes the rules and constraints on CS (here switching between English and Italian):

- Switching rarely involves the insertion of a bound morpheme next to another (*dangerosoly [for dangerously]), whereas I have heard the expression 'very dangeroso!' for stylistic effect.
- Switching rarely occurs through the insertion of function words (closed class words; *I'm going alla swimming pool).

- Switching rarely occurs between a complementiser (that) and its complement (arrived yesterday) in the phrase 'the parcel that arrived yesterday'.
- Switching very rarely violates the morphology or syntax of either of the two languages in question.
- On the other hand, switches often occur with open class words (content words) such as nouns, verbs and adjectives.

These constraints (and lack of constraints) are of great interest to the classroom CS researcher and the language teacher. Not only do they provide a basic framework for CS by the teacher but they also, very importantly, provide a framework for the observation of the developmental processes of the learner. In other words, an L2 learner who can codeswitch while not violating the grammar of either language, or a learner who is able to work within the other constraints above, is demonstrating a far more advanced competence in the L2 – Vivian Cook (1992) would call it a multicompetence of both languages – than simply being able to utter correct forms in the L2 alone. Put differently, classroom CS of the sort that I am describing becomes the raw material in the crucible that is classroom interaction.

Codeswitching for Unknown Lexical Items

We have, nevertheless, a further and very important issue to resolve with regard to switching for unknown lexical items. Recall that, according to the literature on classroom CS, this is the function to which teacher switching is most often put. This particular function, as well as posing a problem, also illustrates vividly the dual purpose of interaction in the L2 classroom. Let us say that, in the process of a teacher explaining how to go about a language task, she utters an L2 word (an English word in the example that follows) which she is sure the learners (Italians learning English) are not familiar with or they signal that they do not understand:

You are to work in groups of four in order to create a fashion show – a show where people come to look at expensive designer clothes ... yes? [some students nodding] ... clothes worn by beautiful women and men ... that have been designed by someone famous ... and they walk up and down [all students nodding] ... okay a fashion show ... we all seem to understand what that is.... You have to do two things ... agree on a commentary for the show and write it out ... agree on a brochure ...

yes? ... a small booklet with illustrations ... pictures ... for the show. You can have some strange clothes or fussy clothes [blank looks] ... fussy clothes? Fussy here means, frilly ... over-elaborate [still blank looks]....

The bilingual teacher now has a choice: she can either keep trying to put across the meaning of 'fussy clothes' in English using paraphrases and contextualisations or she can give the Italian equivalent – *fronzolosi* or *con troppi fronzoli*. What to do?

What would happen in a naturalistic setting? If both interlocutors were bilingual, one speaker might switch the word anyway ('went to this fashion show last week, the clothes were awful, *troppi fronzoli*; I was really disappointed'). If the listener was a less balanced bilingual than the speaker, he might also switch ('Went to this fashion show last week. The clothes were really fussy, *troppi fronzoli*? [gap to await backchannel nod] ... Yeah, I was really disappointed'). So we can find in naturalistic CS switching for lexical items to aid comprehension. However, the bilingual teacher has a further bit of reasoning to perform. Does she simply give the precise Italian equivalent and move on? This would have fulfilled the communicative/comprehension part of her mission. But we have noted above that students are in L2 classrooms not only to communicate but also to learn. So is the teacher to suspend the information about the task and focus on the lexical item 'fussy' in order to convey its somewhat different meaning in this context?

Please note everyone ... this is a different meaning of 'fussy'.... We can say fussy about food, difficult about food, doesn't eat everything....

Does she additionally provide contrastive information in Italian – *molto esigente riguardo al cibo*, and so on?

It seems to me that both the actions related to comprehension and to learning may be justified according to the shared pedagogical perspective of the teacher and the students. In the case of comprehension, switching to the L1 might be justified if providing *troppi fronzoli* allows the task instructions, in the L2, to proceed such that the task can then take place. The switch has been used in order to support communication in the L2 from teacher to learners and subsequently (hopefully) L2 communication between learners.

In the case of 'learning' – that is, the acquisition of a new lexical item and its polysemous nature – there is a discussion to be had regarding whether this temporary 'lexical focus on form' (Laufer & Girsai, 2008) is merited. It would be merited if there is a shared perspective that a particular language task has a dual function: to develop speaking skills and to widen and enrich the mental lexicon.

The Impact of Codewitching on Comprehension and Lexical Acquisition

Studies of the impact of CS on comprehension and lexical acquisition are only just beginning to emerge (Lee & Macaro, forthcoming; Tian & Macaro, 2012), partly because it is difficult to establish what we mean by 'impact'. I am setting aside the notion of impact as a learner preference, learner satisfaction or motivation/engagement: I am specifically talking about impact on comprehension and impact on lexical acquisition.

Let us first take the case of impact on comprehension, where the research question might be 'Do learners more easily comprehend a new lexical item in the teacher's talk if that item is switched to the L1?' I presume that we would immediately mock this research question – 'Of course it is going to be more easily comprehended!' – and probably in 99% of cases we would be right. What about if the research question were 'To what extent is a stretch of teacher talk more easily comprehended if it contains some lexical switches for new or unfamiliar words?' Our mocking reaction might be a little more qualified now. There is considerable research on glossing for unknown words in written texts (although only a few have compared L2 and L1 glosses – see Jacobs *et al.*, 1994) and generally, though not exclusively, the findings suggest that glossing helps comprehension of the text as a whole. It might not help conclusively, because the glosses may not be those related to key words in the text or they may unnecessarily focus learners on words which they then believe are key words. Learners might then build up an erroneous picture of what the text is about. Since we have little direct evidence – to my knowledge, but see Guo (2007) for some insights – of the impact of teacher switching on comprehension of teacher discourse, the last research question may actually be well worth asking.

A research question regarding the impact of teacher switching on lexical acquisition has been 'Does a teacher switching to the L1 for new lexical items in his/her talk facilitate the acquisition of those items better than a paraphrase or definition in the L2?' Here the answers so far have been 'Yes … but'. Firstly, the 'but' is there because, in at least one study, the impact of L1 lexical information on L2 lexical information was clearly found at immediate post-test but was much less clear at delayed test (Tian & Macaro, 2012). Secondly, the 'but' has to be there because of the possible additional research question 'At what cost?' In other words, if the teacher constantly switches to the L1 to provide information about a new lexical item, it is possible that the learners stop using (or do not develop) their inferencing strategies. In some recent research we have carried out at Oxford with 13-year-old learners, we discovered to our consternation how limited

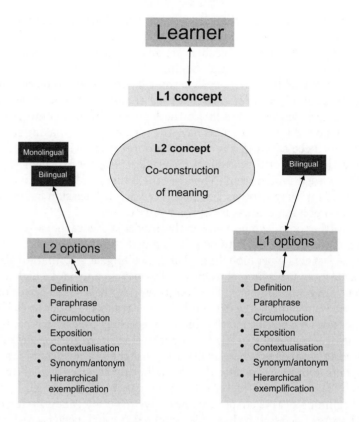

Figure 1 Teacher as dictionary and dictionary designer (Reproduced by kind permission of the publishers: Palgrave Macmillan)

their inferencing strategies were – their constant and only strategy was the 'cognateness' (they were English students studying French) of words in the teacher's L2 paraphrase. So, as in most things related to language teaching, switching to the L1 to provide information for new lexical items may be beneficial for one aspect of learning but it may come at a cost.

In previous writings (Macaro *et al.*, 2009) I have offered a model of the bilingual teacher not only as walking dictionary but also as dictionary designer (Figure 1). Monolingual teachers are able to operate as a walking monolingual dictionary, providing definitions, paraphrases, contextualisations, antonyms and so on. So, in a sense, they are not only a dictionary but also a dictionary designer in that they have to reflect on and select the kind of L2 information about a word which will make that word both understandable and learnable. Bilingual teachers are able to operate both as a walking monolingual dictionary and as a walking bilingual dictionary. In addition, they are a bilingual dictionary designer in that they have to reflect on and select both L2 and L1 information that they, thanks to their knowledge and experience, feel will be of benefit to the learners for both comprehension and acquisition. Bilingual teachers have the further task of making sure that they are not necessarily taking the easy option by providing L1 information, that the shortcut to learning is for real learning not expediency. In the example above, it would seem to me that the bilingual teacher providing L1 information for 'fussy clothes' has taken a principled decision based on the abstract and polysemous nature of the word 'fussy'.

One further point can be made on this model of the teacher as a bilingual dictionary designer. In order to be able to muster all the linguistic resources to provide learners with monolingual and/or bilingual information about a new lexical item, the bilingual teacher really does need to have a high level of proficiency in both languages. The literature that I have come across on the debate between bilingual versus monolingual teachers (Moussu & Llurda, 2008) does not suggest to me that bilingual teachers codeswitch because of low language proficiency in the L2. My intuition, from an overview of the data cited above and elsewhere, is that they 'use the L1' (note that we are not talking here about CS) because they are adopting an inter-lingual teaching approach. This brings us back to the initial two problems which I posited at the beginning of this chapter: what do we mean by codeswitching, and in what sorts of classrooms has codeswitching research been carried out?

Summary

In this opening chapter to what I hope will be a highly influential volume, I have tried to create some sort of theoretical framework for future CS research. I will now try to summarise this framework.

We can observe and document the phenomenon which we call L2 classroom CS:

- if the switching remains within similar grammatical constraints that we observe in naturalistic CS;
- if lexical information in L1 is balanced by L2 information;
- if the L2 is the predominant/matrix language in the interaction – that is, the grammar of the interaction is the L2;
- if the pedagogical objective of the lesson or part of the lesson is to teach/

facilitate communicative skills in the learners (communicative competence);

- if the focus on form (both lexical and morpho-syntactic) is kept at a level where it supports communication rather than overshadows communication;
- if the above interaction and pedagogical approach is sanctioned by all the participants in the classroom discourse.

Within this theoretical framework we can now begin to build a more coherent research agenda to answer research questions on classroom CS. I have hinted above what this agenda might include, but some further thoughts are presented here.

As discussed earlier, one of the often reported functions of CS is to convey the meaning of lexical items. The empirical question here, then, is whether some lexical focus on form using L1 information may be preferable to 'concept checks' using L2 definitions, as has been demonstrated to a limited extent by the research cited above. Further evidence is required to underscore this research and particularly on whether the benefits of CS for vocabulary acquisition apply regardless of variables in the population. For example, is CS beneficial to all age groups? Do young learners benefit more than adults from CS for lexical items? Do adults have more strategies for dealing with L2-only explanations? Is CS for the purposes of lexical explanation beneficial for all types of vocabulary, or is it the case that its benefits correlate with the abstractness of the word?

Linked to the exploration of CS for vocabulary are research questions regarding the teacher's ability to put across the meaning of new items using L2-only resources. We might usefully investigate how teachers differ in their attempts to paraphrase and contextualise new vocabulary in order for their students to understand them without CS. Is the success of their attempts linked to their depth of knowledge of the lexical item in question? Or, regardless of their depth of knowledge, is their success dependent on their level of experience, their ability to think creatively round a problem, their knowledge of the students in front of them, and so on?

Another often reported function of CS is to provide instructions for carrying out a task. Hypothetically, the switch might occur because the language needed for the instructions is perhaps above the level of the task itself, as in the fashion example above. This function can be investigated empirically and in relation to task-based learning literature which claims that it is the task itself that drives acquisition. Therefore any pedagogical activity which delays starting the task (e.g. negotiation of meaning for instructions for that task) might be counterproductive. So the research question might be 'Do brief switches in teacher instructions result in more student–student L2 interaction and, consequently, language development?' In this chapter I have focused almost exclusively on teacher CS. However, another item on the agenda might be related to learner CS in tasks. We need to ask whether some learner CS in tasks might in fact lead to greater acquisition or, more likely, greater fluency. The hypothesis here is that some learners might be more willing to communicate and take risks if they are not forbidden to use brief bursts of their L1. However, willingness to communicate, in my view, is a necessary but not a sufficient outcome. This research would need to measure whether, in the long term, being allowed to codeswitch in task leads to some form of development.

Concluding Remarks

Research on CS in L2 classrooms has mushroomed in recent years. This is to be welcomed because the debate on whether the L1 should be present in the L2 classroom is a matter which needs informed discussion among practitioners and policymakers alike. I have tried to indicate how that discussion could be better informed.

References

Cook, G. (2010) *Translation in Language Teaching: An Argument for Reassessment*. Oxford: Oxford University Press.

Cook, V.J. (1992) Evidence for multi-competence. *Language Learning* 42, 557–591.

Ferguson, G. (2003) Classroom codeswitching in post-colonial contexts: Functions, attitudes and policies. *AILA Review* 16, 38–51.

Guo, T. (2007) A case study of teachers' codeswitching behaviors in mainland China's university EFL classrooms and students' reactions to the code-switching. Unpublished doctoral dissertation, University of Oxford.

Jacobs, G.M., Dufon, P. and Hong, C.H. (1994) L1 and L2 vocabulary glosses in L2 reading passages: Their effectiveness for increasing comprehension and vocabulary knowledge. *Journal of Research in Reading* 17, 19–28.

Kharma, N.N. and Hajjaj, A.H. (1989) Use of the mother tongue in the ESL classroom. *International Review of Applied Linguistics* 26, 223–235.

Laufer, B. and Girsai, N. (2008) Form-focused instruction in second language vocabulary learning: A case for contrastive analysis and translation. *Applied Linguistics* 29, 1–23.

Lee, J-H. and Macaro, E. (2014) Investigating age of population as a factor when considering use of L1 or English only instruction. *Modern Language Journal*.

Levine, G. (2011) *Code Choice in the Language Classroom*. Bristol: Multilingual Matters.

Li Wei, L., Milroy, L. and Ching, P.S. (2000) A two-step sociolinguistic analysis of code-switching and language choice: The example of a bilingual community in Britain. In Li Wei (ed.) *The Bilingualism Reader* (pp. 188–219). London: Routledge.

Long, M. (1991) Focus on form: A design feature in language teaching methodology. In

K. de Bot, R. Ginsberg and C. Kramsch (eds) *Handbook of Second Language Acquisition* (pp. 39–52). San Diego, CA: Academic Press.

Macaro, E. (1997) *Target Language, Collaborative Learning and Autonomy*. Clevedon: Multilingual Matters.

Macaro, E. (2001) Analyzing students teachers' code-switching in foreign language classrooms: Theories and decision-making. *Modern Language Journal* 85 (4), 531–548.

Macaro, E., Guo, T., Chen, H. and Tian, L. (2009) Can differential processing of L2 vocabulary inform the debate on teacher code-switching behavior: The case of Chinese learners of English. In B. Richards, M.H. Daller, D.D. Malvern, P. Meara, J. Milton and J. Treffers-Daller (eds) *Vocabulary Studies in First and Second Language Acquisition: The Interface Between Theory and Application* (pp. 125–146). Basingstoke: Palgrave Macmillan.

Macaro, E., Nakatani, Y., Hayashi, Y. and Khabbazbashi, N. (2012) Exploring the value of bilingual language assistants with Japanese English as a foreign language learners. *Language Learning Journal*, 1–14. See www.tandfonline.com/doi/abs/10.1080/095717 36.2012.678275#.Ug4fqm2BX0w (accessed August 2013).

Moussu, L. and Llurda, E. (2008) Non-native English-speaking language teachers: History and research. *Language Teaching* 41, 315–348.

Myers-Scotton, C. (2001) The matrix language frame model: Developments and responses. In R. Jacobson (ed.) *Codeswitching Worldwide II* (pp. 23–58). Berlin: Mouton de Gruyter.

Raschka, C. , Sercombe, P. and Huang C-L. (2009) Conflicts and tensions in codeswitching in a Taiwanese EFL classroom. *International Journal of Bilingual Education and Bilingualism* 12 (2), 157–171.

Tian, L. and Macaro, E. (2012) Comparing the effect of teacher codeswitching with English-only explanations on the vocabulary acquisition of Chinese university students: A lexical focus-on-form study. *Language Teaching Research* 16 (3), 361–385.

Van Lier, L. (1996) *Interaction in the Language Curriculum: Awareness, Autonomy and Authenticity*. London: Longman.

1 Codeswitching in a University in Taiwan

Case Study: Ching-Yi Tien
Commentary: David C.S. Li

CASE STUDY

Introduction

The belief that 'English only' instruction is the most suitable medium-of-instruction policy in English as a foreign language (EFL) classrooms, has led educators, as well as educational policymakers, in Taiwan to emphasise the importance of the English-only teaching pedagogical methods in the language classroom. As a result, the combined use of mother tongues with the target language – codeswitching (CS) – is often viewed in a negative light. As a practitioner in Taiwanese classrooms for several years, I have observed the tension between the issue of 'English only' teaching and the supportive role that the learners' own language might actually play in the classroom. It is this tension which has prompted me to engage in reflective practice to explore the nature of classroom talk, focusing specifically on how I use more than one language to accomplish lesson objectives.

Over the past decade, the primary focus of the Ministry of Education's educational reform (Ministry of Education, 2003) has been the implementation of the grade 1–9 curriculum (a combination of elementary and junior high-school education) and higher education. Language planning with regard to the English language has been emphasised. Mandarin is taught from grades 1 to 9 and English is taught as a subject from grades 5 to 9. Taiwanese is an optional course in primary school and is taught for one hour per week. At high school and university levels, both Mandarin and English are compulsory courses; Taiwanese is not taught at all. In addition, the Ministry of Education has launched another new policy (Chern, 2010) requiring university students to reach a certain English proficiency level before graduation. Thus, in the upper echelons of the education system, English is the most significant language of instruction.

In line with the Ministry of Education's English policy, the university where I work has embarked on a new policy by which all students, prior to graduation, have to achieve at least a B1 level of proficiency in English according to the Common European Framework of Reference for Languages (CEFR; Council of Europe, 2008 – see the Appendix to this chapter).

Theoretical Orientation: Reflective Practice

Having been a teacher for more than 10 years, I often wonder whether my teaching really meets students' needs, or whether it is appropriate for each course I provide. This is particularly true when an English-only policy is applied. Such a policy is greatly emphasised in Taiwan, especially in the department where I work, so I decided to engage in reflective practice to explore the nature of classroom talk. I decided to focus specifically on how I can use more than one language to accomplish multiple lesson objectives.

Reflective practice, first introduced by Dewey in 1933, is defined as an 'active, persistent and careful consideration of any belief or support form of knowledge in the light of the grounds that support it and the further conclusions to which it tends' (Dewey, 1933: 118). This schema was later extended by Schön (1983), who distinguished between reflection-in-action and reflection-on-action. Reflective practice has been fashionable in the United States since the late 1970s and early 1980s but it fell out of favour in the late 1990s (Farrell, 2004). Nevertheless, it is still favoured and practised in the educational field in many countries (Ashraf & Rarieya, 2008; Leshem & Trafford, 2006; McGarr & Moody, 2010; Minott, 2011; Regan, 2007).

Although, according to Burton (2009), the term 'reflective practice' has sometimes been criticised for being merely a slogan, Finlay (2008: 2) stated that it 'carries multi-meanings that range from the idea of professionals engaging in solitary introspection to that of engaging in critical dialogue with others'. Simply put, it refers to practitioners who learn through, and from, their own teaching experience and gain new insights as a result. Larrivee and Cooper (2006: 4) have presented the following list of definitions of reflective practice over the past two decades. Reflective practice is:

- a dialogue of thinking and doing through which one becomes more skilled;
- a process that helps teachers think about what happened, why it happened, and what else could have been done to reach their goals;
- an enquiry approach that involves a personal commitment to continuous learning and improvement;

- the practice of analysing one's actions, decisions or products by focusing on one's process for achieving them;
- a critical, questioning orientation and a deep commitment to the discovery and analysis of information concerning the quality of a professional's judicious action;
- a willingness to accept responsibility for one's professional practice;
- a systematic and comprehensive data-gathering process enriched by dialogue and collaborative effort;
- the use of higher-level thinking, such as critical enquiry and meta-cognition, which allows one to move beyond a focus on isolated facts or data to perceive a broader context for understanding behaviour and events;
- the capacity to think creatively, imaginatively and, eventually, self-critically about classroom practice;
- an ongoing process of examining and refining practice, variously focused on the personal, pedagogical, curricular, intellectual, societal and/or ethical contexts associated with professional work.

The definitions provided in the list above show that reflection involves the need for perspicacious thinking about how a teacher engages in teaching through the skills of self-enquiry and critical thinking. For this study, to reflect on the course which I am most concerned with I have adopted Burton's (2009: 219) succinct investigative questions of reflective action, which are: 'What do I do?', 'How do I do it?' and 'What does this mean for me and those I work with and for?' Additionally, Richards (1998) proposed a range of reflective procedures, such as using autobiographies, reaction sheets, journals, language learning experience, audio- or video-recordings, when conducting research into self-reflection practices. For the present study, I used audio-recordings of my ordinary regular classes in order to explore the nature of classroom talk, focusing specifically on how I use more than one language to accomplish lesson objectives within classroom instruction.

Setting and Participants

This study was conducted during September 2011 in a linguistics class where the participants were mainly from the College of Language and Communication. I am a full-time lecturer who has taught English at several universities for 16 years. There were 76 student participants in this study (32 males and 44 females), most of them sophomores. They were from the Department of Applied English and were taking the course 'Introduction to

Linguistics', and each class lasted three hours. Apart from seven exchange students from mainland China, the participants were considered to be bilingual speakers of both Mandarin and Taiwanese. It should be noted that it is stipulated that all the courses offered by the Department of Applied English be taught exclusively in English, with the exception of courses related to translation.

Codeswitching in the Classroom: Findings

Three complete consecutive weekly classroom lessons for the 'Introduction to Linguistics' course were recorded and transcribed verbatim at the beginning of the semester in September 2011. Table 1.1 indicates the lecture time and the proportion of teacher talk in L1 and L2 for these lessons.

Extract 1 took place at the beginning of the first class. It is a school policy that every teacher has to explain the syllabus, especially regulations governing course requirements and assessment, to students at the beginning of the semester to help avoid any disputes arising. In this extract, the teacher greeted the students in English and started to explain the syllabus.

Table 1.1 Duration of teacher talk and percentage of teacher talk in L1 and L2 in three classroom lessons

Week	Length of lesson (min/s)	Length of teacher talk (min/s)	Total teacher talking time (%)	Teacher talk in L1 (min/s)	Teacher talk in L1 (%)	Teacher talk in L2 (min/s)	Teacher talk in L2 (%)
1	145'30"	103'55"	71.3%	6'38"	6.2%	97'17"	93.8%
2	148'02"	119'03"	80.4%	17'28"	14.5%	101'75"	85.5%
3	146'58"	107'43"	73.3%	33'08"	30.8%	74'35"	69.2%

Extract 1

01 T   This is a tentative schedule and it's subject to change if necessary. Do you have any questions? 有沒有問題？ *Do you have any questions?* 對這個 syllabus 有沒有問題？ *Regarding the syllabus, do you have any questions?* /// {no responses from the students} Okay, if you don't have any questions, I would like to start today's lecture. /// The first issue I would like to talk about is 'What is language'? Who would like to tell me what language is? /// Anyone? Chu, what do you think?

02 Chu 甚麼？ *What?* {The student looks puzzled and then turns to other students for help}
03 T   What is language? What is your definition of language?
04 S1   Speak.
05 S2   For communication. I think the way we talk to each other.
06 T   {The teacher is making the confirmation to S2.} So, you mean language is a tool for communication?
07 S2   Mm… {S2 nods his head}

In this extract, after introducing the course and explaining the syllabus (before and up to 01), I asked the students 'Do you have any questions?' in English first, and then switched to Mandarin in order to confirm whether or not the students had any questions about the syllabus. The CS here served two functions: to confirm whether students understood the teacher's message in English and to emphasise that students should pay attention to the syllabus. Since the language used in the classroom instruction should have been solely English, the student, Chu, should have responded to the teacher's question in English. Instead, he chose (02) to use Mandarin, 甚麼？ *What?*, and then to seek help from his classmates. In fact, most of the students (except S2) would normally use Mandarin (L1) instead of English (L2) in responding to the teacher, although they know it would be more appropriate for them to do so in English. A reason for this might be that students choose to use their first language (L1) as a 'safe' option, so as not to lose face in front of their peers. However, the case does not apply to S2 since S2 had lived abroad for more than 10 years and was more fluent in English than in Mandarin. Hence, whenever S2 was nominated, he normally spoke English in class as a matter of course. Although Chu was a senior student in the class, his oral English skill was not really commensurate with his level of study. It is likely, then, that a perceived lack of proficiency in English is one reason why Chu chose Mandarin to reply to the teacher's question.

The following extract happened in the third and final hour of the lecture for that class on that day.

Extract 2

01 T   Three types of grammar are introduced in this chapter: descriptive grammar, prescriptive grammar, and teaching grammar.… {The teacher continues to explain the definitions of the three types of grammar in English.} 所以簡單來說 descriptive grammar 就是我們一般所知道的文法。 Prescriptive grammar 就是由文法家所制定的文法。 teaching grammar 就是老師在教室中所教授的文法。這

樣了解了嗎？ *Simply speaking, descriptive grammar is the grammar we know; prescriptive grammar is prescribed by the grammarian; teaching grammar is the grammar a teacher taught in the class. Do you understand?* Do you have any questions? Can you differentiate between the different types of grammar? 知不知道如何分辨這三種不一樣的文法？ *Do you know how to differentiate between these three types of grammar?*

After the long explanation of the three types of grammar in English, I then switched to Mandarin and said: 所以簡單來說 descriptive grammar 就是我們一般所知道的文法。 Prescriptive grammar 就是由文法家所制定的文法。 teaching grammar 就是老師在教室中所教授的文法。這樣了解了嗎？ *Do you understand?* I intended to use Mandarin in order to explain the three types of grammar for the sake of the students' overall comprehension. It is worth pointing out that I did not translate the metalinguistic terms 'descriptive grammar', 'prescriptive grammar' and 'teaching grammar' into Mandarin, primarily because I wanted the students to become familiar with those terms in English directly (and also I could not think of the appropriate Mandarin terms at that time!). It is interesting to note that similar examples occurred on many occasions in the course of the lesson, as in Extract 3.

Extract 3

01 T   According to the book, there are two kinds of aphasias, Broca's aphasia and Wernicke's aphasia. Broca's aphasia 就是如果腦部 Broca area 有受傷對語言所造成的失語現象 *Broca's aphasia is the phenomenon where the Broca's area of the brain has damage that causes loss of language* 。 同樣的， Wernicke's aphasia 就是如果腦部 Wernicke area 有受傷對語言所造成的失語現象…. *Equally, Wernicke's aphasia is the phenomenon where Wernicke's area of the brain has damage that causes loss of language.*

The final extract is from a lesson in the third week. At the beginning of the lesson, I used mainly Mandarin. An example is provided below.

Extract 4

01 T   Good afternoon. // Well, are you ready for the pop quiz? Did you check the blackboard before the class?

02 Ss   No.

03 T   Good. 我之前就告訴過你們會不定時有 pop quiz 。我特別在昨天還在 BB
        上公告說今天會有 pop quiz 。你們果然沒有看。 *I mentioned to you all*
        before that I may have pop quiz some time in this course. I particularly
        made an announcement on the BB yesterday to indicate that there will
        be a pop quiz today. Not surprising to me at all, you didn't check it.
04 S1   老師，在哪裡看？ *Teacher, where can we check that?*
05 T   在 BB 阿。 *On BB.* I made an announcement on the blackboard.
        You should check it from time to time, especially the day before
        the class. I may have some announcement. Anyway, take
        out a piece of paper. Write down your name and student ID
        number. /// 趕快拿出紙來，寫下姓名及學號。 *Hurry up! Take out a*
        piece of paper and write down your name and student ID number. ///
        Question 1, what's Noam Chomsky's famous theory in this
        chapter?

In this extract, after the greeting in English (01), I purposely used
Mandarin (03) to banter with the students about how they had not paid
attention to my previous reminders regarding the quiz policy. The use
of Mandarin enabled me, more easily than would have been possible in
English, to express my disappointment in a jocular manner. The reason
why S1 employed Mandarin (04) instead of English was possibly that the
teacher initiated the question in Mandarin and the student simply chose
to follow out of courtesy. I briefly responded in Mandarin (05) and then
switched back to English when emphasising that students should pay more
attention to course-related matters. The reason I did so was to focus on
English as the medium of instruction after the previous informality and also
to demonstrate my authority position in the classroom. Even so, I switched
back to Mandarin in the same turn.

Reflection

I carried out this study as an exercise in reflective practice to examine
my own educational practice. I was interested in finding out whether I was
able to deliver the lecture by using English-only instruction; or, if not, why
and how frequently I codeswitched. After re-examining the audio data,
I found that CS between English and Mandarin in the content course is
multifunctional in nature. It is used for explaining linguistic terms (e.g.
Lin, 1990, 1996; Macaro, 2003, 2009; Tien, 2004, 2009), confirmation,
emphasis, dealing with unknown equivalent lexical items (e.g. Li, 2010), out
of concern for rapport and solidarity in the classroom (e.g. Martin, 2003a,
2003b), expressing my emotional feelings, and symbolically asserting my

authority. As this was a linguistics content course rather than an English language skills course, the usually common function of using CS to explain grammatical points was not found in the study.

Yet I was still caught in the dilemma of not meeting the departmental requirement, which is to use English-medium instruction only, and the adoption of the learners' mother tongue, which produces better teaching and learning outcomes. Since English is the lingua franca in the Taiwanese educational context, if CS is proven to be a better pedagogical approach for purposes of classroom instruction, it should not be overlooked or dismissed as a restricted basilect. Some teachers treat CS merely as translation or a shortcut, particularly in language skills teaching and learning. For communicative effectiveness, Jenkins (2010) points out that non-native English speakers codeswitch to promote solidarity with their interlocutors and to ensure comprehensibility of the message. Therefore, for courses such as 'Introduction to Linguistics', the content of which makes many of my Taiwanese students anxious, I believe that the appropriate use of CS does help students understand the content of the course and also reduces the students' fear of English-only instruction. At this stage, not all the students have reached the CEFR B1, which is their requirement for graduation, as noted above (see also Appendix).

To find out my students' views towards the use of their L1 and CS in my linguistics class, I asked them some questions at the end of that semester. The majority responded that they thought L1 was very helpful not only to unpack the technical meanings of linguistic concepts in the textbook and to make the lesson more comprehensible, but also to build up their confidence in passing the course. Some students even indicated that they were, in fact, quite worried when lessons were conducted only in English. Such feedback calls to mind Macaro's distinction in the Overview chapter of this book between 'maximal' and 'optimal' positions. One of the foreign teachers in our department once complained to me that after spending three hours explaining the concept of marked as opposed to unmarked forms to his linguistics class, his students continued to be unsure about what he meant. With my students, on the same topic, it took me only 30 minutes to explicate and illustrate that dichotomy with the help of my students' L1. This shows that CS indeed does have tremendous potential to facilitate the give-and-take in content lectures and to achieve the students' learning outcomes more effectively.

After re-examining the data several times, I was surprised to find that I had increased my personal use of the L1 from 6% to 31% of the content words over the three lessons. Although I had good intentions in using L1 to accomplish the lessons' objectives in terms of transmitting content, and

I strongly believed the L1 could be supportive in certain ways, I should have also kept in mind the stated departmental English-only policy and minimised my use of L1 in the classroom. I also found that students used more Mandarin in responding to my questions than using English. I assume that most students did not want to embarrass themselves by not knowing how to answer correctly in English due to a lack of linguistic competence. Further, though, I sometimes prompted the students to use L1 for the sake of expediency, regardless of their demonstrated proficiency. The more I looked at the data, the more I reflected on the importance of how much I should use the languages (English and Mandarin) in a more systematic way, not only to deliver the lecture 'optimally' (Macaro, 2009) but also to pay more attention to the students' use of the target language. I reflected that I should be in a position to help them both to understand the lecture and to enhance their target language and communicative competence.

Burton (2009: 216) remarks, 'being reflective assists teachers' lifelong professional development, enabling them to critique teaching and make better-informed teaching decisions'. The utilisation of reflective practices in this study has indeed greatly helped me to learn insightfully through my own teaching experience and to gain new perspectives to consider my future teaching efforts.

COMMENTARY

Tien's reflections and classroom CS data at a Taiwanese university epitomise the bilingual teacher's dilemma regarding how to strike a balance between adhering to an English-only instruction policy from above, and the need to ensure her students' understanding and to monitor their learning outcomes. The top-down 'English-only' classroom language policy is premised on the assumption that, class time being limited and precious, any verbal exchange in the instructor and students' shared L1 for whatever reasons will mean less exposure to the target language. Such an assumption is especially widespread in societies where English is used as a foreign language and where local people rarely use English for intra-ethnic communication. This is clearly the case of Taiwan, but it is also true of Hong Kong, albeit to a lesser extent (Li, 2009; Poon, 2010).

In Extract 1, Tien reports switching to Mandarin to monitor her students' understanding of her previous question raised in English, even though no vocabulary problems are in evidence: 'Do you have any questions [about the syllabus]¿' Reflecting on the most likely reason why she switched to Mandarin there, she believes it was out of a concern for ensuring that students who were less proficient in English would understand that question, and be ready to interact with her in Mandarin, their shared ethnic language. Even though both Tien and her students were conscious of the 'English-only' classroom language policy, her switch to Mandarin suggests, symbolically and implicitly, that asking questions in Mandarin would be quite acceptable. This is probably why, even though Tien's question directed to the student (named Chu) was in English – 'Anyone¿ Chu, what do you think¿' – Chu uttered spontaneously in Mandarin: *Shenme¿* ('What¿'). From a conversation analysis perspective (Li, 1994), Chu's code choice could be interpreted as signalling 'dispreference' or reluctance to answer the teacher's question. This is non-verbally supported by his bewilderment (i.e. Chu looks puzzled). Interestingly, of Tien's two questions in Mandarin in turn 01, Extract 1, the second contains the English word *syllabus*. We will come back to this below as an instructive illustration of intra-sentential (as opposed to inter-sentential) CS.

Extracts 2 and 3 have one thing in common: Tien is eager to use Mandarin to unpack the fine and somewhat technical distinction between the three types of grammar (Extract 2) and the two types of aphasia (Extract 3). The function of CS from English to Mandarin here corresponds with the classic case in like circumstances, namely, to use the language that students are more familiar with to explain difficult concepts and to ensure that, relative to the goal of grasping content knowledge at hand, no students would be cognitively 'shut off' by English (compare Lin's 2000 study of Cantonese–English mixed code in Hong Kong). Although no ancillary evidence is provided suggesting students' possible lack of understanding (e.g. in a video-recorded lesson, students' puzzling facial expressions would constitute strong supporting evidence), Tien's code choice or decision to codeswitch to Mandarin might have been triggered by visible signs of some students not being able to cope or getting lost. As a teacher with extensive experience lecturing in English to Cantonese-dominant students in Hong Kong myself, I frequently find myself having to make similar moment-by-moment decisions to codeswitch (to Cantonese) in response to questioning looks on my students' faces. This is especially common if the content of the lesson involves abstract concepts, where sometimes no amount of scaffolding is enough to make them cognitively accessible in plain English, not to mention the challenge of accomplishing this within a tight timeframe. Though unplanned, CS (to Mandarin in Tien's case and to Cantonese in mine) may be regarded as one natural consequence of such challenging teaching situations, which often helps keep students on task – students who otherwise would mentally 'shut off' after getting lost in that alien tongue, whatever the message. Such a concern is especially acute where young students' attention span today is known to be short. Cracking difficult concepts by CS to a language familiar to students is thus one pedagogically sound strategy at the disposal of skilful bilingual teachers to maintain such students' attention and to sustain their interest and motivation.

Extract 4 also contains several instances of CS, from English (E) to Mandarin (M), and from Mandarin back to English, schematically as follows:

Turn 01	T	E
Turn 02	Ss	E
Turn 03	T	E/M
Turn 04	S1	M
Turn 05	T	M/E/M/E

The function or motivation of CS in Extract 4 is rather different. Unlike Extracts 1–3, where a switch to Mandarin is arguably driven by the 'referential function' (Chen, 2003), in Extract 4 the switch is motivated by other concerns. As Tien explains, switching to Mandarin in turn 03 allowed her to express her 'disappointment in a jocular manner'. How is it possible? The key here is that using or switching to a shared (first) language is a simple way to index speaker identity symbolically and such other subtle but highly conspicuous interactional meanings as 'shared group membership' and 'rapport cum in-group solidarity'. Switching to Mandarin to deliver those 'harsh' words with immediate punitive consequence (doing the pop quiz) allows Tien to tone down the forcefulness of her reprimand considerably – something that could not be accomplished in English, which would have foregrounded and reinforced the teacher's authority symbolically. In other words, by using the 'we code' (Mandarin) rather than the institutionally required 'they code' (English), the teacher appeals to solidarity and rapport, and plays down her authority as the teacher. Incidentally, the switch back from Mandarin to English in turn 05 (ending with 'take out a piece of paper. Write down your name and student ID number') coincides with directing students' attention 'to course-related matters' and, as such, offers an instructive illustration how English helps reinforce the teacher's authority, albeit symbolically. Interestingly, this last instruction is repeated immediately in Mandarin, suggesting a tension or mental struggle between asserting teacher authority (by using English) and displaying rapport and solidarity (by using Mandarin). Turn 05 ends with Tien enacting her role as teacher by dictating the first question in English ('Question 1, what's Noam Chomsky's famous theory in this chapter?'). Apart from showing that code choice is semantically meaningful, Tien's examples and reflections suggest that CS is not at all random and that, if used judiciously, is a pedagogically sound and productive teaching strategy.

As for theoretical import, Tien's CS data lend support to Li's (2011) 'medium-of-learning effect' hypothesis. First, there is asymmetry in her data: English utterances are free from Mandarin (i.e. no need to switch to Mandarin), while her Mandarin utterances frequently involve English expressions of various lengths (or fragments). The latter results in intra-sentential CS. In summary, the English 'fragments' in Tien's utterances in (otherwise pure) Mandarin occur as follows:

Extract 1 syllabus;
Extract 2 descriptive grammar/prescriptive grammar/teaching grammar;
Extract 3 Broca's aphasia/Broca area/Wernicke's aphasia/Wernicke area;
Extract 4 pop quiz/BB [blackboard].

It can be seen that all of these English fragments in Tien's Mandarin utterances are either linguistic or school jargon. This is consistent with Li's (2011) findings in his study of CS in Hong Kong and Taiwan:

> the use of English as the medium of teaching and learning is one important factor behind Chinese–English CS in Hong Kong, and to a lesser extent in Taiwan. A substantial part of English lexical items that occur in Chinese–English CS in Hong Kong and Taiwan are technical terms or academic jargon taught or introduced to students in English, resulting in cognitive salience with regard to the relative ease with which cognitive retrieval of these terms takes place. This psycholinguistic CS motivation … is clearly a consequence of the medium of learning, hence the 'medium-of-learning effect'. (Li, 2011: 233)

A similar 'medium-of-learning effect' hypothesis is in evidence in Chen's (2003) discussion of the 'referential function' of code-switching in Taiwan:

> Chinese people in Taiwan study most academic subjects in higher education using English textbooks. They therefore may be more familiar with academic or technical terms in English than in Chinese. In addition, the Chinese translations in those registers are not always consistent; the same English word may have different Chinese translations which affects communication. These experiences contribute to using code-switching for this referential function. (Chen, 2003: 135)

In the 'Reflection' section, Tien expresses a concern for being caught in a dilemma: on the one hand, 'meeting the departmental requirement, which is to use English-medium of instruction only', and, on the other, 'the adoption of the learners' mother tongue, which produces better teaching and learning outcomes'. She seems to be blaming herself for not being able to follow the English-only mode of teaching and learning. I think such a guilty feeling is unnecessary. A more productive way forward would be to investigate, as she has done in this chapter, the types of circumstances that lead to CS, and the pedagogical import and impact of CS on students' learning. Rather than agonising for compromising the English-only classroom language policy that could not be helped, if CS is shown to be inevitable and ubiquitous in English content lessons (e.g. Tien's observable increase in the percentage of Mandarin content words from 6% to 31% over three lessons), it is imperative that we gain a better understanding of the multifarious reasons why CS is so irresistible and difficult to avoid in English content lessons, by researching best practices in terms of how it facilitates teaching and learning and enhances the quality of give-and-take in the classroom.

As a first approximation, based on Tien's CS data, some of the commonly encountered circumstances in which a bilingual Taiwanese teacher might want to switch to Mandarin in the middle of an English content lesson would include the following:

(1) Low English proficiency makes it difficult for students to listen to lectures and follow instructions entirely in English. This is especially true in the case of teaching abstract concepts in an English content lesson (e.g. the 'Introduction to Linguistics' course). Switching to Mandarin helps allay such students' fear and anxiety, and makes the content more accessible to them.

(2) Low-proficiency students prefer to use Mandarin in their inter-action with the teacher or with peers because they want to avoid losing face in front of their interlocutors. Here, students' L1 has a place in English (L2) content lessons, in that it is an important resource for less proficient students to (double) check their understanding of L2 content (Cook, 2002).

(3) Depending on the classroom function (e.g. reprimanding students, maintaining discipline, showing the teacher's care or concern to individual students), switching to the students' L1 is a simple way to index speaker identity and/or display rapport and in-group solidarity; conversely, keeping to English could be communicatively less effective, or even counterproductive, if the interactional goal is showing solidarity, or rapport, or individual concern, for the teacher would likely be heard as reinforcing his/her authority.

As shown in Tien's reflections, English–Mandarin CS is peda-gogically conducive to teaching and learning in many ways. The supportive role of L1 in English-medium classes is insufficiently recognised by language policymakers at the national and/or institutional level. There is a widespread but misguided belief that CS to the students' L1, including in informal social interactions, is symptomatic of a malaise, namely the mixed-code users' inability to interact in the target language (here, English). The supportive nature and functions of classroom CS remain inadequately understood.

As Tien has made clear with reference to Macaro's distinction between 'maximal' and 'optimal' positions, classroom CS has the potential to facilitate the unpacking of abstract and technical constructs such as the marked/unmarked dichotomy. Such a cognitive challenge goes way beyond CS being triggered by lexical items which are unfamiliar or unknown to teacher and/or students, even though 'lexical gap' has been attested to be one important factor triggering classroom CS (cf. Macaro's Overview of this volume). What is expected of a resourceful teacher here is careful deconstruction of one or two relevant linguistic examples to help students conceptualise that somewhat abstract technical distinction. To students who are coping with both cognitive *and* linguistic complexities, as in the case of students taking content courses in English, the give-and-take can take place more efficiently if the lecturer has the option of switching to the students' L1. Tien's comparison is indicative of a trend: whereas the meaning of the marked/unmarked dichotomy continued to elude the students of linguistics after their English-only lecturer had tried to 'crack the code' in three hours, Tien, with the help of CS, was able to make clear that dichotomy to her linguistics class within about 30 minutes. The advantage of CS seems obvious from a pedagogical point of view.

Apart from the reflective approach using self-report data, other research methods may be used to better understand the motivations of context-specific CS in the classroom and beyond (compare Li & Tse, 2002; Lin, 2000). So long as CS to students' first language is empirically shown to be pedagogically sound and effective under a broad array of circumstances, the English-only classroom language policy should be relaxed or revised. The last thing the university management wants is for teachers to feel bad or embarrassed for breaching a university regulation that is difficult (if not impossible) to adhere to, or one that can be achieved only at the expense of pedagogical soundness and learning outcomes. In this light, Tien might want to explore the possibility of teaming up with other like-minded colleagues to conduct theoretically informed empirical research on classroom CS, with a view to uncovering a broad range of best practices involving Mandarin–English CS. However well intentioned, a dogmatic English-only classroom language policy which does teachers and students more harm than good should give way to empirically tested, pedagogically sound practices of classroom CS, in Taiwan as elsewhere.

Like those of its East Asian neighbours, the education authorities in Taiwan are very eager to enhance university students' competitiveness by helping them improve their English. However, a quick-fix approach such as the English-only classroom language policy is counterproductive; far from being a catalyst for better English, such a policy stifles learning among students whose English is not strong enough to benefit from English-only instruction. Research in sociolinguistics and classroom CS suggests that, if implemented dogmatically, such a classroom language policy is detrimental to teaching effectiveness and learning outcomes. The education authorities in Taiwan would be wise to rethink whether the English-only classroom language policy is practicable and desirable, and to support 'best practices' research into CS involving any of the local languages, including English.

References

Ashraf, H. and Rarieya, J.F.A. (2008) Teacher development through reflective conversations – possibilities and tension: A Pakistan case. *Reflective Practice* 9 (3), 269–279.

Burton, J. (2009) Reflective practice. In A. Burns and J.C. Richards (eds) *Cambridge Guide to Second Language Teacher Education* (pp. 298–307). Cambridge: Cambridge University Press.

Chen, S.C. (2003) *The Spread of English in Taiwan: Changing Uses and Shifting Attitudes.* Taipei: Crane Publishing.

Chern, C.L. (2010) General English programs at universities in Taiwan: Curriculum design and implementations. *Chang Gung Journal of Humanities and Social Sciences* 3 (2), 253–274.

Cook, V.J. (2002) Language teaching methodology and the L2-user perspective. In V.J. Cook (ed.) *Portraits of the L2-User* (pp. 327–343). Clevedon: Multilingual Matters.

Council of Europe (2011) The Common European Framework of Reference for Languages (CEFR). See https://wcd.coe.int/ViewDoc.jsp?id=1279435 (accessed November 2011).

Dewey, J. (1933) *How We Think*. Buffalo, NY: Prometheus Books.

Farrell, T.S.C. (2004) *Reflective Practice in Action: 80 Reflection Breaks for Busy Teachers*. Thousand Oaks, CA: Corwin.

Finlay, L. (2008) *Reflecting on 'Reflective Practice'*. PBPL Paper 52, CETL. Milton Keynes: Open University.

Jenkins, J. (2010) Accommodating (to) ELF in the international university. *Journal of Pragmatics* 43 (4), 926–936.

Larrivee, B. and Cooper, J.M. (2006) *An Educator's Guide to Teacher Reflection*. Boston, MA: Houghton Mifflin.

Leshem, S. and Trafford, V.N. (2006) Stories as mirrors: Reflective practice in teaching and learning. *Reflective Practice* 7 (1), 9–27.

Li, D.C.S. (2009) Towards 'biliteracy and trilingualism' in Hong Kong (SAR): Problems, dilemmas and stakeholders' views. *AILA Review* 22, 72–84.

Li, D.C.S. (2010) Medium-of-instruction-induced code-switching: Evidence from Hong Kong SAR and Taiwan. Paper presented at the 15th English in South East Asia (ESEA 2010) Conference, University of Macau.

Li, D.C.S. (2011) Lexical gap, semantic incongruence, and medium-of-instruction-induced code-switching: Evidence from Hong Kong and Taiwan. In E.A. Anchimbe and S.A. Mforteh (eds) *Postcolonial Linguistic Voices: Identity Choices and Representations* (pp. 215–240). Berlin: Mouton de Gruyter.

Li, D.C.S. and Tse, E.C.Y. (2002) One day in the life of a 'purist'. *International Journal of Bilingualism* 6 (2), 147–202.

Li, W. (1994) *Three Generations, Two Languages, One Family: Language Choice and Language Shift in a Chinese Community in Britain*. Clevedon: Multilingual Matters.

Lin, A.M.Y. (1990) *Teaching in Two Tongues: Language Alternation in Foreign Language Classrooms*. Hong Kong: City Polytechnic of Hong Kong.

Lin, A.M.Y. (1996) Bilingualism or linguistic segregation? Symbolic domination, resistance and code switching in Hong Kong schools. *Linguistics and Education* 8, 49–84.

Lin, A.M.Y. (2000) Deconstructing mixed code. In D.C.S. Li, A.M.Y. Lin and W.K. Tsang (eds) *Language and Education in Postcolonial Hong Kong* (pp. 179–194). Hong Kong: Linguistic Society of Hong Kong.

Macaro, E. (2003) *Teaching and Learning a Second Language: A Guide to Current Research and Its Applications*. London: Continuum.

Macaro, E. (2009) Teacher codeswitching in L2 classrooms: Exploring 'optimal use'. In T. Yoshida, H. Imai, Y. Nakata, A. Tajino, O. Takeuchi and K. Tamei (eds) *Researching Language Teaching and Learning: An Integration of Practice and Theory* (pp. 293–304). Frankfurt-am-Main: Peter Lang.

Martin, P.W. (2003a) Interactions and inter-relationships around text: Practices and positioning in a multilingual classroom in Brunei. *International Journal of Bilingual Education and Bilingualism* 6 (3–4), 185–201.

Martin, P.W. (2003b) Bilingual encounters in the classroom. In J-M. Dewaele, A. Housen and Li Wei (eds) *Bilingualism: Beyond Basic Principles* (pp. 67–87). Clevedon: Multilingual Matters.

McGarr, O. and Moody, J. (2010) Scaffolding or stifling? The influence of journal requirements on students' engagement in reflective practice. *Reflective Practice* 11 (5), 579–591.

Ministry of Education (MOE) (Taiwan) (2003) *General Guidelines of English Curriculum of High School Education.* See http://hrd.apec.org/images/4/43/47.3.pdf (accessed September 2013).

Minott, M.A. (2011) Reflective teaching, critical literacy and the teacher's tasks in the critical literacy classroom. A confirmatory investigation. *Reflective Practice* 12 (1), 73–85.

Poon, A.Y.K. (2010) Language use, and language policy and planning in Hong Kong. *Current Issues in Language Planning* 11 (1), 1–66.

Regan, P. (2007) Interpreting language used in reflective practice. *Reflective Practice* 8 (1), 109–122.

Richards, J.C. (1998) *Beyond Training: Perspectives on Language Teacher Education.* Cambridge: Cambridge University Press.

Schön, D. (1983) *The Reflective Practitioner.* New York: Basic Books.

Tien, C.Y. (2004) Code-switching in two freshman English classrooms in a university in southern Taiwan. Unpublished PhD thesis, University of Leicester.

Tien, C.Y. (2009) Conflict and accommodation in classroom code-switching in Taiwan. *International Journal of Bilingual Education and Bilingualism* 12 (2), 173–192.

Appendix. Common European Framework of Reference: Learning, Teaching, Assessment

Global Scale

Proficient user	C2	Can understand with ease virtually everything heard or read. Can summarise information from different spoken and written sources, reconstructing arguments and accounts in a coherent presentation. Can express him/herself spontaneously, very fluently and precisely, differentiating finer shades of meaning even in more complex situations.
	C1	Can understand a wide range of demanding, longer texts, and recognise implicit meaning. Can express him/herself fluently and spontaneously without much obvious searching for expressions. Can use language flexibly and effectively for social, academic and professional purposes. Can produce clear, well-structured, detailed text on complex subjects, showing controlled use of organisational patterns, connectors and cohesive devices.

Independent user	B2	Can understand the main ideas of complex text on both concrete and abstract topics, including technical discussions in his/her field of specialisation. Can interact with a degree of fluency and spontaneity that makes regular interaction with native speakers quite possible without strain for either party. Can produce clear, detailed text on a wide range of subjects and explain a viewpoint on a topical issue giving the advantages and disadvantages of various options.
	B1	Can understand the main points of clear standard input on familiar matters regularly encountered in work, school, leisure, etc. Can deal with most situations likely to arise whilst travelling in an area where the language is spoken. Can produce simple connected text on topics which are familiar or of personal interest. Can describe experiences and events, dreams, hopes & ambitions and briefly give reasons and explanations for opinions and plans.
Basic user	A2	Can understand sentences and frequently used expressions related to areas of most immediate relevance (e.g. very basic personal and family information, shopping, local geography, employment). Can communicate in simple and routine tasks requiring a simple and direct exchange of information on familiar and routine matters. Can describe in simple terms aspects of his/her background, immediate environment and matters in areas of immediate need.
	A1	Can understand and use familiar everyday expressions and very basic phrases aimed at the satisfaction of needs of a concrete type. Can introduce him/herself and others and can ask and answer questions about personal details such as where he/she lives, people he/she knows and things he/she has. Can interact in a simple way provided the other person talks slowly and clearly and is prepared to help.

Source: http://www.coe.int/t/dg4/education/elp/elp-reg/Source/Key_reference/Overview_CEFRscales_EN.pdf.

2 Codeswitching in Two Chinese Universities

Case Study: Lili Tian
Commentary: Claudia Kunschak

CASE STUDY

Introduction

Teachers' use of codeswitching (CS) in second language classrooms has been widely researched in various contexts. This case study reports on CS use in two English language classes in a Chinese university. The extent and functions of CS will be examined, together with teachers' comments on the reasons for their CS.

For Chinese learners of English at university level, English study is compulsory, in terms of both institutional requirements and personal needs. The College English Test plays a significant role as an English proficiency criterion for employers at all levels to recruit university graduates. Most universities currently offer both English language skills courses and English courses for specific purposes such as Business English, Journalism English, Tourism English and so on.

Requirements for English language teachers are also demanding in terms of classroom language use. The prevailing belief among teachers, students and assessors for English language lessons in Chinese universities is that English teachers should use as much target language as possible in their classroom and students should be encouraged to use as much target language as they can (Gao & Dai, 2007). A greater use of the mother tongue is believed to reflect a lack of proficiency among teachers in the target language. It is an underlying perception that the more teachers use the Chinese language, the less competent and qualified they are as English teachers at university level. However, guidelines for classroom language use are absent in the College English Curriculum Requirements issued by the Chinese Ministry of Education (2007).

Theoretical Framework

The observational data in the present study were analysed in two ways: firstly, by a quantitative examination of the extent of CS in the two classrooms, and then by a consideration of the pedagogic functions for which the two teachers used the first language. The categories for the latter analysis were derived from the data by a grounded analysis. The teachers were each individually given semi-structured interviews to elicit the rationale for their use of CS in the classes observed. The interviews were conducted in Chinese, the mother tongue of the two teachers, for the sake of clearer expression of the issues.

Before proceeding further, it may be useful to provide a brief introduction to the Chinese language. Mandarin Chinese (or *Putonghua*) is the official language of the People's Republic of China. As a non-alphabetic language, Chinese has many differences from English. Each Chinese character (or *Hanzi*) comprises a variable number of interwoven strokes within an imaginary rectangular block. Visually each written Chinese character is of similar length. Aurally each character is also of similar length. The Chinese phonetic transcription system (or *hanyu pinyin*) uses the letters of the Roman alphabet with diacritics for tones to represent the phonology of Standard Chinese. Each Chinese character is pronounced as one syllable that is normally made up with one consonant (the initial) and one vowel (the final), plus a tone.

A Chinese word does not resemble the notion of an English word, which is another major difference between the two languages. Although a character in Chinese is monosyllabic, a word may be polysyllabic, depending on how many characters are required in that word. Each *hanzi* represents a monosyllabic morpheme, that is, the *hanzi* maps onto language at the morpheme level and onto spoken language at the syllable level (Bassetti, 2009: 758). Chinese lexical items or words (or *Ci*) can be mono- or polymorphemic; in written Chinese they are correspondingly mono- or multi-*hanzi*. For instance, 爱 means love, and 爱人 means spouse (Bassetti, 2005: 339).

The Setting

This case study comprises lessons from two teachers in a prestigious university in Beijing. The university ranks among the top 15 universities in mainland China. Like other universities in China, its English teaching for non-English majors also covers both language skill courses and advanced content courses for specific purposes. The two teachers, Ring and Jeng (pseudonyms), from the two different types of English courses, volunteered to participate in the project. They both have masters degrees in English and doctoral degrees in literature and journalism respectively, and both have over 10 years' teaching experience. Ring teaches Intensive English Reading, one of the English language skill courses, while Jeng teaches Journalism English, one of the advanced content courses for specific purposes.

The lessons from the two teachers were video-taped. Ring's Intensive Reading lesson was on how to cultivate Emotional Quotient (EQ), and lasted 127 minutes. Jeng's lesson on American television was 90 minutes long. All the lessons are of a communicative nature. Each lesson involves about 30 first-year non-English-major undergraduates ranging in age from 18 to 22. Timed analysis (Macaro, 2001) was employed to examine the amount of L1 and L2 use in the classroom. The video was stopped every five seconds to record the language type being used by the teacher. In addition, functional analysis was conducted to explore the reasons and functions of CS use. The amount of L1 use in different types of functions was collected by counting the number of Chinese characters in each function. As a Chinese word may comprise more than one character, counting the number of characters rather than words for each CS episode was considered appropriate for this study to examine the frequency distribution of CS use. A brief interview in Chinese was carried out with the two teachers after their lessons to further explore their reasons for CS use.

Findings

Timed analysis

Table 2.1 reports the amount of teacher talk in different languages calculated by timed analysis.

During the 127'08" of Ring's lesson time, total teacher talk occupied 79.2%. During the 100'07" of total teacher talk in her lesson, she talked in the target language most of the time (90.5%) and spent only 9'06" (9.5%) in

Table 2.1 The amount of teacher talk

Teacher	Length of lesson (min/s)	Length of teacher talk (min/s)	Total teacher talking time (%)	Teacher talk in L1 (min/s)	Teacher talk in L1 (%)	Teacher talk in L2 (min/s)	Teacher talk in L2 (%)
Ring	127'08"	100'07"	79.2%	9'06"	9.5%	91'10"	90.5%
Jeng	90'00"	66'05"	73.4%	7'30"	11.1%	58'35"	88.9%

switching from English to the students' mother tongue, Chinese. Similarly, Jeng also talked most of the time (73.4%) during her lesson, 88.9% of which was in target language, English. She spent only 11.1% of her total talk switching to Chinese. On the whole, an average of 10% CS was used by both teachers during their total teacher talk and an average of 7.9% CS during their total lesson time.

Analysis of CS functions

A further linguistic analysis of the CS episodes during the two lessons was conducted to explore the different functions of CS use. Table 2.2 shows different types of CS functions identified in this study. Both teachers switched to Chinese to provide Chinese equivalents for English words, or to provide English ones for Chinese words, to explain grammar or vocabulary, to give information and to make personal comments. The number of Chinese characters was then counted in order to calculate the percentage of CS distribution across the different functions (see Table 2.3).

Table 2.2 Different functions of teachers' CS use

CS functions	Definitions	Examples
Translation L2–L1	L2 words/phrases/sentences + L1 equivalents	Do you know the word 'moral'? ... 寓意 (moral)
Translation L1–L2	L1 words/phrases/sentences + L2 equivalents	See Extract 3
Grammar teaching	Explaining grammatical points	See Extract 4
Explaining vocabulary	Explaining the usage of vocabulary	suggest 又是表述观点的 (also express opinion)
Personal comment	Making personal comments on certain topics	See Extract 5
Information giving	Giving information on Chinese programme names	Chinese TV programme names, such as 非诚勿扰 (*You Are the One*)、星光大道 (*Shining Roads*)
	Giving information when assigning homework	See Extract 6

Table 2.3 Numbers (and percentages) of Chinese characters across the CS functions (as defined in Table 2.2)

	Translation L2–L1	Translation L1–L2	Grammar teaching	Explaining vocabulary	Personal comment	Programme names	Assigning homework
Ring	618 (45.0%)	547 (39.9%)	152 (11.1%)	45 (3.3%)	10 (0.7%)	0	0
Jeng	380 (72.3%)	5 (1.0%)	0	0	0	30 (5.7%)	110 (21.0%)

As can be seen from Table 2.3, the most frequent use of CS by both teachers was translation from L2 to L1, that is, the provision of Chinese equivalents for English words or phrases.

Observational data

Extract 1

01 T   I want each group to translate the story into English first. // and then tell me what's the moral of the story? / Do you know the word 'moral'?

02 Ss   {murmuring}

03 T   寓意. *Moral*. And which are the four skills here used?

In this extract, Ring was giving instructions for an activity and then paused to check her students' understanding of the meaning of the key word 'moral' (01). When only some students murmured the meaning of the word (02), the teacher gave its Chinese equivalent, 寓意, then moved on with the activity (03). Similarly, in her lesson Jeng also switched from English to Chinese in order to provide Chinese meanings for target English words. For example, in Extract 2, Jeng directly gave students the Chinese translation 美国偶像 for the American television programme *American Idol*, and later she provided the Chinese equivalent for the term 'nationwide auditions', 海选.

Extract 2

01 T   Okay now go ahead. American Idol 美国偶像 *American Idol* American Idol, if you can search online you can easily find this programme American Idol. // American Idol is a reality TV competition to find new singing talent, new singing talent. /

It was first on screen in 2002 on Fox. / So the show has since become one of the most popular in the history of American television. It is currently the highest-rated TV programme in America. / So this programme aimed to discover the best singer over the country through a series of nationwide auditions, a series of nationwide auditions, 海选 *nation-wide auditions*

02 Ss   {murmuring}

The interviews with both teachers later showed that they provided Chinese equivalents instead of English explanations for target English words or phrases for the sake of better understanding for the students. For example, Ring said:

I gave Chinese meanings because the Chinese equivalents correspond well with these English words, and if I used English explanation for these English words I'm afraid that the students would be even more confused.

An English explanation for the word 'moral' would be 'the significance of a story or event', in which the word 'significance' might be difficult and confusing for some students. The definition is also long and time-consuming. Jeng similarly mentioned that 'even if I provided the English explanation the students would not necessarily understand'. It can be seen that both teachers were faced with a decision between the Chinese equivalent and the English definition, and they chose to provide Chinese equivalents based on their own judgements for students' better understanding. A Chinese equivalent might help relieve the cognitive load on students (Cook, 2001; Macaro, 2005) and establish a quick link between the target word and its concept (Jiang, 2000; Kroll & Stewart, 1994).

A further analysis on the provision of Chinese equivalents for English words or phrases shows that both teachers provided Chinese equivalents for only some English words, while they provided English meanings for others. Extract 3 is a case in point to illustrate teachers' pedagogical decision-making on whether to switch to Chinese for vocabulary explanation.

Extract 3

01 T   In this paragraph I noticed a strange word. In paragraph 9, literally. // have you seen this word before?
02 Ss   {murmuring} Yeah.
03 T   What's the meaning?

04 Ss   {murmuring} 字面地 *literally*.
05 T   Yes, 字面地, *literally* right↗ / For example, 大学生字面上讲就是大学里的学生 *college students are literally students at college*. Can you translate into English↗
06 Ss   {murmuring} College students are....
07 T   <Teacher and students together say aloud the following translation> College students are literally students at college.
08 T   We know literally means 字面地 *literally*, but here literally doesn't mean 字面地 *literally*: it means in fact or actually. / So literally means actually.

In this extract, Ring first focused students' attention onto the word 'literally' in the textbook (01) and checked their understanding of its meaning (03). When only some students answered (04), she then nodded and repeated its Chinese equivalent 字面地 (05). However, since this meaning is not the actual meaning of the word 'literally' in this specific context in the textbook, she pointed out the mismatch and provided its appropriate meaning 'actually' in English (08). For the same word 'literally', the teacher provided the Chinese equivalent for one meaning and the English synonym for another. Such decision-making was explained by Ring during her interview:

> for the English explanation (actually), the English synonym of the word is quite familiar to the students, so it is not necessary to use Chinese explanation. But students probably are not familiar with the other meaning of the word (字面地 *limited to the explicit meaning of a word or text*) and it would take quite long time to provide an English explanation. A Chinese equivalent is then to the point and saves lesson time. The purpose is to let students understand accurately its meaning, and the Chinese equivalent could better serve this purpose here.

When asked whether there was a principle underlying such decision-making during the lessons on the meanings of target words or phrases, Ring stated:

> If there is a criterion for me to choose between Chinese and English explanation for English words or phrases, it is to judge students' needs upon their English proficiency level. Another reason is that this text is the last one of this term and using Chinese equivalents could save lesson time.

Ring's decision-making on such vocabulary explanation clearly illustrates the notion of teacher as a dictionary and dictionary designer (Macaro *et al.*, 2009). Teachers function as dictionaries as they have a variety of explanations for target words at their disposal; they also function as dictionary designers as they decide and design which meaning to offer to their students.

Jeng also provided English explanation for some English target words, for example 'self-reliance means you rely on yourself' and 'thought-provoking means causing deep thinking'. When asked for her reasons for such decision-making, she explained in the interview that 'the Chinese equivalents of these words are not as clear as English explanation for students, thus better effects could be achieved by using English ones'. It is true that English explanations are quite easy for these undergraduates to understand and pick up. The Chinese equivalent for thought-provoking is 启发思考的, a long Chinese phrase which is a loose combination of two set Chinese phrases. Thought is the equivalent of 思考 and 启发 is the equivalent of provoking, and 的 denotes the grammatical function of an adjective. It can then be concluded from the comments of both teachers that the decision-making on the provision of vocabulary explanations is mainly based on teachers' judgements on students' better understanding and greater effects.

As well as providing Chinese equivalents for target words, Ring also switched to Chinese to explain their usage. For example, she stated, 'suggest 又是表述观点的 (*also express opinion*)'. When mentioning the word *suggest,* the teacher switched to Chinese to point out that the word is used to express one's viewpoint.

Both teachers also displayed different features when switching to Chinese during their lessons. As can be seen from Table 2.3, two major differences of CS use emerged from this case study. Firstly, Ring sometimes switched from Chinese to English to provide English translations for Chinese phrases or sentences, so as to exemplify the new vocabulary in a translation exercise, while Jeng rarely did so. For example, in Extract 3, after providing the Chinese equivalent for the English word 'literally', Ring presented a Chinese sentence for her students to translate into English using the word (05). She also translated the sentence together with her students in order to emphasise its meaning (07). She justified her practice in the interview:

> I just want to let my students memorise these words and phrases.... Sometimes, such translation exercise from Chinese into English could let my students better understand the usage of these words or phrases.

Clearly it is her belief that such a translation exercise could help her students with better understanding and effective memorisation of vocabulary.

Secondly, the other difference in CS use between the two teachers lies in explaining grammar. Table 2.3 shows that 11.1% of CS use by Ring was to explain grammatical points in her lesson, whereas Jeng did not switch to Chinese for such a purpose at all. Ring either used only a Chinese phrase when referring to an English grammatical term or explained the English grammatical point in long Chinese sentences. For example, in Extract 4, Ring raised the question as to the form of predicate when a singular subject is followed by a prepositional phrase 'together with' (01). Even though the students have no problem in getting the correct answer (02–04), the teacher still proceeded with eliciting the underlying grammatical rule (05) and provided the rule clearly in detail in Chinese (07). When asked for a reason, Ring explained in the interview that she wanted to explain the English grammatical rules in a language (Chinese) familiar to her students in order to help them understand.

Extract 4

01	T	So let's look at next one. The expert together with his assistant is or are required to¿
02	Ss	Is .
03	T	Are you sure¿
04	Ss	Yes.
05	T	So what's the grammatical rule¿
06	Ss	{murmuring}
07	T	Together with, along with, as well as, as much as, no less than 这些词, 如果主语是单数的话, 尽管跟上这些词引导的短语, 谓语依然用单数, 谓语跟着主语走, 这些词是插入语. *For these words, if the subject is singular, although the subject is followed by the phrases led by these words, the predicate should still be singular. The predicate should follow the subjects, and these words are only parentheses.*

There are some further differences in CS use between the two teachers. For example, Ring switched to Chinese to provide a personal comment on a grammatical point. In Extract 5, when referring to the grammatical function of one phrase in the text 'that done' as 独立主格 (*subjunctive mood*), she stated that this grammatical point is too difficult for herself (03), which is certainly an exaggeration because she definitely knew this grammatical point, as admitted by herself in the interview. She explained that the purpose of such a personal comment is to acknowledge the difficulty of such a grammatical point and develop a more informal relationship with her students.

Extract 5

01	T	That done, what is 'that done' here¿ It's strange. // That done.
02	Ss	{murmuring}

03 T   独立主格吧？ *Is it subjunctive mood¿* 叫独立主格吧？ *Is it called subjunctive mood¿* 这个对我来说太高级了 *This is too difficult for me.*

04 Ss   {laughing}

In her Journalism English course, Jeng switched to Chinese directly when mentioning the names of some Chinese television programmes, such as 非诚勿扰 (*You Are The One*), 星光大道 (*Shining Roads*) and so on, which are quite familiar to Chinese students. Besides, when pressed for time, Jeng switched to Chinese in order to save time and make her point clearer. In Extract 6, when the bell rang, the students lost their patience and started to chat. Jeng asked them to wait and switched to Chinese when assigning homework (01). As she stated in the interview, switching to Chinese is a necessity in such a situation in order to make her point clearer and save time.

Extract 6

01 T   {Bell rings and students start chatting and waiting for the lesson to be over} Please wait for a moment. Topic for discussion, Media is the carrier of culture. American TV and film are the carriers of American culture. Please find the American culture conveyed by TV and film. (Teacher raises her voice) 美国的电影和电视，它们是文化的载体，它们承载的是美国的文化，那么到底有什么样的文化被美国的电视和电影所传载？美国的 culture 美国的 value 我们都很感兴趣，最简单的是 reality show 一个是 Big Brother 一个是 Who Wants To Be Millionnaire 还有一个 American Idol 这三类节目的背后是什么样的价值观？因为 ordinary people 是主角，他们传递什么样的价值观？ *American film and TV are the carrier of culture, and what they carry is American culture. So what kind of culture is carried by American TV and film¿ We're all quite interested in American culture and American value. A simple example is reality show, one is Big Brother, another is Who Wants To Be Millionaire, and American Idol. What kind of value exists behind these three programmes¿ Because ordinary people are the protagonists, what kind of value do they carry¿*

02 Ss   American dream.

03 T   Yes, American dream. Okay, this is the topic for Group 7 next Friday.

Reflection

This case study on CS use from the two lessons in a Chinese university context reveals an average of 10% CS use during total teacher talk and 7.9% of total lesson time via timed analysis at five-second intervals. Further analysis on word count distribution for CS episodes identified frequencies of different functions of CS use. The most popular use of teachers' switching to Chinese was translating from English to Chinese. That is, both teachers tended to switch to Chinese to provide Chinese equivalents for English words or sentences, so as to assist with students' understanding of the target language. It should be noted that these teachers provided Chinese equivalents only for some English words, while they provided English explanations for other English words. Such decision-making on the provision of vocabulary explanations was mainly based on the two teachers' judgements on students' better understanding and greater effects. These teachers' explanations of English vocabulary reveal the teacher's role as dictionary and dictionary designer, having several choices at their disposal.

This case study then provides further evidence for Macaro's discussion of bilingual teachers in his Overview chapter in this book. The bilingual teachers in this case study all switched to Chinese to provide L1 equivalents for some unknown English lexical items, and one of the teachers (Ring) also exemplified the new vocabulary in translation exercises. They not only operated as walking bilingual dictionaries, but also as bilingual dictionary designers in that they selected both L1 and L2 information for both comprehension and acquisition. More importantly, they both had high levels of proficiency in the two languages; therefore, their choice of CS was a principled decision to bring about real learning rather than an easy shortcut.

There were, however, also major discrepancies over CS use between the two teachers. Ring switched from Chinese to English a lot in order to exemplify the new vocabulary in translation exercises and to explain grammatical points, while Jeng rarely did so. Besides, Ring also switched to Chinese to provide personal comment on grammatical points to develop an informal relationship with her students. Jeng switched to Chinese directly to give information, when mentioning some Chinese names of American television programmes and assigning homework when time was short. The above differences over CS use between the two teachers could be ascribed to the different lesson types. Ring's lesson was part of an intensive reading course focusing more on target language learning, while Jeng's lesson introducing American television was more informative. Ring's use of CS for translation from L1 to L2 and grammatical explanation indicates the nature of her lesson, while Jeng's CS use on giving information reveals hers. Ring switched to Chinese to help students understand and grasp new vocabulary and grammar in her English language skills course. Although Jeng also provided Chinese equivalents for English words, she focused more on presenting the meanings of these words rather than their usage. However, Ring focused on both meaning and form, as she also switched to Chinese to practise the usage of vocabulary in translation exercise. There might be other factors diversifying the CS use of university teachers in their second language classrooms, and further research is needed to explore teachers' different decision-making.

COMMENTARY

Codeswitching (CS) has a long and controversial history in applied linguistics, educational policy and sociolinguistics. Multilingualism (Herdina & Jessner, 2002) and CS (Jorgensen, 2005) have become recognised by researchers in the field as a special competency and a phenomenon that has been increasing in our globalised world. However, policymakers, teachers and societal stakeholders still mostly frown upon such phenomena, considering them a sign of a deficient kind of monolingualism rather than a demonstration of competent multilingualism. Especially in language teaching, and in particular in the case of English as a foreign language (EFL) and English as a second language (ESL), standard inner-circle monolingualism has been the point of reference. Only relatively recently have approaches such as EIL (English as an international language; e.g. McKay, 2002), ELF (English as a lingua franca; e.g. Seidlhofer, 2010) and EAL (English as an additional language; e.g. Creese, 2010) made some inroads among policymakers and practitioners.

This commentary will focus on the situation in China, comparing the data discussed in Lili Tian's study with other research on CS in Chinese university EFL classrooms as well as data collected by the author at a medium-size public university in southern China located in a special dialect area. Most students attending this university speak Cantonese as their main language and have learned Putonghua (Mandarin) in school as the national language. In addition, a local dialect, Teochew, is spoken in the area. Most faculty and students thus naturally switch between the different dialects of their L1 and incorporate English smoothly into their repertoire (e.g. 'bye-bye'). Even though signs exhorting people to use Putonghua abound on campus, faculty will teach in Cantonese as long as all their students are able to follow. Conversely, upwardly mobile parents talk to their children in Putonghua, the standard dialect, in order to avoid later discrimination.

The English Language Centre (ELC) at the university has a faculty of 50 teachers, half of whom are Chinese, both local and from further afield, and half from abroad, native speakers and non-native speakers alike. The ELC offers classes to the entire university, both English major and non-English major students. Students are placed into levels according to a diagnostic assessment based on their writing and speaking abilities, the latter being computerised. The language of instruction is English, following a communicative approach, and all administrative business, including faculty meetings, is conducted in English. While there is no official English-only policy in writing, emphasis both in and out of class is placed on the development of skills by using English to accomplish tasks irrespective of language proficiency. In fact, an English Enhancement Programme was established in 2003, bilingual and English content classes are being offered throughout the university, and an ESP (English for Special Purposes) bridge programme was set up in 2009.

In this commentary, data from a survey conducted among the Chinese teachers at the university, the author's former workplace, will be analysed, compared with Tian's case study and another study, carried out at Jilin Normal University (Van der Meij & Zhao, 2010). Jilin Normal University is a teacher training institution with a somewhat different population of students, whereas the other two universities are both top-tier universities and share some characteristics of curriculum, expectations and methodology. The survey questions (see Appendix) were designed to investigate teachers' self-reported use of CS, similar to Tian and to the comparative study of Van der Meij and Zhao. The survey was administered via email and elicited a response rate of 30%. Respondents had a wide range of experience (years of teaching), educational background (degree from abroad or from China) as well as courses taught (major/non-major, proficiency level).

The seven main questions of the survey were designed to gauge the applicability of Tian's findings to the setting of this southern Chinese university. Consequently, the first question presented respondents with a quotation from Gao and Dai (2007) about the general consensus among English language teachers in China – that the target language should be used as much as possible by both teachers and students. Of the respondents, 75% *strongly agreed* with that statement and 25% *agreed*. This finding is consistent with the general claim repeated in the literature that target language use, though hardly ever stipulated in writing, is the expectation for English language teaching at the tertiary level in China. As mentioned above, this university does not have an explicit English-only policy but does place heavy emphasis on target language use in and out of the classroom through its hiring policy (50% foreign faculty), textbook choice (imported) and extracurricular activities (where students can practise everything from public speaking to poetry). This kind of implicit language policy seems to be effective, judging by the response of teachers in this study. Interestingly, no respondent even chose the middle ground of *it depends* besides obviously eschewing more radical disagreement as expressed in the options *disagree* and *strongly disagree*. This initial response seemed to set the scene for a negative attitude towards CS among teachers. However, further responses showed that CS was not only used by teachers but also subscribed to as a valid practice.

Following the findings of Tian, the second question explored the extent of CS that teachers believed they engaged in while teaching. Since this question was not corroborated by any empirical data, it may well be corrupted by the effect identified by Van der Meij and Zhao (2010), who found that teachers seriously underestimated the extent of their CS. While Tian reported an average of 10% of L1 use timewise between her two classes, Guo (2007) reported a wide range of variability, averaging out at 19%. Based on the options given in the present questionnaire, ranging from 0% to 25% and more, 75% of respondents chose the option of 5%. Though this is half the time measured by Tian, it may well be that teachers engage in the same 10%, or even more, in actual practice. However, the choice of 5% may provide an indication about the extent of CS considered appropriate by these teachers. In addition, it is worth bearing in mind that

Van der Meij and Zhao's figure of 25% was obtained at a provincial teacher training college, whereas Tian's 10% was registered at a key Beijing university and the present figures emerged from a provincial key comprehensive university with a special English Enhancement Programme.

Tian identified six categories of CS (translation L1–L2, translation L2–L1, grammar teaching, explaining vocabulary, personal comment and information giving), whereas Van der Meij and Zhao (2010) limited themselves to distinguishing between short CS (a phrase or sentence) and longer CS episodes (lasting over two minutes). The present study gave respondents a choice between *single words or phrases, whole sentences* and *multiple sentences*. The first category, intra-sentential CS, was the one favoured by respondents, with an average of 85% reported by teachers. Based on sample data from Tian, this category may be considered to correspond to her categories of translation. These were also the most popular categories in her study, accounting for 85% on one course and 73% in the other. The data in the present study, although self-reported, again seem to confirm Tian's findings.

Tian's categories were defined and examples from the transcripts afforded additional insight into the meaning of those categories, so the next question in the present questionnaire asked respondents to choose among specific functions of CS, such as *state equivalent, illustrate usage, teach grammar, provide information, make personal comment* and *assign homework*. The categories most chosen and ranked most highly were *state equivalent*, which encompasses L1–L2 as well as L2–L1 translation, and *illustrate usage*, which most closely relates to vocabulary. In the option *other*, explaining writing and expressing one's opinion were suggested by respondents. In this respect also, findings from Tian's study and data from the present survey coincide.

As far as justifying the use of CS, besides achieving better understanding and obtaining greater effects, saving lesson time was identified by Tian in the follow-up interviews to her observations. Mirroring these findings and expanding upon them, respondents in the present study were asked to choose among *improving students' understanding, increasing teaching effectiveness, facilitating memorisation, making students feel comfortable, training translation skills* and *saving time*. In line with findings from Tian's study, *improving students' understanding* was ranked first by respondents, followed by *facilitating memorisation*, a category which was also derived from Tian's interview data. It seems, therefore, that categories and justifications for the use of CS can be generalised beyond Tian's study.

Another major issue, addressed in some studies but not satisfactorily resolved thus far, is the question of factors influencing the choice of CS – which, according to Van der Meij and Zhao (2010), are mainly language policy, teacher, student and lesson variables. In the present study, respondents were asked to rank factors that influenced their use of CS in class, choosing from: students' language level; students' explicit request for L1; students' facial expressions; type of class; and specific learning objectives. Contrary to the findings of Van der Meij and Zhao, respondents in this study chose *students' language level* as the main decisive factor, followed by *students' facial expressions*. This finding points to a more integrative orientation among teachers, as opposed to instrumental categories such as *type of class* and *specific learning objectives* that emerged as significant in other studies.

The final question tried to explore teacher variables, specifically their general attitude towards CS, by asking respondents to express their feelings about CS in their non-teaching lives, in relation to their various dialects and English. On a five-point scale, ranging from *I just love it* to *never*, 75% of respondents chose *I try not to* as characterising their own CS behaviour. This points to an underlying negative attitude towards CS, as something that can be used for the purpose of improving student learning but is not seen as a desirable competence to be developed or supported. Factors contributing to this defensive stance vis-à-vis CS may be the rather fierce language competition between Putonghua and Guangdonghua/Cantonese as well as the guiding principles of communicative language teaching of providing the right level of comprehensible input (Krashen, 1994) and facilitating opportunities for meaningful output (Swain, 2005). It would of course be desirable to check these findings against actual language use and the CS behaviour of teachers.

In the comments section of the questionnaire, teachers were invited to provide further explanations of their CS principles and behaviour. Some of the factors described by respondents were the necessity of using CS in certain areas such as translation, writing and the explanation of complex or abstract concepts, which might actually tie into the category of specific learning objective or type of class that teachers did not choose in the earlier question. Another comment emphasised the need to use different approaches in ESL versus EFL settings. Overall, many respondents concurred with the need for flexibility, mentioning, for example: avoiding but not prohibiting CS; the teachers' ability to carry out English-only instruction versus the effectiveness of such an approach; and the desirability of being able to adjust to different contexts according to student- and course-related variables. In line with Tian's pragmatic findings, teachers at this university also favoured a descriptivist over a prescriptivist view of language teaching and learning, while trying to remain within the general framework of task-based communicative language teaching oriented to the target language.

Certain limitations exist in the study of Tian and in the present survey: these include the lack of generalisability into language versus content courses based on only one case each; the reliance on self-reported data; and the small sample sizes. Nonetheless, both studies seem to share some commonalities in the beliefs about and use of CS in Chinese university EFL classrooms that are also found in relevant studies published elsewhere. First and foremost, CS is seen not necessarily as desirable but still as a useful tool for improving the effectiveness and efficiency of English language teaching. Secondly, the main levels of CS are clearly defined as single words or phrases translated between the two languages. Thirdly, the reasons for CS also overlap in terms of the goals of improving understanding and facilitating memorisation. The only variable with considerable divergence when comparing Tian's case study, Van der Meij and Zhao (2010) and the present survey concerns the learner variable of proficiency. While Van der Meij and Zhao's subjects deny any meaningful link between proficiency and the extent of codeswitching required or desirable, Tian's respondents mention the fact that not all students would be able to understand equally well without CS, and the respondents in the present survey also considered the students' language level as the main factor that would help them decide on the extent of CS to use.

If we want to consider the potential theoretical implications of these findings, we may have to return to Macaro's basic questions in the Overview chapter of what CS is, and to what extent it is necessary to distinguish between naturalistic and classroom CS. While no linguistic analysis of the grammatical constraints of CS was undertaken, all three studies fall close to the 15% of L1 use suggested by Macaro for classroom CS in a communicative framework. Similarly, although no tokens of communicative functions of CS such as *signalling a topic switch, brief socialising moves* or *expressions of emotions* were tallied in the studies, Tian reported teachers' explanations of CS behaviour. These included developing a more informal relationship with students – a function that can be considered communicative rather than pedagogical or linguistic.

Overall, the teachers' argument in favour of flexibility regarding language use in the classroom (avoiding instead of prohibiting, ability versus effectiveness and a margin for adjustment to student and course variables) strongly supports Macaro's (1997, 2001) category of optimal use of CS in the classroom. To a certain extent, therefore, the teachers' CS in these studies, while principled, seemed to flow in a naturalistic way. However, further research is needed to explore finer distinctions between classroom and naturalistic CS.

At this point, it must be noted that the studies under review had different research designs, pedagogical aims and levels of stringency, which makes a true meta-comparison a shaky endeavour. However, if the collection of case studies and commentaries in this volume can stimulate a few well designed multi-site, multi-method, teacher–student comparisons conducted in various Asian countries, we can look forward to a significant expansion of our understanding of the extent, success and challenges of CS in EFL university classrooms in Asia. Readers of this volume are encouraged to collaborate in the design, implementation and publication of relevant projects in the future.

References

Bassetti, B. (2005) Effects of writing systems on second language awareness: Word awareness in English learners of Chinese as a foreign language. In V.J. Cook and B. Bassetti (eds) *Second Language Writing Systems* (pp. 335–356). Clevedon: Multilingual Matters.

Bassetti, B. (2009) Effects of adding interword spacing on Chinese reading: A comparison of Chinese native readers and English readers of Chinese as a second language. *Applied Psycholinguistics* 30 (4), 757–775.

Chinese Ministry of Education (2007) *College English Curriculum Requirements.* Beijing: Higher Education Press.

Cook, V.J. (2001) *Second Language Learning and Language Teaching.* London: Edward Arnold.

Creese, A. (2010) Two teacher classrooms, personalised learning and the inclusion paradigm in the UK: What's in it for learners of EAL? In K. Menken and O. García (eds) *Negotiating Language Policies in Schools: Educators as Policymakers* (pp. 32–51). Mahwah, NJ: Erlbaum.

Gao, J. and Dai, W. (2007) Research and analysis on codeswitching in language teaching. *Chinese Foreign Language Education* 28 (1), 51–55.

Guo, T. (2007) A case study of teachers' code-switching behaviors in mainland China's university EFL classrooms and students' reactions to the code-switching. Unpublished PhD thesis, University of Oxford.

Herdina, P. and Jessner, U. (2002) *A Dynamic Model Of Multilingualisms: Perspectives of Change in Psycholinguistics.* Clevedon: Multilingual Matters.

Jiang, N. (2000) Lexical representation and development in a second language. *Applied Linguistics* 21 (1), 47–77.

Jorgensen, J.N. (2005) Plurilingual conversations among bilingual adolescents. *Journal of Pragmatics* 37, 391–402.

Krashen, S. (1994) The input hypothesis and its rivals. In N. Ellis (ed.) *Implicit and Explicit Learning of Languages* (pp. 45–77). London: Academic Press.

Kroll, J.F. and Stewart, E. (1994) Category interference in translation and picture naming: Evidence for asymmetric connections between bilingual memory representations. *Journal of Memory and Language* 33 (2), 149–174.

Macaro, E. (1997) *Target Language, Collaborative Learning and Autonomy.* Clevedon: Multilingual Matters.

Macaro, E. (2001) Analyzing students teachers' code-switching in foreign language classrooms: Theories and decision-making. *Modern Language Journal* 85 (4), 531–548.

Macaro, E. (2005) Codeswitching in the L2 classroom: A communication and learning strategy. In E. Llurda (ed.) *Non-native Language Teachers: Perceptions, Challenges, and Contributions to the Profession* (pp. 63–84). New York: Springer.

Macaro, E., Guo, T., Chen, H. and Tian L. (2009) Can differential processing of L2 vocabulary inform the debate on teacher code-switching behavior: The case of Chinese learners of English. In B. Richards, M.H. Daller, D.D. Malvern, P. Meara, J. Milton and J. Treffers-Daller (eds) *Vocabulary Studies in First and Second Language Acquisition: The Interface Between Theory and Application* (pp. 125–146). Basingstoke: Palgrave Macmillan.

McKay, S.L. (2002) *Teaching English as an International Language: Rethinking Goals and Perspectives.* New York: Oxford University Press.

Seidlhofer, B. (2010). Lingua franca English – the European context. In A. Kirkpatrick (ed.) *The Routledge Handbook of World Englishes* (pp. 355–371). Abingdon: Routledge.

Swain, M. (2005) The output hypothesis: Theory and research. In E. Hinkel (ed.) *Handbook of Research on Second Language Teaching and Learning* (pp. 471–483). Mahwah, NJ: Erlbaum.

Van der Meij, H. and Zhao, X. (2010) Code-switching in English courses in Chinese universities. *Modern Language Journal* 94 (3), 396–411.

Appendix. Survey Questions

Years teaching English
- < 5 years
- 5–10 years
- > 10 years

University education
- China only
- China and abroad
- abroad only

Levels/classes mostly taught
- lower
- intermediate
- advanced
  special courses:

1. Please evaluate the following statement

'English teachers should use as much target language as possible in the classroom and students should be encouraged to use as much target language as they can.' (Finding from Gao & Dai, 2007, about teachers' and students' beliefs on university English teaching in China)

- strongly agree
- agree
- depends
- disagree
- strongly disagree

If you chose 'depends', please share some thoughts if you wish:

2. What percentage of your teacher talk would you estimate includes code-switching (use of L1)?

- 0%
- 5%
- 10%
- 15%
- 20%
- 25% and more

3. What percentage of your codeswitching would you estimate involves the following (total = 100%)?

- single words or phrases ___%
- whole sentences ___%
- multiple sentences ___%

4. What functions would you use codeswitching for and what would be the most common function? (Please rank 1, 2, 3, ...)

- state equivalent
- illustrate usage
- teach grammar
- provide information
- make personal comment
- assign homework
- other

5. What might be some of your reasons for using codeswitching and which ones would be most relevant? (Please rank 1, 2, 3, ...)

- to improve student understanding
- to increase teaching effectiveness
- to facilitate memorisation
- to make students feel comfortable
- to train translation skills
- to save time
- other

6. What helps you decide when and how much codeswitching to use in class?

- students' language level
- students' explicit request for L1
- students' facial expression
- type of class
- specific learning objective
- other

7. How would you characterise your own codeswitching behaviour? (Chinese-English, Mandarin-Cantonese ...)

- I just love it
- frequently
- occasionally
- I try not to
- never

Comments:

3 Codeswitching in Two Japanese Contexts

Case Study: Simon Humphries
Commentary: Richmond Stroupe

CASE STUDY

Introduction

Although Macaro in the Overview to this volume discusses the need for research into the merits of principled codeswitching (CS), in Japan there seems to be a tension between policy and practice, caused by conflicting circumstances. Influenced by a business community concerned by globalisation, the Japanese Ministry of Education, Culture, Sports, Science and Technology (MEXT) introduced policies that focus on using English predominantly in the classroom for practical communication (Tanabe, 2004). However, studies have indicated that secondary-school Japanese teachers of English (JTEs) have continued to conduct classes that rely heavily on the use of the L1 through the *yakudoku* (grammar translation) tradition (Gorsuch, 1998; Humphries, 2012; O'Donnell, 2005; Sakui, 2004; Sato, 2002; Sato & Kleinsasser, 2004; Taguchi, 2005; Watanabe, 2004). The non-communicative nature of the university entrance examinations (Amano & Poole, 2005; Gorsuch, 2001; Nishino, 2008; Watanabe, 2004) and MEXT-mandated textbooks (Browne & Wada, 1998; Gorsuch, 1999; Humphries, 2013; LoCastro, 1997; McGroarty & Taguchi, 2005; Pacek, 1996; Rosenkjar, 2009) are two factors blamed for this phenomenon.

The Japanese further education engineering college (*Kosen*) in this study provided a unique context, for two reasons. Firstly, *Kosen* students could study for five years (15–20 years old) and then transfer by recommendation (*henyusuisen*) into the third year of a university course, graduate and find employment, or study for an in-house degree. These options removed the pressure to study for university English entrance examinations. Secondly, the *Kosen*, free from MEXT's control, implemented English-only communicative textbooks such as *On the Go* (Gershon *et al.*, 2004).

Theoretical Framework

Interactions were analysed based on the self-evaluation of teacher talk (SETT) framework developed by Walsh (2006, 2011). The strengths of this framework are its educational focus and flexibility. It recognises that 'interaction and pedagogic goals are inextricably linked [and] the discourse is constantly changing according to the teacher's agenda' (Walsh, 2011: 110). Thus, although SETT is primarily intended for teachers' self-reflection, it provides a robust framework that can be used, as I have done, to explore the classroom interactions of other teachers.

The central feature of the SETT framework is the use of four classroom micro-contexts, called *modes*. Each mode 'has a clearly defined pedagogical goal and distinctive interactional features determined largely by a teacher's use of language' (Walsh, 2006: 62). The four modes are managerial, materials, skills and systems, and classroom context (Table 3.1).

In managerial mode, the teacher aims to organise the learning by providing instructions and explanations; therefore, it is usually characterised by an extended teacher turn and an absence of student involvement. Skills and systems mode and materials mode tend to have similar interactional features, such as: the initiation–response–feedback (IRF) pattern – the teacher asks a question and then gives feedback on the student response (Sinclair & Coulthard, 1975); scaffolding – providing words or structures to assist learners to make longer utterances (Bruner, 1983); and direct repair – where 'errors are corrected quickly ... with little explanation' (Walsh, 2011:

Table 3.1 Modes in a foreign language classroom (adapted from Walsh, 2011: 113)

Mode	Pedagogical goals	Sample interactional features
Managerial	Organisation of learning	• Single extended teacher turn using explanations and introductions • Absence of learner contributions
Materials	Focus on materials being used	• Initiation–response–feedback (IRF) pattern • Scaffolding • Direct repair
Skills and systems	Language practice in relation to language system or skill	
Classroom context	Context determines the interaction: appearance of a naturally occurring conversation	• Extended learner turns and short teacher turns • Content feedback • Clarification requests

218). In skills and systems mode, the focus is practice in relation to the language system (such as phonology, grammar or vocabulary) or skill (listening, reading, writing or speaking). In materials mode, the goals and language use centre on the materials used, such as the class textbook or DVD. In contrast, in classroom context mode, the local context determines the management of turns and topics. This mode creates opportunities for more natural conversations, where learners may have longer turns than the teacher. Rather than form-focused interactions, the teacher may comment on a student's message (content feedback) or ask for clarification (clarification request).

Data Collection

This chapter focuses on observation data from grade 11 classrooms of two male JTEs called Chikara and Akira (pseudonyms), who taught using *On the Go* (Gershon *et al.*, 2004). For each grade 11 class, four classes were video-recorded, and then an independent bilingual speaker transcribed and translated the Japanese data into English. The two JTEs subsequently participated in semi-structured individual interviews in English, firstly to ascertain their attitudes towards the educational change and secondly to understand their reasons for their teaching practices. The interviews were audio-recorded, transcribed and compared with the observational data. Table 3.2 shows the proportion of language use for the class observations that provided the data for this chapter. As indicated, the classes were conducted predominantly in Japanese, but I selected one extract per class, containing higher than average levels of English interaction in the data between the teacher and students. Moreover, as advised by Macaro (this volume), these extracts contain teachers' attempts to encourage students to create English utterances, rather than the frequently observed focus on language knowledge and translation.

Table 3.2 Proportion of language use

Teacher	Length of lesson (min/s)	Length of teacher talk (min/s)	Total teacher talking time (%)	Teacher talk in L1 (min/s)	Teacher talk in L1 (%)	Teacher talk in L2 (min/s)	Teacher talk in L2 (%)
Chikara	35′11″	29′04″	83%	21′03″	72%	8′01″	28%
Akira	40′54″	27′32″	67%	24′46″	90%	2′46″	10%

Case Study 1: Chikara

Chikara, a 55-year-old full-time male professor, had taught at the *Kosen* for six years and was the head of the English department. He held a master's degree in English education and continued his professional development through attending conferences, giving presentations, publishing papers and reading methodology books. Chikara had a high English proficiency level, because he held the first level of the STEP Test (see http://stepeiken.org). His class contained 24 male students in grade 11. Regarding the use of the target language, in his interview Chikara asserted that Japanese students could benefit from speaking in English:

> **Chikara:** It's very good for them, because, without this kind of [speaking] activities Japanese students tend to be silent I mean / they usually don't read English sentences aloud.

However, although he believed in using as much English as possible and encouraged the students to do likewise, Chikara admitted that he used Japanese and explained that his students struggled to produce English sentences:

> **Chikara:** Asking them, sometimes I use English and Japanese, and but for their answers always, I ask them to use English to ask them I use first English and then I will write some Japanese translation.
> **Interviewer:** [And they answer in English.]
> **Chikara:** [But in answering me, I always ask for English.
> **Interviewer:** And they usually answer okay, in English⸮
> **Chikara:** They have difficulty in speak in sentences, so I say it's okay for them to use some words or some phrases.

The following extract comes from the end of a lesson based on the 'Warm Up' activity from page 16 of *On the Go*. Preceding this extract, Chikara had discussed the unit goals and collected the students' answers to some multiple-choice questions based on house rules. Therefore, the preceding activities had been linguistically low-output, because the students needed only to say letters such as 'f' to represent 'smoking inside'. However, during the following extract, Chikara attempted to engage some students in a communicative exercise where they could employ language not contained in the textbook to describe their own backgrounds.

Extract 1a

01 T   Etto / hai, sorekara mouhitotsu kokoni shitsumon arukara hai, imano B no tsuzukidayo. *There is one question here, in section B* 'What other house rules do you have⸮' hokani donna iedewa

iede kimirano iedene donna kimariga aruka chottokangaete kudasai. Kore muzukashiiyona. Kangaerunona. Itsumo atarimaenokoto to shite nankayatterukarane. Nanika kore o shitewaikenai toka gyakuni koreoshinakereba ikenai demo iidesuwa. Gimune. Ano / *Please think about the house rules in your houses. It is difficult to think about it. We don't think about the rules in our life. You can say things you shouldn't do or you should do is okay too. Erm* 'What you must do at home' ne <*Okay*>. Iede shinakereba naranai kotone. <*What you have to do at home. Okay*>. And what you must not do at home ne <*Okay*>. Hai, shinakerebanaranai kotoshitewa ikenaikoto de chotto kangaete kudasai. Shinakerebanaranai kotoshitewa ikenaikoto. Honede eigode ittekudasaine. Kantanna eigode iidesu /// *Please think about it. The things that you must do and you must not do at home. Say it in English please. In easy English is okay.* {Teacher looking around while some students discuss the question at the front of the classroom} Jyamouchotto, kimiranoiede kon nan yattara akanchuunowa arunyanaidesuka? Imanowa nihon futsuu dokodemo souyanai desuka. Doudesuka? Kimirano iede kore senaakayato kakoreoshitewa ikenaito kaiunoittekudasai // Aruiwa, koreoshinakerebanaranai /// E-tto, kimi ittekudasai *There must be something you shouldn't do at home. Everywhere is the same. How is it? Please tell us about your house rules. You, please tell us.* {Pointing at S1} Your opinion na. *Okay.*

This monologue illustrates that it can be difficult to neatly categorise a discourse because it will often have the essential features of both managerial mode and materials mode. It contains managerial mode features, such as the length of the teacher turn and the introduction of the topic. However, Chikara also assumes a direct participant role – in the materials mode – because he asks the question from the textbook.

Chikara's CS helps to distinguish between the modes. Three of Chikara's four English utterances are purely materials mode. Initially, he reads the question contained in the textbook and then reformulates it to include what you 'must' and 'must not' do at home. This strategy helps the students to confirm that they understand the question and gives them time to formulate their answers. He uses Japanese for the managerial mode: guiding the students to the location in the textbook, translating the questions and instructing the students to answer in English. In addition to the pedagogic functions, Chikara's use of Japanese also fulfils inter-personal functions. He empathises that the students might not normally think about the rules in their houses and that they might therefore find the question difficult. Moreover, his advice 'Kantanna eigode iidesu' (*In easy English is okay*) functions simultaneously as a managerial mode instruction and affective advice to soothe students' nerves. Finally, unlike Chikara's earlier three English utterances, which were in materials mode, his closing utterance of turn 01 above ('your opinion') represents managerial mode for nominating a response from S1.

Extract 1b

02	S1	Kusamushiri (xxx) *cutting the grass*
03	T	Aa – You / you must pick up ///
04	S1	Grass
05	T	Grass, grasses aa~ grasses aa~ in the garden. It's your duty ne *okay.* Every month˧
06	S1	{Nodding his head.}
07	T	Yeah, it's your duty. How about other students˧ Shinakereba-naranai, shitewaikenaikoto *Things you have to do or you shouldn't do.* {Teacher holds up his hand and waits for an answer.}
08	Ss	(xxx) {Inaudible Japanese – the teacher listens to them.}
09	T	Aa / you said S2 kun, his house runs a shop, store and you said {Pointing at S2} Please tell me in English.
10	S2	Eh ///
11	T	People who are not eating lunch, people who are not eating lunch must˧ /// People who are not eating lunch must˧ /
12	S2	Must iwaretemo nani kotaetara eeka wakaran *You say 'must', but I don't know what to say.*
13	T	'Must take care of the store.'
14	S2	Aa / souiukotoka *Ah. That's what you mean.*
15	T	In your store / what are they selling˧ What are they selling˧
16	S2	Selling˧
17	T	What are they selling˧ / Soft cream bread or (xxx) what are they selling˧ ///
18	S2	Peach (xxx).
19	T	Aa / fruits. For example, peach or watermelon˧ Watermelon˧ // {After this interaction, Chikara looks at his watch and then tells a short anecdote in English then Japanese about his childhood, visiting a friend's greengrocer shop.}

Extract 1b demonstrates Chikara's attempts to extract English utterances from students S1 and S2. He talks predominantly in the target language and employs all four modes.

There is a focus on the materials mode (03–14) as Chikara encourages the students to answer the textbook question. Interactional features from materials mode include scaffolding (03 and 11) and direct repair (13). (Turn 13 could also be regarded as skills and systems mode, because he directly taught a sentence structure, but answering the textbook question remains the focus.) Chikara also uses content feedback (05 and 07) – 'it's your duty' – which is a feature of classroom context mode. Unlike the managerial mode segments in Extract 1a, which consisted predominantly of Japanese, Chikara uses English to nominate students during turns 07 and 09.

Regarding CS, Chikara uses translation, leading to a hybrid effect between materials and management modes on two occasions. Firstly, Chikara translates the question in the textbook (07). If he had recast it in English, this could place him as a participant in the materials mode, but his use of Japanese indicates his aim to explain (management mode). Secondly, after listening to the students discussing in Japanese (08), Chikara summarises in English (09). If the students had spoken in English, his summary could represent materials mode feedback; however, the switch from Japanese indicates his expectation for them to follow his lead (management mode). During turns 15, 17 and 19, Chikara attempts to switch to classroom context mode. Initially, he tries asking questions not included in the textbook (15 and 17). Finally, after S2 says 'peach' (18), Chikara suggests the superordinate 'fruits' and an alternative plant ('watermelon') (19). His elaboration of the student's answer contains an element of direct repair (skills and systems mode), but he also clarifies the meaning (classroom context mode).

Despite Chikara's attempts to generate English utterances from S1 and S2, the students tended not to use the target language. S1 used Japanese (02) and a non-linguistic strategy by nodding his head (06). Although S2 eventually uttered isolated English words (16 and 18), his use of Japanese was interesting. His use of a clarification request (12) and feedback (14) displayed confidence and empowerment that may not have been possible if the interaction had remained entirely in the target language.

Case Study 2: Akira

Unlike Chikara, Akira's background lay mostly outside education. This 55-year-old part-time lecturer had completed an MA in theology in Scotland and his main career was as a Christian pastor in the local church. Moreover, although he had some educational experience from teaching English classes in private cramming schools, he had no teaching licence and he had taught in the *Kosen* for only one year. However, he explained that his experience had prepared him for teaching:

Akira: I've lived in Britain so long I've got some grasp of it. I tend to use my own [approaches].

Although Akira had developed his own English proficiency in a practical manner through communicating during his 14 years in the UK, he took a more traditional view towards teaching students. He asserted that they needed a foundation in grammar and vocabulary before they could converse in English.

Akira: But you see conversation is okay but … when you have no solid ground for understanding English
Interviewer: Grand⸮ {I misheard 'ground'}
Akira: Grammar or vocabulary

Akira taught lower-middle proficiency students in a class of 24 learners. All of Akira's classes were highly structured, teacher-centred and conducted almost exclusively in Japanese. In the following extract, Akira used a role-play activity from page 14 of *On the Go*. This was the only activity during the observations where he encouraged all the students to produce English. During other activities, he tended to accept Japanese or one-word English responses. This activity showed a map of a fictional campus, which contained the names of facilities and their locations within each building. Rather than let the students divide into pairs and assume the roles of asker and direction-giver, Akira created his own phrases on the blackboard in English and Japanese:

(1) Is there setsubi *facility*⸮ Arimasuka⸮ *Does it have*⸮ Yes it is [*sic*].
(2) Are they open all the time⸮ Zuttoaiteimasuka⸮ {Direct translation} When is it open⸮ Kaikanjikanwa⸮ {Direct translation} Kaikan *opening time*.
(3) Where is it⸮ Sorewa dokoni arimasuka⸮ {Direct translation} Basho *place*.

Akira then guided the students to take turns reading a question and giving an answer based on their seating order. He used three main assistance strategies: (1) pointing to the relevant phrase on the blackboard; (2) standing next to the student and indicating the information in the textbook; or (3) giving a hint or the direct answer. Therefore, he replaced the student–student dialogue with a teacher–student recitation exercise with all turns mediated through the teacher. The following extract illustrates the type of interaction that took place.

Extract 2a

01 T   {Nominating a student} S20, tsugina nikanitsuite kite kudasai
            S20, *please ask about something.*
02 S20   Is there ///
03 T   Is there a / naniga ii? *What do you want to ask about?*
04 S20   / 'Student office'.
05 T   'Student office?' ne *Okay.* Hai *Okay* xxx 'International student
            office' S21, S21. {Walks to S21 and wakes him up.}
06 S21   Hai *yes.*
07 T   xxx Yes, yes {points to 'yes it is' on the blackboard}.
08 S21   Yes, it is.
09 T   Yes, it is desune. Hai *Okay* {nominating a student} S22, S22,
            S22! Hai 'Student office' nitsuite 'When is it open' te kite
            kudasai *For the 'Student Office', please ask 'when is it open?'*
10 S22   When is it open?
11 T   Hai, *yes* When is it open?

Akira tends to feed the answers to the students in English. Although to
some extent such prompting resembles scaffolding in materials mode, here
it becomes merely a repetition exercise (07–08 and 09–10). In the same interaction, he also uses managerial mode, reflected in his switching to Japanese
to provide instructions (01, 03 and 09). S20 utters the English 'Is there' (02)
and then pauses for three seconds. Walsh describes how extended wait-time
(of two seconds or more) from the teacher 'not only increases the number of
learner responses, it frequently results in more complex answers, and leads
to an increase in learner/learner interaction' (Walsh, 2011: 34). Conversely,
however, in this extract and examples from other students during the same
activity, these two strategies are employed by students to draw the correct
answer from their teacher.

Extract 2b below was selected because it contains his interaction with a
problematic female student (FS1). The class of 24 contained only five female
students, four of whom sat at the back corner of the room and tended to
chat off-topic for the majority of each observed lesson. During the interviews, Akira had described his 'battle' with the female students and other
unmotivated individuals:

Akira: It's really bad. So before you start teaching, there's a battle going
on, you know, how mentally making them turn around to listen to
you/to the class, but er you know some kids are not interested in
listening at all.

Extract 2b

11 T   ... hai *yes* When is it open? {Nominating a student} FS1, 'Student office" nokaikanjikan *What are the opening hours for the 'Student office'.*

12 FS1   Kinyoubito /e? *Friday and /* what?

13 T   Kaikanjikan *opening hours.*

14 FS1   Kaikanjikan? *Opening hours?*

15 T   'Student office' ne *Okay.* 'International student office' no kaikanjikan *The opening hours of the 'International student office'*

16 FS1   {FS1 discusses with other FS} / hachijihan <*8:30*>

17 T   De eigode. *in English* from?

18 FS1   Furomu ei emu *from a.m.*

19 T   Eight thirty ne *okay* to?

20 FS1   To

21 T   Six

22 FS1   Sikkusu *6*

23 T   Thirty

24 FS1   Sa-ti- *30*

25 T   p.m.

26 FS1   p.m.

27 T   p.m. desune. Hai, soredewa S23 *it's 'p.m.' isn't it. Okay, next S23* 'where' ['where is it?'

28 S23   'Where] is it?'

During Akira's interaction with FS1, her non-English language use appears to challenge his authority (11–27). After she uses Japanese (12 and 16), Akira instructs her (in Japanese, managerial mode) to use English (17). He then attempts to use scaffolding (materials mode) to prompt her to speak English. Very short turns follow (18–27), where FS1 echoes the teacher word by word. However, rather than attempt to copy his pronunciation, she uses the Japanese *katakana* pronunciation: 'from' becomes 'furomu' (18), 'six' is 'sikkusu' (22) and 'thirty' becomes 'sa-ti' (24). Japanese students commonly write English words in *katakana* for memorisation purposes; however, this approach has been criticised due to the incomprehensibility of the pronunciation to English speakers who are unfamiliar with this phenomenon (Jannuzi, 2001; Martin, 2004). The use of *katakana* by FS1 may be an act of subtle rebellion. Following Akira's request for English (17), it avoids an outright confrontation, but she avoids repeating the expected form.

Reflection

The unique nature of the context and the narrow data sample prevent generalisation of these findings, as is inevitable in reporting any case study. Instead, this section offers a summary and some of my reflections, which will, it is hoped, enable readers to relate the points to their own contexts.

The SETT framework provided a useful tool for analysing the teachers' use of language to achieve their pedagogic goals. Akira switched to Japanese for his managerial mode instructions and explanations. Chikara often did likewise, but he also used Japanese to empathise with the students (Braine, 2010). He sometimes used English in managerial mode to indicate that he wanted students to follow his use of the target language. In the materials mode, both teachers used English, but Chikara used more range in his target language use than Akira. Chikara used interactional features such as scaffolding and direct repair, but Akira tended to supply the answers. Chikara also gave content feedback (classroom context mode) and elaborated a student response (combination of skills and systems mode and classroom context mode).

The use of the framework for this study had some limitations. It has been designed for teacher self-evaluation. Under such an approach, practitioners may gain useful insights into their own teaching and may be able to unpack their thought processes. However, other researchers may challenge the interpretations that I made as an outsider. A further limitation stems from the assumption that the teacher controls the dialogue. Although teacher-centred classrooms were observed, the students' utterances constrained the teachers' attempts to increase the use of the target language.

Four student tendencies emerged: to speak Japanese; to use extended pauses or to stay silent; to utter single English words; and to switch to *katakana* pronunciation. These phenomena existed despite the teachers' attempts to encourage English use, the lack of form-focused entrance test pressure, and the implementation of communicative textbooks.

In addition to previous policies described in the introduction, the latest MEXT plan aimed to see a transfer towards classes conducted entirely in English from 2013 (Fredrick, 2011). As indicated in the introduction, previous research has focused on teachers' continued use of *yakudoku*. Studies from the students' perspective, often critical of teachers, have been retrospective surveys of university students (Falout & Maruyama, 2004; Kikuchi, 2009; Kikuchi & Sakai, 2009; Shimizu, 1995). However, the students' reluctance to use English in this study indicates that we need more research into students' attitudes to CS in their specific contexts, as well as those of their teachers.

In his Overview in this volume, Macaro proposes the benefit of adopting the 'optimal' position that recognises the advantages of a principled approach to CS. Macaro makes this call from a cognitive perspective within research into mainstream second language acquisition. However, more classroom studies from a sociocultural perspective – seeking to understand factors underlying participants' reticence to speak in the target language and the empowerment that could result from using their mother tongue – may help to advance the debate beyond the 'English-only for communication' versus 'mother tongue for grammar' illusion.

COMMENTARY

Introduction

During one of my initial trips to Malaysia many years ago, I was struck by the conversations in which my local friends engaged. While all Malaysian nationals, my friends represented the dominant ethnic groups of the country: Malay, Chinese and Tamil. I quickly realised that while I could understand much of what they were saying because they were predominantly using English, to my astonishment they were also using vocabulary, slang and idiomatic phrases from the three other languages common in the country (often all represented in a single sentence): Bahasa Melayu, Chinese dialects including Mandarin, Hokkien or Cantonese, and Tamil. While the official language in Malaysia is Bahasa Melayu, these other languages are also used by the ethnic groups in the country (Gill, 2005; Ministry of Foreign Affairs, Malaysia, 2012; Shamsul, 2001). When I asked my friends about this practice of mixing languages, they replied that they simply chose the most appropriate linguistic item for the meaning they wanted to convey, not necessarily considering the origin language, since those involved were all familiar with the languages in question. Many years later, after a significant number of years in Japan, while not fluent in Japanese, there are Japanese lexical items that I chose to use with my Japanese colleagues and fellow long-term expatriates, because the meaning expressed in Japanese is not present in an English translation. This mixing of languages, or CS, allows for more effective communication of meaning.

In the EFL context, the use of CS invariably leads to the argument between L1 use in the foreign language classroom and the exclusive use of the target language, such as can be seen in 'direct' or 'natural' teaching methods (Hobbs *et al.*, 2010; Kamwangamalu, 2010; McMillan & Rivers, 2011; Yonesaka, 2005). While a detailed discussion of this debate is beyond the scope of this commentary, it is relevant to point out that such discussions do have an important impact on teaching practice in Japan, where the EFL classroom has been characterised as primarily focused on grammar structure and driven by the national examination scheme, notwithstanding policy initiatives implemented by MEXT (Fujimoto-Adamson, 2006; Hobbs *et al.*, 2010; McMillan & Rivers, 2011; MEXT, 2003; Stroupe *et al.*, 2009; Yonesaka, 2005).

Humphries focused on many of these issues in the research component of this chapter. In the case of the two teachers at the *Kosen* school, the predominant language used during the class was Japanese. These findings are consistent with the commonly held belief that although EFL is included in the curricula of secondary schools in Japan, English as the language of instruction is not typically implemented until the tertiary level (Lee, 2010). Additionally, Humphries focused on the purposes of the CS choices of these instructors, which focused mostly on managing the class, providing explanations and empathising with their students. After reading this research, I considered how these findings would apply to my own teaching context: a language centre responsible for providing communicative language programmes in English (and other languages) within a private university with a diverse faculty of both native Japanese- and English-speaking people providing a wide variety of courses with English as the predominant language of instruction. Building on the work of Humphries, the following research investigates:

- to what extent faculty members with different cultural and linguistic backgrounds implement CS in their classes where the medium of instruction in English;
- for what purposes these faculty members codeswitch;
- on what pedagogical or institutional factors they have based their language use decisions.

Methodology

A group of university instructors were interviewed individually, based on questions focused on years of teaching experience, self-assessment of language proficiency, courses taught, frequency of CS and for what purposes, and pedagogical beliefs or institutional policies that guided their decision-making process.

The purposes of the CS were categorised based on the modes listed in the above case study. Additionally, if teachers reported using Japanese (the students' L1) during their classes, a follow-up question related to the structure of the CS was asked, based on the six models listed in the Appendix. A limitation to the current research is that all data are self-reported: participants were asked to estimate the percentage of class time for which they used Japanese in a typical class. These individually reported percentages were then averaged, resulting in the percentages listed in the current study. While no observations were conducted to validate the reported amount of CS actually occurring in the classroom setting, there was little variation among responses, with reports below 10% in most cases (except on courses in the lowest proficiency level) (see Table 3.4). Often the majority of participants reported no use of Japanese. While not statistically verifiable, the trend in teachers' reported use of students' L1 does indicate a strong perception and propensity to use only English in the language classroom. These findings are in contrast to those of Humphries, where emphasis was placed on the use of students' L1 as the language of instruction.

Results and Discussion

Eighteen experienced university instructors were included in the interview process (Table 3.3). Most of these instructors were part of the language centre of the university and were categorised at the academic rank of 'lecturer'. The largest numbers of participants indicated American or Japanese nationality. The majority of the participants indicated that English was their native language while Japanese was indicated by the second largest group. Participants were also asked whether they spoke other languages, and to self-assess their fluency level for each language, on a scale of 1 (monolingual) to 10 (fully bilingual). Seven participants indicated their L2 was English and seven indicated Japanese as their L2.

Table 3.3 Participant descriptors

Descriptor	No. of participants	Mean	Range	Proficiency (scale 1–10)
Experience				
Total experience (years)		15.1	2–30	
Years at current institution		8.3	1–18	
Gender				
Male	12			
Female	6			
Academic department				
Language support centre	14			
Economics	2			
English literature	1			
Business	1			
Academic rank				
Professor	3			
Assistant professor	2			
Lecturer	10			
Assistant lecturer	3			
Nationality				
Japanese	8			
American (US)	8			
Australia	1			
Belgium	1			
Native language				
English	10			
Japanese	7			
French	1			
Self-reported L2 proficiency				
English	7			7.2
Japanese	7			7.9

Use of students' L1

A reported shift from one language to another, whether limited to a single word or as extended explanation or communication, in or outside of class, between students and teachers, was considered an example of CS. In this case, the most frequently used language was English, as the medium of instruction, and the predominant secondary language was Japanese, here often referred to as students' L1. Overall, instructors reported that they used very little Japanese during their classes. Many instructors responded that they never used students' L1; in this regard there was no association with the instructors' nationality, ethnicity or years of experience. Of those who did indicate that they made use of the students' L1, the majority indicated that the overall percentage of use was less than 10% in most situations. However, there were notable exceptions. Instructors indicated that their decision regarding the use of L1 on any course was related to the type of course and the level of the students enrolled. Instructors reported teaching a variety of courses, at varying levels (Table 3.4).

Instructors of students at lower proficiency levels often indicated the students' need for L1 instruction at different times during their class. This reflects the trend found by Humphries; the teaching context characterised by a low proficiency level led instructors to depend more heavily on students' L1. Through the interviews, the majority of participants in the current study indicated that their

Table 3.4 Percentage L1 use by course level

Level	TOEIC range	No. of sections at level*	Percentage of L1 use reported
Advanced II	~625	8	2.0
Advanced	570–620	24	2.7
Upper intermediate	490–565	5	2.3
Intermediate	425–485	10	2.3
Elementary	285–420	19	6.0
Basic	~280	9	30.4

*Total number of sections taught by multiple instructors included in this study at a given level.

Table 3.5 Percentage L1 use by course content type

Course content type	No. of sections per content category	Percentage of L1 use reported
Content	33	2.9
Content-based	9	4.2
English instruction (communication)	47	5.6
English instruction (test preparation)	12	20.4

inclination to use students' L1 decreased as the level of the class to which the instructor was assigned increased (students are enrolled in classes based on TOEIC scores). Instructors teaching classes at the Advanced or Advanced II levels used students' L1 2.0% and 2.7% of the class time, respectively. In contrast, at the elementary level, the percentage reported was 6.0%, and at the basic or lowest level, participants reported using students' L1 during 30.4% of class time.

The type of course content also influenced the instructors' decisions on the extent to which to use students' L1. In general, instructors used students' L1 less than approximately 5% of class time, unless the course was for test preparation (Table 3.5). Repeatedly during the interviews, instructors distinguished this type of course from others, indicating the ease and in some cases the importance of utilising students' L1, particularly for lower-evel students, when explaining grammatical structures or test-taking strategies.

Purposes of using the students' L1

During the interviews, when instructors reported the use of students' L1, they were additionally asked to indicate the primary purpose for this language choice, followed by the secondary purpose, and so on, in descending importance. As was found by Humphries, most instructors reported using students' L1 for managerial purposes, that is, to organise the class, to provide instructions, or to maintain the pace of activities (Table 3.6). However, the instructors included in these interviews often distinguished between providing (general managerial) extended directions in L1 from using only a single word to aid students' understanding, the most commonly reported reason for using students' L1. This pattern of use of students' L1 falls in

Table 3.6 Purposes of using the students' L1

Ranking of purpose	Frequency (n)
Primary purpose	
Managerial (limited to single vocabulary or similar)	29
Managerial (general)	20
Solidarity: rapport/affective functions	5
Emphasis/clarification	4
Materials: scaffolding	3
Personal (instructor) study	3
Skills and systems: scaffolding	2
Skills and systems: grammar instruction	1
Secondary purpose	
Solidarity: rapport/affective functions	15
Managerial (general)	7
Elaboration	6
Managerial (limited to single vocabulary or similar)	4
Skills and systems: grammar instruction	4
Materials: scaffolding	2
Solidarity: solidarity	1
Skills and systems: scaffolding	1
Tertiary purpose	
Solidarity: rapport/affective functions	12
Personal (instructor) study	4
Managerial (general)	2
Skills and systems: grammar instruction	1

line with Macaro's distinction in his Overview between utilising CS for a communicative function – 'for the purpose of maintaining L2 communication' – rather than focusing primarily on developing knowledge about the language as a subject of study. More general managerial strategies in Japanese were also cited by the instructors in the current study as primary, secondary and tertiary purposes, but at lower frequencies. Additionally, many instructors reported using students' L1 to lighten the atmosphere of the class or to reduce the affective level of students through joking or other methods in order to build rapport.

When asked how they integrated students' L1 into their speech during class, instructors most often indicated they presented a concept in English first, and at times followed that with the Japanese equivalent of a concept or lexical item, and then continued in English (i.e. model 2 in the Appendix). This supports the assertion that the most common purpose for teachers' use of Japanese in their classrooms was to provide instructions and explanations, but using only single vocabulary words to do so. This is also an example of what Macaro has identified as naturalistic CS, where a speaker will utilise lexical items from one language or another in order to assist with comprehension. Other instructors reported using turn-taking with students, alternating between languages. Fewer instructors reported using extended explanations in students' L1. In contrast, the instructors in the Humphries study typically made use of more extended explanations in students' L1.

Instructors also reported using Japanese outside of the teaching context. In cases of formal meetings, such as students visiting an instructor's office to ask a question, meetings outside of the classroom, or official functions, the likelihood of instructors using students' L1 remained comparatively low, depending on the seriousness of the questions asked and the difficulty the student may have in communicating. In more informal situations, including casual meetings and discussing non-class-related activities, the use of L1 increased. In such cases where students presented personal problems, instructors were more inclined to communicate in students' L1. In fact, related to this final category, many of the non-native Japanese-speaking instructors suggested that they would direct the student to a Japanese colleague, as they may not have been confident in their own foreign language abilities related to such topics.

Pedagogical or institutional factors influencing L1 use

When asked about institutional or administrative factors that influenced instructors' decisions related to use of students' L1, there was little emphasis on 'written rules' or administrative dictates related to language of instruction of courses. Likewise, there was no indication of punitive measures that could be taken if an instructor used Japanese in class. Rather, there was a sense of a professional community among instructors within the language centre at the university who shared a pedagogical approach that emphasised L2 use in class. One instructor pointed to a standard comment on the language centre's online syllabi in a section dedicated to advice for students (rather than to instructors) which stated that 'Courses taught by [language centre] faculty are taught in English...'. This instructor indicated that this influenced her decisions when first joining the university. Many other instructors spoke of a clear sense of a consensus among language centre instructors, and other departmental faculty teaching English-medium courses, that English should be used at all times, with few exceptions. One teacher went further and suggested that the 'English-medium environment' which existed at the institution was different from what she had experienced at other universities. As a new instructor, she recalled having to adjust to these new, clear, yet 'unwritten' expectations, but as this approach coincided with her own language teaching beliefs, she experienced few difficulties making this transition.

Other instructors recalled their educational experiences during their teacher training, naming particular advisers, practicum supervisors, writers or methodological approaches that had influenced their decision to attempt to provide an 'English-only classroom'. Many pointed to the fact that, in the Japanese context, there are few opportunities to use English outside of the classroom, therefore it seemed important to provide opportunities to use the language effectively in a simulated environment, which in turn would lead to increased motivation and achievement on the part of students. One instructor suggested that, if presented appropriately and scaffolded, Japanese students could 'flourish' in an English-only environment. As language learners themselves, a number of instructors indicated that they had felt disadvantaged during their own studies when instructors had translated for them, feeling they had been 'robbed' of an opportunity for a successful learning experience. One instructor indicated that switching to students' L1 is 'insulting their intelligence', assuming that they cannot understand the topic under discussion in English. One teacher pointed out that students had also indicated on course evaluations that they preferred to be taught in English.

For native Japanese-speaking instructors, much of their decision process was based on their own experiences as language learners, but also on themselves as models of successful L2 speakers for their students. One Japanese instructor said that she knew the errors that students made, why they were made and how they could be corrected, based on her own experience. Additionally, Japanese students rarely have confidence in speaking English, and a number of other Japanese instructors saw their opportunity to provide a model of success for students as central to their decision-making process. Both these qualities were seen as unique to non-native English-speaking instructors. Nevertheless, here again instructors also highlighted the need to be flexible, based on the students' needs and context: discussing personal issues, explanation of complex grammatical points, and working with quite low-level students were all seen as areas where L1 use may be more appropriate.

Identity

An unexpected theme emerged from some instructors during the interview: their language choice was related to their identity and, in varying ways, was based on their individual backgrounds. A new Japanese instructor who had spent significant time abroad suggested that she was able to be more intimate with students in Japanese, to understand the nuances of the language and to communicate more effectively. At first, she was not confident enough to use only English even in informal situations, but as she became more confident she used English more often. This same instructor also suggested that students could recognise confident teachers easily, those who demonstrate control over the classroom. In her case, she needed first to accomplish this through the use of Japanese; however, as she has gained experience, she came to use English exclusively. Like other Japanese instructors who use only English, when they do use Japanese, students seem surprised, and assumed that even native Japanese teachers were not 'Japanese' if they had not been using the language in their classes. Students might also assume that such teachers were 'returnees', that is, Japanese people who had received much of their elementary and/or secondary education abroad, thereby developing a bicultural perspective, and then returning to Japan.

One native Japanese instructor commented on students' reactions when they enrolled in his class. While he grew up in the United States, indicating that his L1 was English, he was fluent in Japanese, his L2, and was a Japanese citizen. While this instructor saw himself (and his colleagues saw him) as bicultural, his students saw him initially as ethnically Japanese, and he reported noticing disappointment on their part, thinking that they 'got the Japanese guy' when in reality they had been hoping to enrol in a class with a foreign teacher. In such cases, this instructor used his fluency in English to identify himself as a 'foreign-like' teacher to his students, yet also had the ability to utilise his Japanese language abilities with lower-level students if he so chose.

Another instructor had faced similar responses. He was Japanese-American, ethnically Japanese, an American citizen, with English as his L1 and Japanese as his L2. This instructor suggested that 'I look Japanese, therefore the assumption is that I know Japanese', although he did not always speak Japanese accurately. He went on to say 'by speaking English, I reinforce the perception that I am American'. This instructor suggested that if he spoke Japanese, he lost the effort that some students would make in his class to speak in English, because they assumed that he would translate what he had said into Japanese. This instructor self-identified as American, but 'in Japan, if you look Japanese, there is a whole set of expectations that goes along with that'. Therefore he used English to emphasise his identity as a Japanese-American.

A final instructor grew up in an environment where, although he identified his L1 as English, he naturally codeswitched with family members (his mother was Japanese, his father Asian-American of Hawaiian, Chinese and Japanese decent). This instructor also emphasised the 'unwritten rule' within the institution of ensuring as much exposure to L2 as possible to prepare students for study abroad or their professional life. Nevertheless, this instructor reported that if he could use Japanese to save a few minutes in class, to avoid 'verbal gymnastics' when describing abstract or technical terms, he did so. However, he stated that he did 'not want to be identified as Japanese'. When using Japanese, he saw himself (and others saw him) as a different person than when he is using English. He identified more closely with his 'English self', that is, how he and others perceived him culturally and individually as a native English speaker when he spoke English. Using Japanese resulted in Japanese cultural expectations with which he was uncomfortable.

In these cases, the instructors' choices about language use and CS were not based on teaching methodology or learning objectives, but rather they were using language as a tool to manipulate the perceptions of others. In his Overview to this volume, Macaro indicates that such CS can occur when bilinguals are making a sociolinguistic statement. In the current study, this statement seemed to revolve around how language choice more clearly identified the speakers as Japanese, or not, based on the situation and context, their choice of language use, and the way in which they wanted to be identified by others.

Conclusion

Language choice is a complex process, yet is one through which bilingual and multilingual speakers progress naturally and frequently. The process increases in complexity in the language learning environment, when multiple languages and cultural expectations are present. Additionally, questions arise to the appropriateness of L1 and L2 use in the EFL classroom, and the balance, utility and emphasis of each. In the current commentary, the results mirror those of Humphries, in that language is seen as a tool for classroom management and for explanation of complex ideas, as an efficient method to transfer knowledge. Nevertheless, what has also been indicated in the current research is that there are other variables, namely the official and unofficial expectations of a professional community, that may impact on decisions regarding language selection. And for some instructors, language choice is closely related to identity, both as a professional and as a member of a national or ethnic community. What does seem clear is that polarised views on language use in the EFL classroom, whether the emphasis is on L1 or exclusive use of L2, are not relevant to the practical experience of EFL teachers, whether in Japan or elsewhere. What is apparent is that the investigation of the conscious or unconscious decision process regarding language use can lead to the appropriate and effective use of languages in the learning environment, with the overall goal of providing effective learning opportunities and experiences for students.

References

Amano, I. and Poole, G.S. (2005) The Japanese university in crisis. *Higher Education* 50, 686–711.

Braine, G. (2010) *Nonnative Speaker English Teachers: Research, Pedagogy, and Professional Growth*. New York: Routledge.

Browne, C.M. and Wada, M. (1998) Current issues in high school English teaching in Japan: An exploratory survey. *Language, Culture and Curriculum*, 11(1), 97–112.

Bruner, J. (1983) *Child's Talk*. Oxford: Oxford University Press.

Falout, J. and Maruyama, M. (2004) A comparative study of proficiency and learner demotivation. *The Language Teacher* 28 (8), 3–9. See http://jalt-publications.org/tlt/articles/447-comparative-study-proficiency-and-learner-demotivation (accessed August 2007).

Fredrick, C. (2011) English translation of the MEXT guidelines. See http://ajet.net/2011/02/24/english-translation-of-the-mext-guidelines (accessed November 2011).

Fujimoto-Adamson, N. (2006) Globalization and history of English education in Japan. *Asian EFL Journal* 8 (3). See http://asian-efl-journal.com/quarterly-journal/2006/09/29/globalization-and-history-of-english-education-in-japan/ (accessed August 2013).

Gershon, S., Mares, C. and Walker, R. (2004) *On the Go: English Skills for Global Communication*. Hong Kong: Pearson Education Asia.

Gill, S.K. (2005) Language policy in Malaysia: Reversing direction. *Language Policy* 4, 241–260.

Gorsuch, G. (1998) *Yakudoku* EFL instruction in two Japanese high school classrooms: An exploratory study. *JALT Journal* 20 (1), 6–32.

Gorsuch, G. (1999) Monbusho approved textbooks in Japanese high school EFL classes: An aid or a hindrance to educational policy innovations? *Language Teacher* 23 (10), 5–15.

Gorsuch, G. (2001) Japanese EFL teachers' perceptions of communicative, audiolingual and yakudoku activities: The plan versus the reality. *Educational Policy Analysis Archives* 9 (10). See http://epaa.asu.edu/ojs/article/view/339 (accessed August 2007).

Hobbs, V., Matsuo, A. and Payne, M. (2010) Code-switching in Japanese language classrooms: An exploratory investigation of native vs. non-native speaker teacher practice. *Linguistics and Education* 21, 44–59.

Humphries, S. (2012) From policy to pedagogy: Exploring the impact of new communicative textbooks on the classroom practice of Japanese teachers of English. In C. Gitsaki and R.B. Baldauf, Jr (eds) *Future Directions in Applied Linguistics: Local and Global Perspectives* (pp. 488–507). Newcastle: Cambridge Scholars Publishing.

Humphries, S. (2013) Western-published versus MEXT-mandated: A comparative textbook analysis. *Doshisha Studies in English* 90, 217–238.

Jannuzi, C. (2001) Do students need Katakana Eigo to learn and to read English? *Language Teacher*, 25 (4). See http://jalt-publications.org/old_tlt/articles/2001/04/jannuzi (accessed September 2011).

Kamwangamalu, N.M. (2010) Multilingualism and codeswitching in education. In N.H. Hornberger, and S.L. McKay (eds) *Sociolinguistics and Language Education* (pp. 116–142). Bristol: Multilingual Matters.

Kikuchi, K. (2009) Listening to our learners' voices: What demotivates Japanese high school students? *Language Teaching Research* 13 (4), 453–471.

Kikuchi, K. and Sakai, H. (2009) Japanese learners' demotivation to study English: A survey study. *JALT Journal* 31 (2), 183–204.

Lee, J.J. (2010) The uniqueness of EFL teachers: Perceptions of Japanese learners. *TESOL Journal* 1 (1), 23–48. See http://onlinelibrary.wiley.com/doi/10.5054/tj.2010.214881/abstract;jsessionid=B41A2A73075FABFDE714F3688DD0E2CA.d02t02 (accessed August 2013).

LoCastro, V. (1997) Politeness and pragmatic competence in foreign language education. *Language Teaching Research* 1 (3), 239–267.

Martin, A. (2004) The 'katakana effect' and teaching English in Japan: Are there fundamental impediments to greater ELT success in Japan? *English Today* 20 (1), 50–55.

McGroarty, M. and Taguchi, N. (2005) Evaluating the communicativeness of EFL textbooks for Japanese secondary schools. In C. Holten and J. Frodesen (eds) *The Power of Context in Language Teaching and Learning* (pp. 211–224). Boston: Heinle and Heinle.

McMillan, B.A. and Rivers, D.J. (2011) The practice of policy: Teacher attitudes toward 'English only'. *System* 39, 251–263.

MEXT (Ministry of Education, Culture, Sports, Science and Technology) (2003) Regarding the establishment of an action plan to cultivate 'Japanese with English abilities'. See http://www.gifu-net.ed.jp/kyoka/eigo/CommunicativeEnglish/Regarding%20the%20Establishment%20of%20an%20Action%20Plan%20to%20Cultivate%20%A1%C8Japanese%20with%20English%20Abilities%A1%C9.htm (accessed August 2013).

Ministry of Foreign Affairs, Malaysia (2012) *Malaysia: Country Profile*. See http://www.kln.gov.my/web/gha_accra/history (accessed August 2013).

Nishino, T. (2008) Japanese secondary school teachers' beliefs and practices regarding communicative language teaching: An exploratory survey. *JALT Journal* 30 (1), 27–50.

O'Donnell, K. (2005) Japanese secondary English teachers: Negotiation of educational roles in the face of curricular reform. *Language, Culture and Curriculum* 18 (3), 300–315.

Pacek, D. (1996) Lessons to be learnt from negative evaluation. *ELT Journal* 50 (4), 335–343.

Rosenkjar, P. (2009) Adapting a Japanese high school textbook to teach reading microskills communicatively. In L. Savova (ed.) *Using Textbooks Effectively* (pp. 63–72). Alexandria, VA: TESOL Inc.

Sakui, K. (2004) Wearing two pairs of shoes: Language teaching in Japan. *ELT Journal*, 58 (2) 155–163.

Sato, K. (2002) Practical understandings of communicative language teaching and teacher development. In S.J. Savignon (ed.) *Interpreting Communicative Language Teaching: Contexts and Concerns in Teacher Education* (pp. 41–81). New Haven, CT: Yale University Press.

Sato, K. and Kleinsasser, R. (2004) Beliefs, practices and interactions of teachers in a Japanese high school English department. *Teaching and Teacher Education* 20, 797–816.

Shamsul, A.B. (2001) A history of an identity, an identity of a history: The idea and practice of 'Malayness' in Malaysia reconsidered. *Journal of Southeast Asian Studies* 32 (3), 355–366.

Shimizu, K. (1995) Japanese college student attitudes towards English teachers: A survey. *Language Teacher*, 19 (10). See http://jalt-publications.org/old_tlt/files/95/oct/shimizu.html (accessed August 2013).

Sinclair, J.M. and Coulthard, M. (1975) *Towards and Analysis of Discourse: The English Used by Teachers and Pupils*. London: Oxford University Press.

Stroupe, R., Fenton, A., MacDonald. L. and Riley, M. (2009) A comparison of learner attitudes and perceptions. Paper presented at the JALT 35th Annual International Conference and Educational Materials Exposition, Shizuoka, Japan.

Taguchi, N. (2005) The communicative approach in Japanese secondary schools: Teachers' perceptions and practice. *Language Teacher* 29 (3), 3–12.

Tanabe, Y. (2004) What the 2003 MEXT Action Plan proposes to teachers of English. *Language Teacher* 28 (3). See http://jalt-publications.org/tlt/articles/730-what-2003-mext-action-plan-proposes-teachers-english (accessed August 2007).

Walsh, S. (2006) *Investigating Classroom Discourse*. London: Routledge.

Walsh, S. (2011) *Exploring Classroom Discourse: Language in Action*. New York: Routledge.

Watanabe, Y. (2004) Teacher factors mediating washback. In L. Cheng, Y. Watanabe and A. Curtis (eds) *Washback in Language Testing: Research Contexts and Models* (pp. 129–146). Mahwah, NJ: Erlbaum.

Yonesaka, S. (2005) A proposal to use classroom discourse frames to investigate patterns of teacher L1 use. *Studies in Culture* 32, 31–57.

Appendix. Models of CS

English text

One of the basic principles of economics, supply and demand, can be used in many different circumstances. The concept of supply and demand shows the relationship between the demand of consumers and supply of products.

Model 1: L1 use integrated into L2

One of the basic principles of economics, supply and demand, can be used in many different circumstances. 需要・供給の概念 *The concept of supply and demand* shows the relationship between the demand of consumers and supply of products.

Model 2: L1 use integrated into L2, repeated single idea/item

One of the basic principles of economics, supply and demand, can be used in many different circumstances. The concept of supply and demand, 需要・供給の概念 *The concept of supply and demand*, shows the relationship between the demand of consumers and supply of products.

Model 3: One sentence in L1, extension in L2

One of the basic principles of economics, supply and demand, can be used in many different circumstances. 需要・供給の概念は、消費者側の需要と生産者側の供給との関係を表します。 *The concept of supply and demand shows the relationship between the demand of consumers and supply of products.*

Model 4: One sentence in L1, repeated in L2

One of the basic principles of economics, supply and demand, can be used in many different circumstances. The concept of supply and demand shows the relationship between the demand of consumers and supply of products. 言い換えると、需要・供給の概念は、消費者側の需要と生産者側の供給との関係を表します。 *In other words, the concept of supply and demand shows the relationship between the demand of consumers and supply of products.*

Model 5: Turn taking in L1 and L2

A One of the basic principles of economics, supply and demand, can be used in many different circumstances.

B 分かりました。この概念は消費者の需要に基づいているのですね。 *I understand. This concept is based on the demand of consumers.*

A That's partly right. The concept of supply and demand shows the relationship between the demand of consumers and supply of products.

Model 6: Any other method used by a teacher

4 Codeswitching in Universities in Thailand and Bhutan

Case Study: Chamaipak Tayjasanant
Commentary: Matthew G. Robinson

CASE STUDY

Introduction

The fact that English has recently been the main language of instruction in various school and university programmes has largely caused Thai teachers of English as a foreign language (EFL) to feel obliged to use as much English as possible. Research into codeswitching (CS) in Thai EFL classes is rare, mostly because teachers are encouraged to use English as the sole medium of classroom instruction. This has led to low recognition of classroom CS – the use of the foreign language in class with occasional use of the students' native language to provide some explanations (Coulmas, 2005).

This case study discusses the role of English at various educational levels in Thailand, and presents a case study of CS in EFL classrooms at a Thai university, based on observational and interview data. Findings reveal similarities and differences between the two participant teachers, regarding the extent and purposes of CS, their beliefs about CS in general and in classrooms, and the reasons they give for its use in the observed classes.

The Role of English in Thailand

English has considerable power in south-east Asia, as in many other parts of the world. Although all the region's countries share similar cultural elements, they have no common language, and thus have to use English as the lingua franca. Thailand, unlike many of its neighbouring countries, such as Brunei Darussalam, Malaysia and Singapore, which have shared a history of British colonisation, is the only country in the region which was not a colony of any western nation. Thus, English is not as highly integrated into Thai life and it remains a foreign language, rather than a second language, as it is in the aforementioned countries where it is more widely spoken, especially in the main urban centres. Nonetheless, since the reign of King Rama III (1824–51), when a trend towards western-style education started, English has been recognised as a tool for modernising the country (Durongphan et al., 1982).

English was introduced as a school subject immediately after the First National Education Scheme was announced in 1932. In school curricula between 1937 and 1960, English was a compulsory subject, beginning from the fifth year of primary education. Before the 1960s the written language was taught through traditional methods of rote learning and grammar translation. Yet when the need to use the language for communication was highlighted in the 1960 curriculum, the four language skills were integrated and taught using the audio-lingual method, by which teacher-centred repetitious practice was emphasised.

Since the mid-1990s, EFL has been a compulsory school subject for all primary students (from year 1). Recent curricula have followed the fashion of student-centred learning, and promoted analytical thinking and problem-solving activities to enable students to apply knowledge in real life. The four language skills are now to be taught for functional-communicative purposes, with the aim of leading students towards learner autonomy (Wongsothorn et al., 2002). Bilingual education programmes, where the content of various subjects is taught in both Thai and English, have also become popular in many private schools. Yet the availability of such content-based instruction is limited in Thailand, because of a shortage of bilingually competent teachers and the high cost of hiring English-speaking instructors.

Like primary and secondary schooling, higher education in Thailand did not originate from western colonisation. Instead, the country has chosen to adopt various foreign models since the attempts made by King Rama V (1853–1910) to promote the country's overall socio-economic advancement, for instance in infrastructure, banking and education (Sinlarat, 2004). Since then, the country's universities have conserved the Thai language as the main medium of instruction. This, together with the fact that 'the development of Thai universities was in line with the Thai approach, which favors the middle path and one not marked by extreme changes' (Sinlarat, 2004: 211), has perhaps made university education in Thailand less competitive than it is in many neighbouring countries which promote western-style education and the use of English as the medium.

However, the increasing impact of globalisation has recently influenced many universities to offer international programmes to compete with other world-class universities, and this inevitably requires staff to teach and research in English. This also coincides with the country's move towards the ASEAN Economic Community (AEC) in 2015, where English is used as its lingua franca to promote sociocultural, economic and security integration among ASEAN countries. This has led the Thai government to feel the need to declare English as a second medium of instruction in all educational institutions, to enable new-generation Thais to communicate with regional and world communities in English. Yet its plan to make an official announcement to this effect was vetoed and finally abolished, with a claim that the change was likely to create social disputes and sensitivities in terms of administration and a possible misunderstanding that Thailand had been colonised in the past. Thus, while English will not be the main language of instruction in the short term, it will remain one of the most important foreign languages in schools and universities.

The Present Study

Setting and participants

The present study was carried out at an English language department in a university in Thailand, where instructors (both Thai and native speakers of English) are responsible for teaching a variety of EFL courses to both English major and non-English major students. Generally, an English language course totals 45 hours and lasts 15 weeks in regular terms, but there are also weekend courses and intensive programmes during summer breaks (from one to six weeks in April–May).

Two Thai instructors volunteered to participate in the study. 'Elspeth', in her late 20s, was awarded a BA in English in Thailand and her MA in linguistics abroad, while 'Bessie', in her early 40s, obtained both her BA and MA in English and her qualification in teaching English as a foreign language (TEFL) from two prestigious universities in Thailand, and had experience teaching at both private and public universities.

Research questions

The present study intended to answer the following research questions:

(1) To what extent do the teachers' switch codes and what functions are served by CS?
(2) What are their beliefs about language teaching and learning, with an emphasis on the teacher talk and CS?
(3) What are their reasons for CS at particular instances?

Data collection: Audio-recordings of classes and individual interviews

During the six-week summer term in April 2011, two audio-recordings of each teacher's one-hour class were made to obtain classroom discourse data. The focus was on classroom language use, types of CS in the teachers' talk, and key functions of their switches in relation to contexts and pedagogic purposes. Elspeth's recorded lessons were part of an elective course in English for specific purposes (ESP), highlighting reading English-language newspapers. Most of the students were drop-outs from the Faculty of Engineering; some could not graduate within four years. Bessie's recorded lessons were in the Basic English Structure course, which enrolled third-year non-English majors. The number of students in both classes exceeded 40.

In the second phase of data collection, I conducted an individual semi-structured interview with each of the teachers two months later, when they were less occupied with teaching and grading. Each interview, lasting approximately 30 minutes, was divided into two parts. The first aimed to explore their beliefs about EFL teaching and learning, covering the changing role of English in Thailand, language development and the characteristics of good EFL teaching. Within this discussion, I also attempted to elicit reasons for their expressed beliefs and factors and their explanations of any mismatches between beliefs and practice. The second part of the interview aimed to elicit their reasons for CS at particular instances, by showing key extracts from the lessons. This part also helped me to check the accuracy of my lesson transcription.

Data analysis

All the collected observational data were transcribed, translated into English and subjected to two steps of coding. Open coding was first applied, to identify sections for the main themes: the classroom language use, various patterns of the teachers' CS, different functions of their switches, their beliefs about different aspects of language teaching and learning, reasons for their beliefs, and constraining factors. For the second step of coding, I compared and contrasted my transcripts of the audio-recordings (from the classrooms and interviews) to identify patterns across the datasets, to conceptualise the main themes and to select corresponding quotations.

Findings 1. Observational Data: The Teachers' Classroom Language Use and Codeswitching

The two participant teachers differed in terms of classroom language use in that the transcripts of Elspeth's lessons on classified advertisements revealed extensive use of Thai with little use of English, while those of Bessie's lessons on adverbial clauses revealed extensive use of English with little use of Thai, as shown in Table 4.1.

Three types of CS were evident (Poplack, 2000): *tag-switching* (the switching of a tag phrase or a word); *intra-sentential switching* (switching within a sentence); and *inter-sentential switching* (switching between sentences). As shown in Table 4.2, tag-switching far outweighed intra-sentential switching and inter-sentential switching in all the one-hour audio-recorded lessons, accounting for 91.9% and 78.1% of CS in Elspeth's lessons, and 75.0% and 73.2% in Bessie's lessons. Yet their tag-switching differed, in that Elspeth inserted English words in her explanation, which was mainly in Thai, while Bessie inserted Thai tag words and phrases into her explanation in English, as can be seen in the following extracts:

Table 4.1 The amount of teacher talk

Teacher	Length of lesson (min/s)	Length of teacher talk (min/s)	Total teacher talking time (%)	Teacher talk in L1 (min/s)	Teacher talk in L1 (%)	Teacher talk in L2 (min/s)	Teacher talk in L2 (%)
Elspeth	109'	81'20"	74.6%	65'20"	80.3%	16'00"	19.7%
Bessie	131'	97'30"	74.4%	31'50"	32.6%	65'40"	67.3%

Table 4.2 Types of codeswitching in the teachers' talk and their number of occurrences

Teacher	Tag-switching		Intra-sentential switching		Inter-sentential switching		Total CS use	
	Lesson 1	Lesson 2	Lesson 1	Lesson 2	Lesson 1	Lesson 2	Lesson 1	Lesson 2
	No. %	No. %	No. %	No. %	No. %	No. %	No. %	No. %
Elspeth	79 91.9	121 78.1	5 5.8	18 11.6	2 2.3	16 10.3	86 100	155 100
Bessie	102 75.0	235 73.2	8 5.9	27 8.4	26 19.1	59 18.4	136 100	321 100

Extract 1 (Elspeth, tag-switching)

Un nikue auk naewduengdood jai ka. *This appears attractive.* // Sadangwahaiyeryoo. *It shows the company generously provides many benefits.* Miarai bang. *What are they?* /// Kor mi {pointing at the advertisement in the book} *There is/are* accommodation, mi *there is/are* meals, mi *there is/are* social security. ///// Kor auk puawkprakansankom. *They are mostly social security things.*
(Lesson 2, minutes 3'24" to 3'38")

Extract 2 (Bessie, tag-switching)

And next ka, on page 79 naka. We're gonna do only one example ka – only one exercise ka. ///// Exercise A ka. <Women end a sentence with 'naka' or 'ka' as a discourse marker signalling politeness in Thai.>
(Lesson 1, minutes 29'02" to 29'10")

Elspeth made slightly more intra-sentential switches (5.8% and 11.6%) than inter-switches (2.3% and 10.3%) in both her lessons, whereas Bessie seemed to prefer the inter-sentential type (19.1% and 18.4%) to the intra-sentential switching type (5.9% and 8.4%).

Extract 3 (Elspeth, intra-sentential switching)

Na ka. Kao hai *The book asks you to* write the word for each of the following. // The first one 'uni' // stands for / ?
(Lesson 1, minutes 2'39" to 2'49")

Extract 4 (Elspeth, intra-sentential switching)

Na ka // Kosana nitum hai rao rue waa. *Okay, we can learn from this advertisement that* you can make your house look beautiful and expensive if you use our service.
(Lesson 2, minutes 14'22" to 14'30")

Extract 5 (Bessie, inter-sentential switching)

They still ask you to do a paraphrasing exercise nuh <a sentence ending used to seek agreement or confirmation>. /// Plien nuun plienniiplienpaiplien maa chonkonpliensubson. *Change this, change that. We need to change the same text again and again, and then we get confused.*
(Lesson 1, minutes 14'22" to 14'32")

Extract 6 (Bessie, inter-sentential switching)

Nai cheewit ching nuu mai tong kra tue rue ron kanaad nii naka. In your real life you don't have to be this alert. /// You don't have to stop reading a newspaper and change a phrase to a clause.
(Lesson 2, minutes 26'41" to 26'50")

The following excerpts are among the few examples of Bessie's intra-sentential switching and Elspeth's inter-sentential switches.

Extract 7 (Bessie, intra-sentential switching)

Almost the last week of the term laew *already*, and then you can go back to your baan nok dai loei na ka *hometown in the countryside* after the exam.
(Lesson 1, minutes 8'56" to 9'02")

Extract 8 (Bessie, intra-sentential switching)

Because last time we looked at the layer of modification, laak kwam sampan ah na kor loei mai dai kuen bot mai *drawing lines to show relationships, so we couldn't start the new chapter.*
(Lesson 2, minutes 23'02" to 23'10")

Extract 9 (Elspeth, inter-sentential switching)

We also have a decorating service. Nok chak cha tum tam na tii laew nia yang mii toktang hai duey *Apart from doing our job, we also decorate it for you.* We will design it for you, free of charge. Kor kue mai kid tang loei na ka *This mean we do it free of charge.*
(Lesson 2, minutes 14'41" to 14'51")

Extract 10 (Elspeth, inter-sentential switching)

If you order a full set of furniture, we will decorate your house, free of charge. Un nii mai kiew loei na ka. Kao mai dai bork waa cha tong sang tang chud na. /// Yang nii pen ton tii cha tong du nid nueng. La eid nid nueng na ka. *This one doesn't count. It doesn't say that you need to order a whole set. This is an example to show that you need to pay attention to detail.*
(Lesson 2, minutes 15'08" to 15'24")

As for the key functions of CS in the teachers' talk, the following pedagogical and social functions emerged, as proposed by Adendorff (1996), O'Cain and Leibscher (2009), and Cook (2010).

The switches served four *pedagogical* functions:

(1) *questioning and elicitation* – to get students to give information (e.g. grammar rules, vocabulary items and correct answers in exercises);
(2) *translation* – to ensure students understand unfamiliar words;
(3) *clarification* – to clarify meanings, give students feedback and explain or reinforce important L2 content;
(4) *comprehension check* – to check whether students can still follow the teacher or the lesson.

The following three *social* functions of CS were also evident:

(1) for *compliment and praise* – to promote positive self-esteem in students;
(2) for *encouragement* – to give students (particularly weaker students) confidence in doing difficult activities;
(3) for *casualness* – to reduce the distance between the teacher and her students by means chatting and making jokes.

The two participant teachers differed greatly in terms of CS functions. Elspeth occasionally explained linguistic issues in English, and tended to switch from English into Thai for pedagogical functions, as shown in the following examples. Her switches for social functions were minimal.

Extract 11 (Elspeth, CS for questioning/elicitation)

$110 pw, yor ma jaak? *Shortened form?* {pointing at the advertisement in the book.}
(Lesson 1, minutes 8'30" to 8'35")

Extract 12 (Elspeth, CS for questioning/elicitation)

Business premises, plaewaaarai la? *Is translated into?* {pointing at the advertisement in the book.}
(Lesson 2, minutes 11'06" to 11'09")

Extract 13 (Elspeth, CS for translation)

This is a ground floor opportunity with high income potential. // Rabrong loei tha maa ruam kub rao laew raidai pen kob pen kam naenae na ka *We guarantee a high income if you join us.*
(Lesson 2, minutes 16'26" to 16'36")

Extract 14 (Elspeth, CS for clarification)

For a confidential interview, un ni kue kon tii son jai ruam tha haak yhaak tham thurakij kub rao nia diew maa kui kan *This is for those who are interested. If they want to join the business, they can arrange to talk.*
(Lesson 2, minutes 16'37" to 16'47")

Extract 15 (Elspeth, CS for comprehension check)

Bok pailaew *I have already told you* 'personnel' means⸮
(Lesson 2, minutes 17'07" to 17'10")

On the contrary, Bessie, who predominantly conducted her classes in English, switched to Thai for pedagogical functions at times.

Extract 16 (Bessie, CS for translation)

So sometimes you will understand that it modifies the noun 'country'. But if you translate it into Thai, you will find 'the country'. Prated tii yuu nok phanaek IT plaek plaek chai mai⸮ *The country outside the IT department. Doesn't it sound strange⸮*
Lesson 1, minutes 11'08" to 11'22")

Extract 17 (Bessie, CS for clarification)

If it starts with present participial phrase, you can answer ... two answers are possible – adjective modifies subject, adverb modifies main verb. Tae tha bok *but if we say* adverb clause function tong un diew tao naan kue *there is only one answer,* adverbkhayai *modifies* verb.
(Lesson 1, minutes 17'02" to 11'17")

Yet most of her distinctive switches were for various social functions, as indicated below.

Extract 18 (Bessie, CS for compliment and praise)

Participial phrases and adjective clauses klai pen ruangdekdeklaew *have become very easy* /// Kengkhuennhaa taa mii khwamrootukkonloei *You've done much better. You all look clever.* I'm very proud of you na <informal ending> {laugh}.
(Lesson 1, minutes 20'47" to 21'03")

Extract 19 (Bessie, CS for encouragement)

Very good. Krai nuey laew mai tong *if you're tired, you don't have to break*. Break nai jai kor dai na ka proawaa prayok maan klaiklai kan *quietly because these sentences are similar* /// Kru mai yhak hai tham yer diew ja ngong pai saa plao plao *I don't want you to overdo it, or you'll get confused*. (Lesson 2, minutes 42'56" to 43'08")

Extract 20 (Bessie, CS for casualness)

Krai mai tham mai kroat na ka *For those who haven't done it, I'm not angry.* Tae pruengnii jaa pirotawathang salapankapisai na ka *But tomorrow I'll get so mad* <in highly poetic language> *if you do it again tomorrow* {laugh}. (Lesson 2, minutes 52'39" to 52'45")

Findings 2. Interview Data: The Teachers' Beliefs

The teachers' beliefs about English language teaching and learning will be discussed in terms of the role of English in Thailand, L1 and L2 development, components of good EFL teaching, and classroom language use and CS. These will be followed by the teachers' reasons for their expressed beliefs, and factors causing mismatches between their beliefs and practice.

Both teachers were aware that English had become increasingly essential for work and education. Elspeth felt that this was due to the country's preparation for membership of the AEC in 2015, which highlighted regional economic integration. She said: 'Those with good English will have better job opportunities than others.' Bessie added, 'I think in four years' time, people may need to take more standardised tests in order to get a job. Right now they do in some fields, but I think many more types of businesses will require these tests to select quality people.' Bessie also noticed more changes at various levels in the education sector, where there is an increasing number of international and bilingual courses.

Their views on the development of English as a foreign language were similar: both teachers thought external factors in the globalised world were now forcing students to learn English in classrooms. Nevertheless, they believed that students with an interest in the language should easily succeed in their learning. Additionally, they both encouraged their students to experience the language beyond the classroom: Elspeth suggested that they watch English language films and other kinds of entertainment, while Bessie stressed a mixture of formal learning and socialising with native speakers of English, for example through social networking. With regard to components of good EFL teaching, Elspeth did not favour any particular approach to this. She reasoned that activities and teaching methods were normally determined by student preferences, their nature, proficiency and learning styles, and should be integrated eclectically. Bessie, however, believed that subject contents helped her to decide which approach to use. She advocated communicative methods for teaching the general skills, but teacher-fronted lecturing was still needed for promoting academic language proficiency, such as grammar rules. She argued that authentic texts should be used at all times as an essential element of communicative language teaching.

Classroom talk and CS

Although the institutional norm required them to speak as much English as possible, neither of the teachers agreed with the use of only one language, whether English or Thai. Elspeth maintained, 'using English only is not a good idea either because students are at different levels. Only some students can cope with English-speaking classes, while the others may not be benefited from this.' They also had the same opinion that the amount of L1 and L2 should vary depending on learner levels. Bessie supported the use of as much English as possible for advanced learners, that is, English major students, while CS was required for non-English majors. However, they supported the alternation between English and Thai for different purposes. Elspeth chose to switch from English to Thai when explaining or reviewing grammar rules to students: 'The Thai language serves as a link to make students better understand what they are learning. They may roughly understand what the teacher says in English, but Thai makes them understand things more deeply.' Bessie, on the other hand, stressed conducting classes in English, and speaking Thai just occasionally, to draw the students' attention: 'I codeswitch when students are not so involved in learning. When I speak Thai either to explain or to chitchat; the classroom atmosphere will change. Thai is good for joking. They do not laugh when we make jokes in English.' These stated beliefs also corresponded to their observed practice, as shown in the observational data.

Reasons for the beliefs related to CS

The teachers identified factors which they themselves thought were likely to be linked with their beliefs about CS. Elspeth indicated that her background as a BA student had allowed her to observe her own teachers: 'I was an English major student, my teacher codeswitched.... Especially when I think about my English literature class, there were so many difficult parts that even [a] dictionary could not help. The teacher's translation and interpretation of hidden messages help a lot.' Bessie explained that her belief in communicative language teaching had come from her previous teaching experience. She only occasionally switched codes, but believed that the use of L1 was useful in a quiet classroom atmosphere: 'When I look around in the class and see students quiet, I feel there should be some interaction. So I motivate them to interact with me by talking to them in Thai.'

Constraining factors

Elspeth considered student factors, such as their high ego and lack of interest, and administrative issues as the main obstacles for her to codeswitch properly. She felt many students thought they were good at the language, but were unmotivated. Interaction in class thus was rare and there was nearly no student talk: 'They don't work hard, and become less motivated.... So my relationship with my students is not always good.' The administrative factors she had been facing were too strictly prescribed syllabuses and the requirement by some programme leaders that teachers speak only English (i.e. the prohibition of CS): 'It can be a problem, especially when some programmes have someone observe whether the teacher speaks only English or not.' Bessie also regarded administrative factors as the most constraining. Students might be reluctant to take certain required courses, and thus become unmotivated and rarely talk in the class. Class size also mattered, 'as it is related to the teacher's ability to control the class and motivate students. Large classes need a lot of efforts from the teacher.'

Reflection

In sum, the findings showed that both of the participant teachers in the present study were able to conduct classes both in English and in mixed code. Yet they showed significant differences in their classroom language use, types of CS and CS functions, apparently due to their different characters, as well as their beliefs about language teaching and learning (Borg, 2006, 2009). Elspeth, who had had no teacher training background, mainly spoke Thai in class and codeswitched to English for pedagogical purposes, that is, questioning and elicitation, translation, clarification and comprehension check. She accepted that she adopted the teaching method of her own teachers, who largely codeswitched for knowledge transmission. Bessie, in contrast, largely used English and codeswitched to Thai primarily for social functions, that is, compliment and praise, encouragement, and casualness, due to her strong beliefs in communicative language teaching (CLT) from her teacher training. This study thus sheds some light for EFL teachers on the proper use of students' first language to serve useful pedagogical and social functions, and to assist foreign language teaching and learning.

In the light of Macaro's Overview in the present volume, in which he outlines a framework for CS, both Elspeth and Bessie's classroom CS was by no means 'naturalistic'. This refers back to the role of English in Thai educational institutions, discussed at the beginning of the chapter. Elspeth and Bessie's CS was not deliberately for furthering communication, as English is used very little in everyday situations. It was, rather, for exposing their students to English, to help them make progress in the language. Nevertheless, Elspeth and Bessie differed with regard to the virtual, maximal or optimal CS positions put forward by Macaro in the Overview. Bessie obviously took the 'optimal' position, believing in the value of limited CS, particularly for enhancing learning as well as communication. She used Thai mainly for social purposes, which in some way was to help her students feel more at east. Elspeth, by contrast, did not seem to fit easily into any of the three positions due to her main use of L1. One of the reasons for this discrepancy might be that both teachers, though able to use both languages fluently, possibly considered that their students were not fluent. This led Elspeth to use Thai most of the time. That the teachers might not fit into any of Macaro's three broad categories is only to be expected: such variation is likely owing to individual teacher beliefs as well as to the wider sociocultural and sociolinguistic context beyond the classroom, in Thailand, or indeed anywhere else.

COMMENTARY

Introduction

As mentioned by Chamaipak Tayjasanant, in Thailand little research has been done on the language use of university English teachers, due to a widespread belief that English should be the primary medium in such classes. In that context, new English language policies are emerging which aim to give Thais greater access to international fora and other international opportunities of various kinds. In Bhutan, the widespread use of the English language leaves policymakers more concerned with preserving Bhutan's national language. Issues such as teacher language use and CS in the classroom in Bhutan are thus rarely discussed, and are not perceived as very important. Attitudes, policies and practices presented in this chapter make for interesting comparison, considering that the two Asian countries continue to maintain strong national identities and are among the few nations in the region that were never colonised. Little literature on classroom CS in either context has been published.

After giving some background on the educational and linguistic context of Bhutan, I will report on interviews I held with two Bhutanese university teachers, in which we discussed their approaches to teaching English, the use of CS in their classrooms and the role English in Bhutanese society, in order to shed light on salient similarities and differences between the two contexts. It is also hoped that this commentary will serve to motivate future exploration of related areas of enquiry in the Bhutanese context.

Bhutan: Educational and Linguistic Background

Before the introduction of organised education in Bhutan, Bhutanese people seeking an education would usually go to Tibet to pursue monastic study. The birth of systematic education, both monastic and secular, in Bhutan began in 1914, under the auspices of the first king (Druk Gyalpo) of Bhutan's current monarchy (Tobgay, 2012). The first schools in Bhutan were Hindi-medium. Though not a native language of Bhutan or an international language, 'Hindi was chosen as the medium of instruction because of the ready availability of inexpensive textbooks in Hindi from neighboring India' (van Driem, 1998: 7). The medium of instruction was later changed to English by the third Druk Gyalpo, Jigme Dorji Wangchuk, in the early 1960s.

Until the 1960s, literacy and education of any kind remained unavailable or impractical pursuits for the majority of Bhutanese people. The country remained isolated and had little in the way of infrastructure such as roads, electricity, telephones, hospitals or postal services (Planning Commission, 1999). Jigme Dorji Wangchuk began making sweeping changes throughout the kingdom in order to modernise. Aside from building new infrastructure and increasing international participation, Bhutan's leader instituted a language policy and expanded modern education. There were no teachers in the country and few Bhutanese people had any experience with modern curricula. Even after the medium of instruction changed, the new system relied heavily on the recruitment of Indian nationals, until a new teacher training college was established in 1968 and began producing Bhutanese teachers (Mackey, 2002). At first, this new system was so alien to members of society that some parents kept children at home, felt more comfortable sending children for monastic education, or even tried bribing officials to get their children unenrolled; many viewed the English language as symbolic of a suspicious or sacrilegious invader, as well (Phuntsho, 2000). However, modern education in Bhutan did not take long to achieve a remarkable degree of success, and primary and secondary schools are now operating even in remote regions of the country.

While English instructional materials were being developed for the initial English-medium schools, the country's language policy was also solidifying into its current form. Bhutan's government recognised the need to unify, in terms of language, the nation's multilingual population. There are four principal language groups – Ngalop (now referred to as 'Dzongkha'), Tshangla, Bumthap and Lhotshamkha – and 20 dialects of these languages throughout the country (Dzongkha Development Commission, 2002). Many of these 'dialects', which may include varieties that constitute separate sub-groups of the language family (see e.g. van Driem, 2011), have few speakers. No single language has majority usage: Dzongkha acts as a lingua franca in the west, Tshangla in the east and Lhotshamkha in the south – all having roughly the same number of speakers (van Driem, 1994). Dzongkha, which has the greatest religious and historical significance, was officially chosen as the national language in 1971, although efforts to modernise this language began in the 1960s (Tashi, 2013). Dzongkha and English became the focal languages of communication, education and administration. Perhaps partially due to the lack of materials and technical terminology in Dzongkha (Phuntsho, 2000), educated Bhutanese people (both those educated domestically and abroad) began to embrace English in academic and official settings. In terms of written policy and administrative practices, Dzongkha and English are given equal importance – with the important exceptions of the armed forces and monastic body, both of which use Dzongkha for all official documentation.

While several Bhutanese institutions offering coursework and degrees beyond the secondary level existed in the country previously, a national university system emerged only in 2003 (Royal University of Bhutan, 2010). This tertiary system is now known as the Royal University of Bhutan (RUB), and consists of 11 member colleges located throughout the country. With the establishment of RUB, tertiary institutions in the country no longer rely on Indian curricula, and all degrees are awarded under the regulation of a central RUB body. RUB aims to develop its member colleges as centres of excellence, in both teaching and research, and has begun increasing student numbers in response to increasing numbers of applicants.

The Context of the Present Study

Two RUB lecturers were individually interviewed for this commentary. Each was introduced to Chamaipak's Thai case study, and was asked to peruse the data and findings before the semi-structured interview was recorded. Interviewee responses were transcribed. Both lecturers were shown this chapter before publishing to ensure that their views were not mischaracterised. Both are given pseudonyms here.

One lecturer, Sherab, teaches at an institute training candidates in traditional culture and language. At this institute the medium of instruction is generally Dzongkha, unlike most other institutions in RUB, and most students have a better command of Dzongkha than of English. (Sherab estimates about 80% or more of the courses at her institute are Dzongkha-medium. She explained that most other RUB colleges have only one Dzongkha teacher on the faculty.) The other lecturer, Tshering, teaches at an institute preparing health workers. Tshering's institution is English-medium. While Sherab finished a BA in Bhutan and studied in North America for her MA in English literature, Tshering completed her BS in midwifery in India and an MSc in midwifery in Australia. Both lecturers have native-like English language proficiency. Generally, the medium of instruction at the tertiary level in Bhutan is English. However, as was the case with both teachers in the Thai case study, neither of the English lecturers interviewed taught students who are majoring in English.

While Sherab's classes were mainly aimed at improving the L2 proficiency of students, Tshering's classes were predominantly focused on content. Tshering's English course, which was new and given throughout RUB, was called 'Academic Skills'. She delivered the module to a group of approximately 30 students, though some of her colleagues offering the same course had 40–50 students. Sherab mostly taught English literature to class sizes of approximately 30 students. Both teachers seemed to like the courses they were currently teaching. Sherab found her students had weak reading skills and could benefit from the sorts of activities typical of a literature course. Tshering also seemed to have a favourable opinion of her course, and said it had inspired her to create similar participatory activities in her other subjects – a development that she felt had yielded pedagogic improvements.

It became clear during the interviews that degrees of motivation between Sherab's and Tshering's groups of students varied. Tshering's students were in-service adult learners – a factor Tshering suspected afforded her students more motivation than those in the Thai case study. Tshering saw her students as eager to learn and somewhat easy to manage in the classroom. Sherab, on the other hand, explained that some of her students had motivation problems concerning the study of English. Generally, her students did not study much outside class, nor did they get involved in extracurricular learning activities, which she and Chamaipak's Thai teachers believe to be crucial to learning a foreign language. Sherab described several initiatives she had tried, including listening activities, various media such as news or movies, and even required library hours. However, she lamented, 'we tried to do all these things, but I think it was not effective'.

Interview Data: The Role of English in Bhutan

Both interviewed teachers saw English as playing an indispensable role in Bhutanese curricula. Generally speaking, Sherab noted that Bhutanese people tend to give the development of the English language more importance than the development of Dzongkha, perhaps because there is a widely held belief that if they want to do well in life, they have to know English. Tshering similarly noted that if one's English is poor, one faces problems internationally, for example in presenting at conferences or in seeking employment outside Bhutan. English seems to play an equally vital role domestically, as well. Sherab noted that Dzongkha-speaking teachers at her school often express regret for not having learned English better.

Many Bhutanese people's English is stronger than their Dzongkha, especially, as Sherab pointed out, for professional tasks such as correspondence and office work: 'Informally, people use L1, but for office, people generally use L2.' The dominance of English also exerts itself in academic spheres. Phuntsho (2000) has noted that in Bhutan the concepts of literacy and erudition have become equated with the English language and western standards of scholarship. Sherab seemed to share this notion, stating that 'the educated lot are more exposed to the western system of education and that's why they give more importance to English, and less importance to Dzongkha'. Education has become equated with 'the future' and perhaps people 'feel that Dzongkha is archaic and, I don't know, maybe they have this kind of mental block against Dzongkha'.

'English mentality' is seen to be pervading Bhutan's urban centres. In Bhutan's capital, Thimphu, 'English started taking a strong hold', Sherab explained, 'it's there; it has invaded our household and everything'. Both teachers mentioned that their family elders, who had not received any modern education, used English words interspersed within utterances at home. Both teachers also noted that several families in Thimphu, particularly elite or highly educated families, almost exclusively speak English in their homes. Describing these developments even led Sherab to pose the following question: 'Is that colonisation of the Bhutanese mentality by the English mentality?' Sherab's question seems to imply a form of linguistic imperialism, which has been defined by Ansre as follows:

> the minds and lives of the speakers of a language are dominated by another language to the point where they believe that they could and should use only that foreign language when it comes to dealing with the more advanced aspects of life.
> (Ansre, 1979, cited in Phillipson, 1992: 56)

Asked if this concept, and the above definition, applies at all to Bhutan, Sherab responded 'maybe'. She then noted that perhaps the size and political strength of a country dictate how large a role a national language can play in comparison with English: 'For a small country like Bhutan, yes, English is important. Otherwise we could just disappear. And because Bhutan is very small we have to depend for things on the outside world.' This reliance on the outside world may thus necessitate a nation such as Bhutan putting the benefits of English language influence to work in order to retain independence, counterintuitive though this may initially seem.

Interview Data

Teaching methodology

Neither Bhutanese teacher interviewed expressed an explicit methodological bent. Both did, however, give explanations of and opinions on the teaching context at RUB, how they coped and how RUB should move forward, methodologically speaking.

Chamaipak's finding concerning teacher talk in Thailand was noted as similar to their own teaching contexts by both Bhutanese lecturers. Upon seeing the Thai teachers' classroom data, Tshering commented, 'Ah, here also I think the teacher talks most of the time'. Examining reasons why this might be the case in Bhutan, the two lecturers independently came to a consensus that old pedagogic norms and roles were still playing a part in the new education system. One source of pedagogic influence is derived from monastic education, where respect (even veneration) of the teacher and teachings is expected, and the approach generally aims 'to receive and uphold, to preserve and prolong rather than innovate and invent' (Phuntsho, 2000: 102–103). Some aspects of monastic education therefore differ greatly from the goals and expectations embodied in the western model of secular education, including heavy reliance on memorisation and repetition, and the dominance of examination-based assessment.

Pedagogy derived from the legacy of monastic and Indian influ-ences still appears to affect perceived student and teacher roles. Tshering explained that 'in the Bhutanese system, you might find a scenario where the teacher speaks 100% of the time sometimes, because everything, whatever the teacher said, is right. If the teacher says the moon is square, then, yes, the moon is square.' Teachers' authority can leave students feeling that it is safer to sit quietly and listen rather than to speak during class. Sherab conveyed similar frustration regarding the willingness of her own students to actively participate: 'The problem with our students is they don't want to think, they want somebody else to put something in their head'. She believed the cause of this behavior might be cultural in nature, as Bhutanese children are raised to revere teachers and parents. She recalled seeing serious arguments in the west, resulting from differences of opinion, but said these kinds of argument do not happen in Bhutan because 'it's like going against some kind of system'. Interestingly, Sherab suspected that students' behaviour might be different when a foreigner taught them, perhaps because foreign teachers would not be perceived as part of the old system.

The legacy of these teacher and student roles seems to be in the process of change throughout the RUB colleges, which is a development both Tshering and Sherab believed to be positive. Tshering noted that some new courses, such as 'Academic Skills', were 'designed in such a way that all have equal opportunity to talk'. According to Tshering, students are now willing to challenge lecturers. With this new behaviour among students, teachers had 'to be on our feet, so it helps us also'. To continue this trend, Sherab expressed interest in increasing opportunities for RUB lecturers to participate in systematic professional development. She thought more workshops could keep lecturers up to date on teaching methods and strategies, and prevent them 'holding on to the old ways'.

In terms of requirements and policies of RUB, both lecturers agreed that there was the freedom within syllabuses to adapt to student needs and the teacher's methodological preferences. Tshering believed that as long as students learnt the targeted outcomes of a course, one need not linger on every detail of a syllabus. Similarly, Sherab noted that while covering prescribed course material, she also felt free to supplement her classes with other materials or activities as desired: 'I think flexibility is there in Bhutan for the teacher.' Whether this decision-making freedom exists broadly in Bhutan's tertiary system would need to be verified with additional research.

L1 in the L2 classroom

In terms of the expectations of the authorities, both teachers shared the same assumptions concerning teacher language use in the English classroom. As Sherab pointed out, in the context of RUB, 'it's just known that if you're teaching English you might as well teach in English'. Unlike their Thai counterparts, Bhutanese administrators are somewhat unconcerned with checking teacher language use in English classrooms. The lecturers both indicated that observations to check teacher language use, for example, would be unlikely in their context. Tshering commented that perhaps one reason for this difference between Thai and Bhutanese contexts was related to the medium of instruction: in Bhutan, most subjects have been taught through English for approximately 50 years, whereas in Thailand a big change is desired now and therefore differences of opinion about such issues would be expected. Sherab also conjectured that assessment may play a part, because English is considered 'one of the major subjects; you have to get through English to go to the next grade'. Since evaluation focuses on English to a great extent all the way through schooling, perhaps the result is a broad assumption in Bhutan that teacher language use need not be monitored.

The languages used as the medium of instruction in Bhutanese university classrooms are English and Dzongkha. However, it appears that bits of Tshangla, Lhotshamkha, Hindi and perhaps other languages may also appear from time to time. Sherab pointed out that these other languages are unlikely to occur as a medium of instruction. The two interviewed teachers' beliefs about CS varied. Sherab seemed to be a proponent of 'English only', and would rarely use even a word of L1 in her classroom. She stated that she felt 'comfortable using English; for any conversation or if I meet them on the street, then I'll speak in Dzongkha, but in my English class I make sure that I just speak to them in English'. When asked whether it is alright to use L1 in the classroom, she replied:

> No, because since you are teaching English language, then why would you want to switch over to the other language because they have proficiency over other languages, like Dzongkha and Lhotshamkha and Sharchhop [Tshangla]. So, they speak in these every day of their lives, but they are coming to school to learn

how to speak English. So why speak L1 when they have come to learn L2?

With regard to the idea suggested by the Thai participants in Chamaipak's study that more L1 can be used to support students with lower levels of L2 competence, Sherab believed that a better approach when students struggle to understand would be to restate information and simplify the English being used. She avoided using translation to teach English. She explained that when teaching something complex, though, there may be certain terminology that is difficult to explain. In this case, 'if you can't make them understand in English, then maybe you try to, not explain, but bring in one Dzongkha word'. She gave an example of this strategy in a recent lesson: 'Today I was trying to teach one short story and because they didn't understand I had to tell them a Hindi word, which they know because it's commonly used in Bhutan, and then they understood.' Despite her efforts, though, Sherab also explained that her students were reluctant at times to use English in the classroom, and instead used Dzongkha or Tshangla to ask questions. 'They know that I speak both Dzongkha and Sharchhop [Tshangla], and they take advantage of this.'

Tshering's beliefs about teacher language seemed to reflect a more flexible perspective than those of Sherab. While she used mostly English to teach in her classes, she said that it was not necessary to restrict language use to English all the time. She noted some reservations concerning her Academic Skills course materials, where it was recommended that students speak only in English. She said, 'I later realised that, stressing the importance of what I'm trying to convey, sometimes use of our other languages is also necessary.' She expected that using L1 for such purposes was unlikely to cause a problem with the administrative authorities:

[Since the] medium of instruction is English, I guess I took it for granted that we have to speak English. It's expected of us. But I'm sure they won't take us to prison for using other languages too. For stressing points, for giving examples, sometimes you need to give in other languages too. In fact, if they know how much they learn from using those languages I'm sure they'll encourage it.

Her statement was tempered by her belief that, generally, 'since it is there in the education system that medium of instruction should be in English, we should use English, except for, of course, Dzongkha subjects'.

The interviewees also seemed to disagree in terms of the functions of L1 in the L2 classroom. When shown functions used by the Thai participants of Chamaipak's study, which included explanation and social uses, Tshering said that she used L1 at times for both of these purposes in her classroom. As mentioned above, she sometimes used an L1, usually Dzongkha, to explain something or to stress points. In terms of social uses, she recalled an instance of translating a joke told in English to make sure everyone understood. Regarding social use of L1 in the classroom of this kind, Sherab commented that she would still prefer to use the medium of English, simplifying if needed. Tshering also mentioned another use of L1 in her classroom: when she recounted clinical examples, which come up frequently in her institution, she said that she preferred to deliver them using English, but would quote patients using the language they themselves had used, which usually would be Dzongkha, Tshangla or Lhotshamkha. She explained that 'if I translate what that person said into English, it would be a bit strange and the magic of that understanding or that sentence will be gone'.

In light of data presented here, it would appear that the two informants hold different positions on L1 use (Macaro, 1997, 2001). Sherab was a clear proponent of the 'virtual' position, because her stated beliefs show that she actively avoided using any language other than the target language in her classroom. Tshering, like Bessie in Chamaipak's study, seemed to support the 'optimal' position. While she used primarily L2 in classroom discourse, she appeared to be conscious of the advantages and disadvantages of using L1 in the classroom. Tshering's opinions imply that she feels guilt-free in CS when a purpose surfaces that she feels warrants L1 use. These positions stand in contrast to the unclassified position of Elspeth, who used large amounts of L1 in classroom discourse.

Reflection

Thailand and Bhutan are nations with somewhat similar goals in terms of cultural preservation and modernisation, but it seems that the two contexts differ in many ways. While Thais are now focusing more on English, Sherab explains that Bhutan is now moving in the direction of Dzongkha. Bhutan's policy regarding the English language is very different from that in Thailand, where, Chamaipak points out, no official comment is made on policy regarding the role of English. Conversely, Thai as a national language appears to have a stronger hold in Thai society than Dzongkha in Bhutanese society. However, policies in the two countries seem to be converging, in the sense that the ideal of bilingual competence is taking hold. Bhutanese organisations are increasingly requiring bilingual competence in Dzongkha and English, and government agencies often require official documentation to be bilingual. In Thailand, Chamaipak's case study discussed the increasing popularity of bilingual educational opportunities in the country, and the desire of Thais to participate internationally in a variety of economic, academic and political fora.

The findings reported in this chapter have implications for CS policy and future research. As mentioned in the above discussion on teacher beliefs, each Thai and Bhutanese informant occupied a different position regarding L1 use in the classroom (Macaro, 1997, 2001). This diversity of opinion may merit future investigation, as the lack of a homogeneous belief system regarding CS in these contexts contrasts sharply with the seemingly homogeneous CS policies of universities across Asia. Additionally, Sherab's mention of student L1 use in her classroom raises another topic in line with Macaro's suggested research agenda that merits further investigation in Thailand and Bhutan, as is also suggested in Chapters 7 and 8 of the present book. Future policy stands to benefit from more comprehensive documentation and theorising on teachers' and students' use of, and beliefs about, CS in the L2 classroom.

I might also add that, as mentioned in my introduction, Bhutan is a new context for classroom CS research. Based on these necessarily limited findings, and keeping in mind Macaro's guidance on CS research (this volume), Bhutan appears to be a context ideal for this form of classroom research. Macaro's guidelines on prerequisites for research contexts all seem to fit, as the majority of university classrooms focus on content through the medium of English, which seems to be the language used in the majority of classroom talk time, and CS appears to exhibit naturalistic qualities. These points are conjecture and are in need of verification at this point, in view of the paucity of research and literature on the subject.

References

Adendorff, R. (1996) The functions of code switching amongst high school teachers and students in KwaZulu and implications for teacher education. In K.M. Bailey and D. Nunan (eds) *Voices from the Language Classroom: Qualitative Research in Second Language Education* (pp. 388–406). New York: Cambridge University Press.

Borg, S. (2006) *Teacher Cognition and Language Education: Research and Practice*. London: Continuum.

Borg, S. (2009) Language teacher cognition. In A. Burns and J.C. Richards (eds) *The Cambridge Guide to Second Language Teacher Education* (pp. 163–171). Cambridge: Cambridge University Press.

Cook, G. (2010) *Translation in Language Teaching: An Argument for Reassessment*. Oxford: Oxford University Press.

Coulmas, F. (2005) *Sociolinguistics: The Study of Speakers' Choices*. Cambridge: Cambridge University Press.

Durongphan, M., Aksornkul, N., Sawangwong, W. and Tiancharoen, S. (1982) *The Development of English Teaching in Thailand: A Rattanakosin Experience*. Bangkok: Aksorn Charoentat for Thai/TESOL.

Dzongkha Development Commission (2002) *The New Dzongkha Grammar*. Thimphu: Dzongkha Development Commission.

Macaro, E. (1997) *Target Language, Collaborative Learning and Autonomy*. Clevedon: Multilingual Matters.

Macaro, E. (2001) Analyzing students teachers' code-switching in foreign language classrooms: Theories and decision-making. *Modern Language Journal* 85 (4), 531–548.

Mackey, W. (2002) How it all began – A note on development of education in Bhutan. In National Institute of Education (ed.) *The Call: Stories of Yesteryears* (pp. 6–8). Paro: Center for Educational Research and Development.

O'Cain, J. and Leibscher, G. (2009) Teacher and student use of the first language in foreign language classroom interaction: Functions and applications. In M. Turnbull and J. O'Cain (eds) *First Language Use in Second and Foreign Language Learning* (pp. 131–144). Bristol: Multilingual Matters.

Phillipson, R. (1992) *Linguistic Imperialism*. Oxford: Oxford University Press.

Phuntsho, K. (2000) On the two ways of learning in Bhutan. *Journal of Bhutan Studies* 2 (2), 96–126.

Planning Commission (1999) *Bhutan 2020: A Vision for Peace, Prosperity and Happiness*. Thimphu: Planning Commission Secretariat.

Poplack, S. (2000) Sometimes I'll start a sentence in Spanish y termino en español: Toward a typology of code-switching. In W. Li (ed.) *The Bilingualism Reader* (pp. 221–256). London: Routledge.

Royal University of Bhutan (2010) *The Royal University of Bhutan: Prospectus 2010–2011*. Thimphu: Royal University of Bhutan.

Sinlarat, P. (2004) Thai universities: Past, present, and future. In P.G. Altbach and T. Umakoshi (eds) *Asian Universities: Historical Perspectives and Contemporary Challenges* (pp. 201–220). Baltimore, MD: Johns Hopkins University Press.

Tashi, T. (2013) Voice of the fort: How Dzongkha became the national language (11 April). News site, Kuensel Online. See http://www.kuenselonline.com/voice-of-the-fort/#. UiVXAGRHikI (accessed 3 September 2013).

Tobgay, L.S. (2012) The blazing trail of Bhutanese education: Part 1 (12 May). News site, Kuensel Online. See http://www.kuenselonline.com/2011/?p=31031 (accessed 14 April 2013).

van Driem, G. (1994) Language policy in Bhutan. In M. Aris, and M. Hutt (eds) *Bhutan: Aspects of Culture and Development* (pp. 87–105). Gartmore: Paul Strachan-Kiscadale.

van Driem, G. (1998) *Dzongkha: Languages of the Greater Himalayan Region, Volume 1.* Leiden: Research School CNWS, Leiden University.

van Driem, G. (2011) Tibeto-Burman subgroups and historical grammar. *Himalayan Linguistics* 10 (1) (special issue in memory of Michael Noonan and David Watters), 31–39. See http://www.linguistics.ucsb.edu/HimalayanLinguistics/articles/2011/ HLJ1001B.html (accessed August 2013).

Wongsothorn, A., Hiranburana, K. and Chinnawongs, S. (2002) English language teaching in Thailand today. *Asia Pacific Journal of Education* 22 (2), 107–116.

5   Codeswitching in Universities in Vietnam and Indonesia

Case Study: Le Van Canh
Commentary: Fuad Abdul Hamied

CASE STUDY

Introduction

Although codeswitching (CS) in second language education has recently attracted a considerable amount of scholarly attention, more empirical research on this linguistic behaviour in pedagogic discourse is needed to gain insights into teachers' motivation for language switches. Macaro (2001; and in this volume) reports that teachers take three different positions on CS: the 'virtual position', which completely rejects CS; the 'maximal position', which views CS as necessary because of students' low proficiency in the target language; and the 'optimal position', according to which CS may be both facilitating or hindering student learning. Unfortunately, studies that are aimed at uncovering teachers' motivations for CS are few, particularly in the context of English as a foreign language (EFL). This chapter reports the results of a single case study conducted in a Vietnamese university, a context in which this issue remains under-explored. The study explores the functions of a teacher's use of CS and her motivation for it in classroom discourse. I believe that a thorough understanding of teachers' CS motivations is the first step towards the theorisation of CS in the second/foreign language classroom. This study is a modest step towards that goal.

Codeswitching in Asian Contexts

There are relatively few empirical studies that consider CS in EFL contexts in Asia. Liu *et al.* (2004) studied the CS practices of 13 South Korean high school teachers in the context of the enforcement of the English-only policy by the South Korean Ministry of Education. They found that the teachers used Korean more frequently than English, and for several purposes, the most salient of which were: explaining difficult vocabulary and grammar; giving background information; overcoming communication difficulties; saving time; highlighting important information; and managing students' behaviour.

In the Vietnamese EFL context, Kieu Hang Kim Anh (2010), who administered a questionnaire to 12 university EFL teachers in Ho Chi Minh City and interviewed four of them, reports that the teachers showed great support for the use of Vietnamese in English language teaching. The three most common functions of CS, as stated by the teachers, were explaining grammar, explaining vocabulary and checking comprehension. Very recently, I conducted a multi-method case study with eight Vietnamese high school teachers, investigating their beliefs and practices regarding form-focused instruction (Le Van Canh, 2011). As revealed in that study, teachers often switched to Vietnamese to explain grammatical rules and to check students' understanding of meta-language. They tended to use English first and then translate the message into Vietnamese, as they believed that such CS was necessary to help the students whose English proficiency was too low for them to understand grammar thoroughly when explained in English.

A review of the classroom-based literature reveals three major limitations of the studies on CS. First, 'there is still very little research about teachers' codeswitching' (Macaro, 2001: 532), 'especially in the EFL context' (Liu *et al.*, 2004: 610). Secondly, few studies on teachers' CS attempt to uncover the teachers' epistemological knowledge that underlies their alternative use of L1 and L2. Finally, most of the investigations cited so far did not use a multi-method approach, especially the combination of classroom observations, stimulated recall interviews and teacher reflection to uncover the complicated issues governing teachers' switches. This study, motivated by the inadequacy of research on teacher CS behaviours in the Vietnamese context, where a monolingual approach has always been prioritised, is a modest attempt to fill some of this research gap.

The Study

This qualitative case study was designed to seek answers to the following questions:

(1) What types of CS are frequently observed in a teacher's classroom talk in the university EFL context?
(2) What functions does the teacher's CS serve in this context?
(3) What motivates the teacher's CS practice?

The study was conducted in a university in Hanoi where English is taught as a minor but compulsory subject to all students. As prescribed in the university curriculum, the English course is spread over four semesters with 60 classroom hours allocated in each semester. The students are taught four hours of English per week. This is augmented by a 30-hour online course provided by an international partner university in an attempt to give the students more exposure to the target language. Communicative language teaching is prescribed as the dominant teaching methodology and the course books are the *New Headway* English course series (Soars & Soars, 2009). By the end of the fourth semester, the students are expected to achieve B2 level of proficiency in English as defined in the Common European Framework of Reference for Languages (Council of Europe, 2001; see the Appendix to Chapter 1, pp. 41–42) so that they can move on to a 60-hour course on English for specific purposes.

Following the recommendation by Liu *et al.* (2004), data for research into teachers' CS should come from observations and interviews with few participating teachers and each teacher should be observed more than once to achieve the greater depth, this case study examined the CS practices of a single teacher, a woman with three years of teaching experience. She had a university degree in teaching English as a foreign language and was completing her masters degree in the same field with a local university. She was selected purposefully in that she was teaching English as a foreign language in a Vietnamese university and was accessible, easy to contact and well known to myself. In order to avoid any possible effect upon the observed teacher's use of language, she was told only that I was interested in teacher–student classroom interaction.

Data collection procedures

For this study, I adopted a qualitative case study approach (Yin, 2009) without predetermined hypotheses or experimental manipulation. In keeping with the qualitative nature of this study, data were collected in the form of audio-recorded classroom observations, stimulated recall interviews and the teacher's reflection. The teacher was observed teaching four 45-minute lessons over four consecutive weeks. These lessons were audio-recorded because the teacher was reluctant to allow her lessons to be video-taped. The audio-recorder was placed on the teacher's table at the front of the classroom as agreed by the teacher, and the audibility of the teacher's recorded voice was satisfactory. After the first observation, I listened to the recording carefully and identified all the CS episodes which occurred in the lesson. This helped me to draw up points on which I focused in the stimulated recall session (Gass & Mackey, 2000), which was conducted three hours after the observation.

The face-to-face stimulated recall sessions lasted 30 minutes each, during which time the recorded lesson was replayed and paused at meaning-ful episodes, that is, the episodes containing the teacher's codeswitches. Since, while observing the teacher, I found that she was not quite fluent in English (although she was a university teacher of English), I decided to use Vietnamese in the stimulated recall session, believing that this might help the teacher to feel more comfortable, and to be able to articulate her thoughts more accurately (Le Van Canh & Maley, 2012).

The focus of the stimulated recall sessions was to elicit from the teacher her comments on her use of Vietnamese in the lesson just observed, stimu-lated by extracts from the recording so that I could obtain the information about her reasons for CS as well as the functions she believed CS served. So, every time the recording was paused, she was asked (in Vietnamese), for example, 'Can you tell me what you thought when you codeswitched from English to Vietnamese?' Depending on her responses, I might continue with questions such as 'Why did you switch to Vietnamese here?' or 'I wonder if you could have achieved the same purpose if you had used English instead?', or, where she used English, I asked, for instance, 'I don't know if you think it might have been better if you had used Vietnamese in this utterance?' so that I could gain more accurate information about her CS behaviours.

I then transcribed those episodes which contained codeswitches and returned them to the observed teacher to verify them. The teacher was also asked to write a reflective account about whether she would have done the same thing again, or whether the episode might better have been in English.

Data analysis

Data-driven methods of analysis were used, involving 'making sense of, sifting, organizing, cataloguing, [and] selecting determining themes' (Holliday, 2007: 99). I first read and reread the transcripts thoroughly in order to identify patterns; this allowed me to organise them manually into some initial categories. After that, I assigned abbreviated codes of a few letters, placing them next to the themes I found (Miles & Huberman, 1994: 54). Having examined these general categories carefully, I created a descriptive label for each. However, the categories were reviewed with reference to the research questions as well (Duff, 2008: 160) for analysis and interpretation. The observed data were analysed at the sentence level using extracts of verbatim teacher language. Analysis was (subsequently) carried out at the 'functional' level, with a focus on the teacher's moving from one function (e.g. explaining vocabulary) to another (e.g. explaining grammar). By following this inductive approach to data analysis, I was able to interpret the motivations behind her CS practice.

Findings and Discussion

The present study is not aimed at evaluating the teacher's CS practice, but to raise issues about CS practice in a Vietnamese university context where English is taught as a compulsory component of the curriculum. In what follows, I first present the types and functions of CS, and the factors that motivate the teacher's switches between languages.

Length of teacher talk in L1 versus L2

Table 5.1 presents the length of teacher talk in L1 against her talk in L2. As can be seen, the teacher talking time across four lessons did not vary remarkably except for lesson 2, when the teacher talked the least. This was a listening comprehension lesson, and most of the classroom time was spent on students' listening to recordings. Regarding the teacher's CS, in most of the observed lessons the teacher codeswitched to L1 for up to about a third of her total talking time, although in lesson 3 the teacher talk in L2 took up just 14.6% of her total talking time.

Although the recorded total teacher talking time in these lessons seemed to allow plenty of opportunity for students to talk in the target language, the observation notes showed that they were often asked either to read the course book or to do the forms-based exercises silently.

Table 5.1 Teacher talk in L1 versus L2

Lesson	Length of lesson (min/s)	Length of teacher talk (min/s)	Total teacher talking time (%)	Teacher talk in L1 (min/s)	Teacher talk in L1 (%)	Teacher talk in L2 (min/s)	Teacher talk in L2 (%)
1	45'	17'03"	37.9%	3'55"	23.0%	13'08"	77.0%
2	45'	10'10"	22.6%	3'05"	30.3%	7'05"	69.7%
3	45'	20'32"	45.6%	3'00"	14.6%	17'32"	85.4%
4	45'	19'04"	42.4%	6'03"	31.7%	13'01"	68.3%

Types of codeswitching

In the following extract, the students were asked to listen to a recorded story and then to decide which of the sentences given in the course book were not correct according to the story.

Extract 1

Now you hear some sentences about the story and you have to correct some. Trong phần này các bạn sẽ phải nghe một số câu về câu chuyện này sau đó các bạn sẽ phải sửa lỗi sai. Maybe I think that you need some more minutes to read once more the main content of the story. Có lẽ các bạn phải cần thêm vài phút để đọc lướt lại một lần nữa và nắm được nội dung chính của câu chuyện trước khi quyết định câu nào sai.

First, the teacher gave the instruction in English and switched to Vietnamese to repeat the instruction. She then switched back to English and once again she repeated the sentence in Vietnamese. In another extract, the teacher was explaining how to use English indefinite pronouns, such as 'something':

Extract 2

Now we move to 'something, somebody, anything, anybody, nothing, nobody'. You use these words quite similar with 'some' and 'any'. And remember that these words always go with a singular verb. Do you understand? Với các từ như something, somebody, anything, anybody, nothing, nobody nên nhớ là tất cả các từ này đi với động từ số ít. Okay? Bây giờ các bạn chỉ việc điền vào thôi. *Three minutes for you and then we'll listen and check.*

As in the previous extract, the teacher used English to transmit the information about how to use the target grammar point. Then she translated the information into Vietnamese before she switched back to English. Here, as elsewhere, the CS was largely at the inter-sentential level. This type of CS was observed even when her English utterances were simple enough for the students to understand. For example:

Extract 3

Now we talk about an unforgettable memory tức là chúng ta sẽ nói về một kỷ niệm không thể quên được *maybe it's a bad thing or it is a good thing* có thể là tốt có thể là xấu. We're practising the past tense so we talk about an unforgettable memory and you have some minutes to prepare before you talk about your experience nói về sự trải nghiệm của mình. *It is a memory so you should use the past tense.*

Although the students' English was limited, they were unlikely to have any difficulty understanding the English phrases such as 'unforgettable memory' or 'maybe it's a bad thing or it is a good thing', or 'your experience'. It is interesting that she used English for the more complicated utterance to remind the students to use the past tense to talk about their unforgettable memory.

In Extract 4, the teacher even switched to Vietnamese to explain the meaning of the question 'What did you buy yesterday when you went shopping?', which is certain to be simple enough for these students, who had been studying English for two semesters at the university, and for several years before that at high school.

Extract 4

So tell me what did you buy yesterday? What did you buy yesterday when you went shopping? Do you understand? Hôm qua các bạn đi chợ các bạn mua cái gì? *What did you buy? What did you buy?*

Although all three types of CS identified by Poplack (1980) – tag-switching, intra-sentential switching and inter-sentential switching – were observed, the last type seemed to dominate. The teacher frequently said something in English, then translated her utterances into Vietnamese.

Functions of codeswitching

The following extract offers an example of the multi-functional use of classroom CS. The teacher was instructing the students to do a grammatical exercise which required them to match the given nouns with either 'how much' or 'how many', as demonstrated in the conversation in the course book.

Extract 5

So look at the conversation. Nhìn vào phần conversation. Ah, how much milk do you need? How many eggs? How many potatoes? How much butter? These are examples of 'how much' and 'how many'. Đây là những ví dụ về 'how much' và 'how many'. So exercise 2. Match the quantity

quantity do you know quantity từ chỉ số lượng *the word denoting quantity* two hundred grams, four packages. Work in pairs and three minutes for you to decide.

In this extract, the teacher first switched (*Nhìn vào…*) for classroom management. She wanted to make sure that the students understood and followed her instructions. The second switch (starting Đây là những…) is pedagogical, that is, content-related. She wanted her students to 'notice' the count/non-count distinction. The third switch (từ chỉ số lượng) is a comprehension check for the word 'quantity'. The teacher at first was speaking English, requesting the students to look at the conversation in the course book. As soon as she finished the sentence, she switched to Vietnamese to repeat the command. Then she exemplified the use of 'how much' and 'how many' in English and repeated the utterance in Vietnamese. After giving another command in English, she defined the word *quantity* after repeating this word three times. The extract indicates that the teacher first switched for classroom management. She wanted to make sure that the students understood and could follow her instructions. Switch 2 was pedagogical, that is, content-related. She wanted her students to 'notice' the count/non-count distinction. Switch 3 was a comprehension check for the word 'quantity'. Thus this extract provides examples of three major classroom CS functions: classroom management, pedagogical and comprehension check.

The teacher often switched from English to Vietnamese to define words. For example:

Extract 6

I think if you want to talk about anyone, for example your father, your mother, anyone you want to talk about, you should give information about job, appearance, appearance, ngoại hình, for example, tall, short, black hair or straight hair or curly hair or slim, slim, mảnh dẻ, mảnh khảnh, or fat, and maybe about their job, their hobby or maybe how often you and that person do something together. Okay? And you may talk about the future, yeah?

In the above extract, the teacher switched to Vietnamese to define the words 'appearance' and 'slim'. Similar to Extract 5, she first repeated the words that she believed to be problematic to the students before switching. In the stimulated recall interview, she said that she was asking the students to talk about someone's appearance, but the students did not understand the words 'appearance' and 'slim'. Therefore, she defined the words in

Vietnamese. She also said that in teaching vocabulary, if she could not use synonyms or antonyms she tended to translate the words into Vietnamese. Again, CS serves a pedagogical function, and this is further illustrated in Extract 7, in which the teacher switched quite often to highlight important points, especially to explain grammar or pronunciation rules.

Extract 7

Can you tell me the differences between the pronunciation of the ending –ed⸮ Các bạn có thể cho biết sự khác biệt trong cách phát âm cuối –ed được không? Điểm khác biệt là gì? Ví dụ khi nào đọc là /t/ khi nào đọc là /d/, khi nào đọc là /id/. Các bạn có nắm được quy tắc này không nhỉ? What's the difference⸮ For example, when –ed is pronounced as /t/, when as /d/ and when as /id/. Do you know this rule⸮

In the stimulated recall session she explained her rationale for this practice:

This is an explanation of the grammar rule. I usually switch to Vietnamese to explain grammar or pronunciation because if I use only English the students cannot understand, especially the terminology. If there are words the students don't know in the rules, I define the words in Vietnamese. If the students don't understand the grammar point, I explain everything in Vietnamese. If I am correcting the grammar exercises, I use English first and then translate it into Vietnamese.

Then she added:

In teaching grammar if only English is used, the students just sit quietly with a vague look. They understand nothing. Therefore, when I finish one sentence in English, I repeat it in Vietnamese otherwise the students would lose concentration on what I'm saying. They cannot pay attention long if I speak only English.

The teacher believed that her students' English was not good enough to understand the lesson in English. If the students could not understand what the teacher was talking about, they were likely to get bored and lose concentration. This is quite a reasonable pedagogical function of CS. Not only did the teacher switch for classroom management, but she also used Vietnamese to elicit the students' comprehension of the reading text. In the following extract, she was guiding the students to do the true/false exercise in a reading comprehension lesson.

Extract 8

01 T   Find out the key words for me. You know 'key words'؟ Cố gắng
        tìm những, key words, những từ chính của câu.
02 Ss   Waiting for husband.
03 T   Key words here are 'waiting for her husband', đợi chồng.
04 T   Look at the first paragraph. Can you see the words 'watching
        him walk up the path'؟ Vậy là cô ấy đang nhìn anh ta đi bộ trên
        đường, đúng không? Now continue reading. Đọc tiếp đi nào.
05 Ss   {Read the text.}
06 T   Can you find something؟ Các bạn có nhận thấy gì không? Tại sao cô
        ấy lại đang đợi chồng như vậy? Can you notice something؟ Why
        was she waiting for her husband ؟
07 S   It's their wedding anniversary.
08 T   Was she waiting for her husband to kill him؟ Vậy có phải cô ấy
        đợi chồng về để giết anh ấy không? No. So is it true or false؟
09 Ss   {In chorus} False.

Even when the students were able to identify the key phrases in the text
(i.e. 'Waiting for her husband'; 'It's their wedding anniversary'), the teacher
translated what the students had said into Vietnamese. Similarly, the word
'husband' would be quite familiar to the students, but she translated this
also. When asked for the function of her CS in the above lesson extract, the
teacher said she wanted to help the students to comprehend the text by
understanding the meaning of the key words in the text. While reflecting on
her CS practice, she wrote:

> I believe that if I did not translate the sentences containing key infor-
> mation, the students could not understand or misunderstand the text.
> My teaching experience tells me that in some cases if I tried to explain
> in English, the students would get confused. Consequently, they could
> not answer the comprehension questions correctly. In my opinion, the
> students' reading comprehension would be improved if I explained
> the important information or difficult sentences in the reading text in
> Vietnamese.

All in all, data from classroom observations and stimulated recall indicate
that the teacher switched codes for three major functions: classroom management, pedagogical treatment and comprehension checking. Of these
three, the pedagogical function (particularly explaining grammar or new
words) is deemed to be the most important, that is, facilitating the students'
understanding of the lesson input and their task completion. These findings

lend further support to previous studies on Vietnamese teachers' CS (Kieu Hang Kim Anh, 2010; Le Van Canh, 2011). However, while observing the teacher, I realised that she switched even when there was no sign of the students' failure to understand the point or to complete the learning tasks. The teacher seemed to underestimate the students' ability in the target language. In the following section, I look further into the issues that motivated the teacher's switches.

Factors Motivating the Teacher's Codeswitching

While it has been well reported in the CS literature (e.g. Cook, 2001; Kharma & Hajjaj, 1989), that teachers' switches are to serve a variety of pedagogical functions, such as the three illustrated above, factors that motivate their CS practice remain inadequately explored. It is not quite clear whether their switches to the students' native language are shaped by their students' and their own beliefs and attitudes towards the use of the native language, their underestimation of the students' target language proficiency, the institutional policy on the use of the target language in the classroom, or their teaching methods. Yet, a plausible interpretation can be made of the motivates for the teacher's CS practices in Extract 9 below. In this extract, the teacher was asking the students to identify which items given in the shopping list are countable and which are uncountable.

Extract 9

01 T   Okay. Answer my question. Can you count milk? Do you un-
         derstand? The word 'count', do you understand it? Đếm. Can
         you count milk? Vậy mình có đếm được sữa không? Yes or no?
02 Ss No
03 T   Oh no. Can you count eggs?
04 Ss Yes.
05 T   Certainly. Now tell me what are the countable nouns on the
         shopping list. Vậy bây giờ nói cho cô biết những danh từ đếm được
         trong cái shopping list này and, vice versa, what are uncountable
         nouns on the shopping list và ngược lại đâu là những danh từ
         không đếm được trong cái shopping list này. Okay? One minute
         for you to decide. Một phút để các bạn quyết định.

When asked why she translated the word 'count' into Vietnamese, she said that the students did not know it. In other words, she switched to define the word that the students supposedly did not know. However, even after she had already translated the word 'count', she continued to repeat the question 'Can you count milk?' in Vietnamese. In the stimulated recall session, she gave more thought to this and said that the translation was unnecessary. Evidently, in this case the teacher underestimated the students' ability in the target language and this judgement is justified by the students' correct response to her second question, 'Can you count eggs?' Then, even though she had explained the meaning of the word 'count' in Vietnamese, she switched to Vietnamese again to define the word 'countable' in the question 'What are the countable nouns on the shopping list?', reasoning that the students knew the word 'count' but they did not know the meaning of the word 'countable'. When I asked her if she thought she could have explained the words 'countable' and 'uncountable' in English by pointing out the suffix and prefix, she said that she had used English but felt that the students did not understand, so she switched to Vietnamese to help them. But when asked how she had known the students did not understand, she just laughed. So, another factor that governs the teacher's switches is her teaching method and her belief that the students' English was inadequate, as opposed to the reality of her students' actual English capabilities. This is further justified by her responses to questions about why she switched: she admitted that her CS behaviours were often just habitual and automatic.

To gain more evidence of the teacher's motivations for CS, following the classroom observation and stimulated recall, I gave the observational transcripts to her and asked her to reflect on her switches at home, and to decide which of her switches she thought were appropriate and which inappropriate, and whether she would switch to Vietnamese if she taught the lesson again, before filling in the worksheet with her reflective responses. These reflective responses were sent to me via email. Out of 58 CS events that had been identified in her four observed lessons, she decided that 16 were either inappropriate or unnecessary. For example, she wrote:

After looking through the lesson transcripts I found that some switches to Vietnamese were not necessary. For example, I could have used the synonym 'thin' to explain the word 'slim' [Extract 6]. Or I did not need to translate sentences 'What did you buy yesterday when you went shopping?' [Extract 4] or 'Look at the conversation' [Extract 5] into Vietnamese. I think the students could understand these sentences in English.

These findings support those reported by Liu *et al.* (2004), that the teacher's switches appeared not to be governed by her stated principle of CS to explain difficult material. More often than not, the teacher in the present study switched from English to Vietnamese 'to say something very simple, which [she] could have said easily and [in a] less time-consuming [way] in English' (Liu *et al.*, 2004: 623). Ellis (1988: 133) calls this type of CS practice 'misguided'. The results also support the scholastic claim that teachers' CS practice is motivated by their unfounded worry that the students' proficiency in the target language is not adequate to understand the teaching material, and that CS in the second language classroom is likely to be driven by the teacher's teaching methods. In other words, the teacher in this study adopted what Macaro (2001) called an 'unhealthy deficit model' of CS, or the maximal position.

Reflection

This qualitative case study has yielded some interesting findings about the teacher's CS in the discourse of a Vietnamese university classroom. Especially, the findings reveal some factors that motivate the teacher's CS practices, an issue that remains under-explored in the literature on foreign language education. The study indicates that CS is a normal feature of the foreign language classroom where the teacher and the students share a native language. This implies that the promotion of the English-only policy in a context where English is being taught as a foreign language is unrealistic and perhaps ethnocentric. In an informal chat with the teacher participant in this study after the data collection had been completed, she told me that teachers in her university used Vietnamese far more frequently when they were not observed. My experience tells me that this was true.

The major functions of the teacher's switches included classroom management, explaining grammar, pronunciation and lexis, enhancing motivation and checking students' comprehension. Other functions such as establishing teacher–student rapport and maintaining discipline (Cook, 2001; Kharma & Hajjaj, 1989) were not found in this study. However, the most significant finding of this study is that it shows the complexity of teacher CS in the EFL classroom. That complexity is evident in the many reasons the teacher gave for her CS behaviours, which were largely motivated by her beliefs, which she acknowledged to be mistaken, about the students' target language ability and her teaching methods. This leads to the fact that many of her switches to Vietnamese were automatic, habitual, unconscious and unprincipled, evidenced in her reflective acknowledgement of many inappropriate and unnecessary switches to Vietnamese.

The present study focused on just one teacher working in one university. Despite its limitations, though, two suggestions can be made, one for future research and the other for teacher education programmes.

Since arguments for or against CS in the foreign language classroom are beyond the scope of this single case study, further research is needed to identify the factors that govern teachers' CS practices and the effect of their CS on the students' learning. Suchinvestigations will help to theorise CS, in an attempt to develop effective CS strategies that can be transferred to teacher education programmes. Methodologically, future research should go beyond survey methods to uncover the teachers' thoughts and beliefs that underlie their CS behaviours. As revealed in this study, stimulated recall interviews and teacher reflective accounts, in addition to observations, are useful instruments, which both enable the researcher to gain in-depth insights into factors that govern teachers' CS practices and provide participant teachers with good opportunities to reflect on their own CS behaviours. Such reflection is helpful to teachers in that they become aware of when and how CS can be effective and when it is not.

For teacher education programmes, instead of promoting a deficit view of CS, it is necessary to introduce codified effective CS strategies to both pre-service and in-service teachers. This could be implemented by allowing teachers in training to watch videos which record teachers' CS practices in real classrooms, and then discussing the appropriateness and effectiveness of the recorded CS behaviours. The videos could function as cultural artefacts which mediate teachers' cognitive transformation (Vygotsky, 1978). In other words, this video-based training approach will not only raise the teachers' awareness of CS but challenge their existing beliefs regarding how to switch codes appropriately in the classroom so as to change their practices as well.

COMMENTARY

Introduction

As reported by Le Van Canh, empirical studies in Asia on CS in university EFL contexts are still very few. Canh sees three major limitations of the studies on CS: they are few in number, rarely focus on the epistemological knowledge of the teachers, and none has adopted a multi-method approach. The major functions of CS, such as classroom management, explaining grammar, pronunciation and lexis, enhancing and checking students' comprehension, were found in the Canh's case study. Other than the complexity of CS, Canh reports that CS is a normal phenomenon in a foreign language classroom when a common first language is shared by the teacher and students.

Similar to what is reported here by Canh, studies on CS in the Indonesian context have also been relatively scarce. I will review several which have some relevance to Canh's findings. The first one is by Safitri (2011), who, after analysing the lyrics of selected Indonesian pop songs, found both intra-sentential and inter-sentential switches. Nafila (2009) did research on CS from Indonesian to Javanese or Sundanese by selected Javanese speakers staying in a community of predominantly Sundanese speakers. She found that all types of CS did take place, with intra-sentential CS occurring most frequently. Susanti (2010) conducted a case study on the functions of CS in EFL teachers' classroom instructions. She found six functions of CS, namely personalisation, reiteration, emphasis, clarification and topic shift; reiteration was the most frequent.

So far, no research has yet been conducted on CS within tertiary education contexts in Indonesia. Therefore, commenting on Canh's research by presenting and discussing data that occured in a context somewhat similar to that in Indonesia could provide new insights regarding this sociolinguistic phenomenon, especially as regards types and possible benefits or drawbacks of CS for educational purposes.

This commentary will address some findings and reflections put forward by Canh using my own data as a comparative source, especially as regards the purposes of CS and why it was carried out as perceived by the teacher himself. Somewhat different from what Canh did, this commentary will also include students' perceptions regarding CS occurrences as they took place in the class session reported here.

An Observational Study

To provide a commentary on Canh's case study, initially I video-taped three different class sessions from three different courses: statistics for language studies, speaking in professional contexts, and psycholinguistics. In the last two video-taped classes, very little CS was identified. So only the first was used as a comparative resource for this commentary. The video-taped classes were all conducted at the Department of English Education, Indonesia University of Education at Bandung, Indonesia, where all department courses offered should be taught in English, including the statistics for language studies course, a 100-minute session of which was video-taped and selected for the purposes of this commentary on the Vietnamese case study.

The participating teacher was a 31-year-old man with seven and a half years of teaching experience at the university. He had a masters degree in educational research methodology from an Australian university. Other than statistics for language studies, he also taught EFL methodology, speaking and intercultural com-munication. The video-taping was initially consented to by the teacher for the purpose of teaching improvement, as mandated by the department chair, not for CS analyses; it is therefore likely that there was no major effect of video-taping on the teacher's use of language, especially with regard to CS during class. The 55 students were undergraduates in the second year of their four-year first-degree programme at the Department of English Education.

Data and Discussion

The data shown below are extracts purposefully taken from the video-taped material, which are used here for providing comments on what has been done and found in the Vietnamese study. Thus, the selection of these extracts was mainly triggered by findings in Canh's study. The extracts are sequenced below as they take place in the video; therefore, commentaries are not in the same order as Canh's, namely types followed by functions. The analysis of the data, like Canh's, was also data-driven with an inductive approach and as a result the analysis repeatedly addresses the same issues as they arose in the extracts selected. For the benefit of readers, an English translation of what is uttered in Indonesian is given in italics after each extract from the video-taped material, with the transcript conventions followed elsewhere in this volume (see p. xv).

A few days after video-taping was over, a questionnaire was administered to the participating students asking how they perceived CS as it took place in the statistics for language studies class, with regard to whether the codeswitches to Indonesian were generally appropriate, what purposes they thought the CS occurrences took place for, and whether they were effective in helping their understanding of the subject taught. The teacher was given a similar questionnaire but in addition I conducted a post-lesson discussion with him regarding his perception of CS issues.

Canh reported that CS occurrences were largely at the inter-sentential level. This phenomenon is similar to what takes place in the Indonesian context, as shown in the following selected extracts.

Extract 1 (05:22, video 1)

To take an example, what is actually the mean of gender in your classroom? It is impossible to do because the type of variable is nominal. Jadi akan susah kalau ada yang nanya, Itu rata-rata jenis kelamin di kelasnya, laki-laki perempuan? *So it would be difficult if there is a question about the average of sex in class, male or female?*

Another somewhat frequently occurring phenomenon in Canh's data is repetition. This also happens in the Indonesian context, as shown in the above extract. Using inter-sentential CS, after saying that it is impossible to get the mean out of a nominal variable, the teacher turned to Indonesian to reiterate the impossibility. This type of CS here seems to have been carried out to provide clarification of a newly introduced concept, namely the mathematical concept of 'mean'. According to the teacher, the switch in the above extract was appropriately inserted, intended to explain the concept, and it was effective in helping students to gain a better understanding.

With reference to Extract 3 in his study, Canh indicates that CS did take place 'even when her English utterances were simple enough for the students to understand'. This type of switching also took place in my study, as indicated in the following extract.

Extract 2 (10:47)

Now, measure of dispersion also indicates how close data are, the values are clustered about a measure of central tendency, which is mean. Jadi kalau anda ingin melihat sebaran … itu seperti apa terhadap mean. *So if you want to see how the distribution … is like what to the mean*. We can use measure of … Pasti konsepnya belum nempel tapi *For sure the concept is not understood yet, but …* step by step we will go there.

There is some evidence here that the teacher somewhat underestimated the students' ability to understand him, as indicated by his saying 'Pasti konsepnya belum nempel', which means 'for sure the concept is not understood yet'. However as admitted by the teacher afterwards, the switch was actually done due to a change from the topic, the mean, to a different topic, measure of dispersion. The same type of CS occurred in the Vietnamese context in Canh's Extract 9: 'in this case the teacher underestimated the students' ability in the target language'.

Explanation in the students' language was in many cases given not only to clarify difficult concepts but also to add examples in reference to a simple word, such as the word *inconsistent* in the following extract.

Extract 3 (13:20)

Well, even though we don't calculate the values, the measure of central tendencies, at least we can say that consultant X is highly inconsistent in terms of seeing the client. Ada yang harus nunggu tiga menit, ada yang harus sampai setengah jam. *There are those who should wait three minutes, there are those who should (wait) up to half an hour*. Now why that different phase with consultant Y in this case? You can see here that clients wait about more or less ten minutes.

The Indonesian expression in the above extract 'Ada yang harus nunggu tiga menit, ada yang harus sampai setengah jam' is put forward to refer to its antecedent 'inconsistent'. This type of switching is not reiteration, as there is no relevant English utterance given by the teacher ahead of or following the L1 switch. The teacher believed that the switch was appropriately inserted to explain the abstract concept, which actually is simple enough to be rendered fully in English.

As regards switching for a simple matter, Canh has indicated (quoting Liu) that 'More often than not, the teacher in the present study switched from English to Vietnamese "to say something very simple, which [she] could have said easily and [in a] less time-consuming [way] in English".' This phenomenon of switching was also seen in the Indonesian context, as shown in the following extract.

Extract 4 (13:26)

Because you can see here, nine minutes least, and thirteen minutes most. Ya kurang lebih kalau sembilan menit kan kurang satu menit, tiga belas kelebihan sedikit. *Yes, more or less, if nine minutes, it is one minute less, thirteen is a little more....* But then, you can see here that in terms of consistency, consultant X is more consistent.

In the above extract the switching seems to function simply for reconfirmation of what has been stated in English. The switch to 'Ya kurang lebih kalau sembilan menit kan kurang satu menit, tiga belas kelebihan sedikit' is a repetition of the preceding phrase, 'nine minutes least, and thirteen minutes most'.

In pedagogy, examples are commonly positioned to assist understanding on the part of the students. Canh has indicated that, of three major functions – classroom management, pedagogical treatment and comprehension checking – 'the pedagogical function ... is deemed to be the most important' in facilitating the students' understanding of the subject taught.

Extract 5 (21:35)

Now, so, deviation actually the distance of individual values to the mean. Misalkan, nilai rata-rata kelas ini dalam mata kuliah Grammar adalah tujuh puluh, kamu dapat berapa? Oh, saya dapat enam puluh. Si A? *For example, the average score of this class in the subject of Grammar are seventy, what did you get?* Oh, *I got sixty. A?* Any deviation? … Kalau skor rata-rata di kelas ini Grammar-nya tujuh puluh, si A dapat skor enam puluh. Meny-impang apa tidak untuk si A? Menyimpang sebanyak? Sepuluh point negatif ya dari tujuh puluh. Si B dapat skornya delapan puluh. Menyimpang? Sepuluh point lebih positif. Kalau yang dapatnya tujuh puluh, sama dengan rata-rata kelas? Berarti? *If the average score on the Grammar of this class is seventy, and A got sixty. Any deviation or not of A? Deviation how much? Yes negative, ten points from seventy. Person B got eighty. Deviant? Ten more positive points. If a scoref of seventy, same as the average score? Meaning?* No deviation at all.

The above CS event is the longest in my video-taped data. It obviously functions to provide examples demonstrating the concept of deviation. According to the teacher, the switch was appropriately inserted because he feared students' failure to understand him. This extract is another example of 'the multifunctional use of classroom CS', to borrow Canh's words, which could consist of classroom management, pedagogical concern and comprehension check.

Pedagogical switching occurs as is indicated by content-related words and phrases referring to the topic being discussed, such as 'deviation' and 'menyimpang'. Rising intonations taking place in the above extract are indicators of CS for the purpose of comprehension check, as seen in 'Menyimpang apa tidak untuk si A? Menyimpang sebanyak? … Menyimpang? Sepuluh point lebih positif. Kalau yang dapatnya tujuh puluh, sama dengan rata-rata kelas? Berarti?' The concept 'deviation' in the first sentence in the above extract functions as an antecedent to the succeeding CS.

Teacher Reflections

To get further elaboration regarding beliefs and motivations for the teacher's CS, a set of questions were posed to him regarding the appropriateness of inserting the switches occurring in the extracts above and their purposes. The teacher's position and self-evaluation have been indicated in the commentary section above for some extracts. Overall, the teacher believed that the insertion of switches was appropriately done in all extracts above and mostly carried out in case students failed to understand him. He also felt that those switches were effective in helping students to understand better what was being explained.

The teacher was also asked to put forward (in writing) his own view regarding CS and its significance in teaching content subjects in higher education. Fairly similar to what has been cited by Kieu (2010), who did research in a Vietnamese context, the teacher in the present study elaborated his belief that using L2 only is impractical for non-native speaker learners, and L1 is more effective in explaining difficult concepts. In Canh's words, it is 'unrealistic and perhaps ethnocentric'. In this regard, the Indonesian teacher wrote:

> In general, I see the use of codeswitching more as one of the ways to ease the process of communication. In teaching students by using a language that does not become their mother tongue, I believe that the ability to use properly constructed codeswitching in giving elaboration is needed by teachers or lecturers. Since meanings in certain concepts are often culturally and contextually specific, the use of codeswitching may ease the process of understanding them.

He believes here that as English is not the students' mother tongue, CS should be carried out in a proper way as a tool for more effective communication, especially when dealing with the meaning of difficult and contextually specific concepts. So, the key issue here is student understanding of what is being taught. When asked further about the specific purposes of CS, he clarified the issue by writing that:

> The codeswitching I often practise in my classroom is mainly intended to increase the students' understanding on the topic being discussed, especially on some seemingly difficult concepts to understand. I usually use codeswitching together with some repetitions just to make sure that students get 'what I really want them to have in their minds'. I may not know for sure whether they really understand, but, at least from the gesture they show me, I can predict that they get the thing that I want them to know.

Table 5.2 Percentage of students' perceptions as regards the appropriateness and function of CS performed by their teacher

	Appropriately inserted words in the context	Explain abstract con-cepts	Or-ganise tasks	Establish student–teacher rapport	Maintain class-room disci-pline	Build soli-darity as users of Indo-nesian	Automatic and un-conscious	For fear of students' failure to under-stand	Show topic switches	Teachers' insuf-ficiency in English	Helps students better under-stand the subject
Strongly disagree	0	0	1.8	1.8	1.8	12.7	3.6	5.5	0	3.6	0
Disagree	0	1.8	7.3	14.5	23.6	18.2	12.7	12.7	34.5	16.4	0
Slightly disagree	1.8	1.8	16.4	14.5	10.9	10.9	34.5	29.1	32.7	9.1	1.8
Slightly agree	18.2	12.7	23.6	34.5	38.2	27.3	30.9	14.5	16.4	34.5	9.1
Agree	70.9	54.5	45.5	34.5	21.8	20.0	14.5	23.6	16.4	21.8	47.3
Strongly agree	9.1	29.1	5.5	0	3.6	10.9	3.6	14.5	0	14.5	41.8

Students' Perceptions

In order to see how students perceived CS as it had taken place in their classroom, I administered a questionnaire to the whole of the video-taped class. The 55 students were asked to respond to questionnaire items regarding appropriateness of CS performed by their teacher, the way CS was done, the purposes for which they thought the teacher had used CS and the effectiveness of CS in their own mastery of the subject being taught.

The questionnaire also asked the students to self-report their academic achievement as well as their level of proficiency in English. Categorised as *very high*, *high*, *slightly high*, *slightly low*, *low* and *very low*, on average the students' academic achievement was *slightly high*, with 3.6 out of a possible highest score of 6.0. Their reported proficiency in English, classified as *excellent*, *very good*, *good*, *fair*, *bad* and *very bad*, was categorised as *good*, again at an average of 3.6.

The student questionnaire classified the appropriateness and functions of CS as identified in Canh's report: to explain difficult concepts, to organise tasks, to establish student–teacher rapport, to maintain classroom discipline, and to show a switch from one topic to another. Overall, the students had a very positive perception of how the teacher managed his CS. Table 5.2 shows percentage figures of the students' perceptions in each of the appropriateness and function aspects of CS phenomena during the class session.

When asked about appropriateness of switching to Indonesian by their teacher, the students showed their very firm agreement with the appropriate insertion of Indonesian in the dicourse (70.9% agreed and 9.1% strongly agreed that the switches were appropriately inserted by the teacher). As regards functions, the data show that most of the switches were for the purpose of explaining abstract words or concepts, and 96.3% of the students at least slightly agreed that the CS was appropriate for clarification of difficult words or concepts.

As to how switches were performed, the students were equally split (51% and 49%). In other words, about half of the students agreed that the teacher codeswitched automatically and unconsciously, but the other half disagreed. Basically the students were uncertain about this issue, as most either slightly disagreed (34.5%) or slightly agreed (30.9%) with the proposition.

Interestingly, a very high proportion (70.8%) of the students thought CS took place due to the teacher's insufficiency in English. However, from what I gather based on my daily interaction with the teacher, his proficiency in English is far above what is required to conduct teaching a subject fully in English. This is also supported by the teacher's response to the question regarding English insufficiency for all extracts selected in the data analysis. The teacher confirmed that the CS which occurred was definitely not due to his inability to express complex ideas in English.

Conclusion

Overall, CS in the discourse of Indonesian and Vietnamese higher education occurred in a somewhat similar fashion, despite the fact that there were differences as regards the nature of each of the subjects taught and the proficiency in English of the teachers involved. 'Unnecessary' switches did take place in the two contexts, and there were signs that teachers underestimated their students abilities in some extracts by their switching to L1 even when the topic was actually simple enough to be put forward fully in English. The Vietnamese teacher did acknowledge this by saying 'I found that some switches to Vietnamese were not necessary'. I regard this phenomenon as an indication of 'linguistic fatigue' on the part of the teacher. When a speaker is tired, physically or psychologically, especially after talking for a rather lengthy period, he would naturally resort to his L1 to comfort himself if the context and the people around permitted. In these two classroom contexts, both teachers were certainly aware that the contexts and the students would have no objection to their use of L1. Any teacher in a similar context could argue that providing comprehensible inputs to the students should not be automatically categorised as underestimating them.

As to the methodological aspects, I fully agree with Canh that CS research would be better carried out using a multi-method approach, due to the intricacies involved. I am not satisfied myself with my questionnaire-based discussion regarding the students' perceptions of CS, but I think what I have revealed here with some limited quantitative data could provide a different angle on complex CS phenomena. Certainly, a thorough investigation and in-depth analysis are needed in future research, and one area worth investigating is the effectiveness of CS in enhancing students' comprehension and acquisition of the subject matter and of the target language.

References

Cook, V.J. (2001) Using the first language in the classroom. *Canadian Modern Language Review/La revue canadienne des langues vivants* 57 (3), 402–423.

Council of Europe (2001) *Common European Framework of Reference for Languages: Learning, Teaching, Assessment*. Cambridge: Cambridge University Press.

Duff, P.A. (2008) *Case Study Research in Applied Linguistics*. New York: Lawrence Erlbaum Associates.

Ellis, R. (1988) *Classroom Second Language Development*. New York: Prentice Hall.

Gass, S.M. and Mackey, A. (2000) *Stimulated Recall Methodology in Second Language Research*. Mahwah, NJ: Lawrence Erlbaum Associates.

Holliday, A. (2007) *Doing and Writing Qualitative Research* (2nd edn). Thousand Oaks, CA: Sage.

Kharma, N.N. and Hajjaj, A.H. (1989) Use of the mother tongue in the ESL classroom. *International Review of Applied Linguistics in Language Teaching (IRAL)* 27 (3), 223–235.

Kieu Hang Kim Anh (2010) Use of Vietnamese in English language teaching in Vietnam: Attitudes of Vietnamese university teachers. *English Language Teaching* 3 (2), 119–128.

Le Van Canh (2011) Form-focused instruction: A case study of Vietnamese teachers' beliefs and practices. Unpublished PhD thesis, University of Waikato.

Le Van Canh and Maley, A. (2012) Interviews. In R. Barnard and A. Burns (eds) *Researching Language Teacher Cognition and Practice: International Case Studies* (pp. 90–108). Bristol: Multilingual Matters.

Liu, D., Ahn, G., Baek, K. and Han, N. (2004) South Korean high school English teachers' code-switching: Questions and challenges in the drive for maximal use of English in teaching. *TESOL Quarterly* 38 (4), 605–638.

Macaro, E. (2001) Analyzing students teachers' code-switching in foreign language classrooms: Theories and decision-making. *Modern Language Journal* 85 (4), 531–548.

Miles, M. and Huberman, A.M. (1994) *Qualitative Data Analysis* (2nd edn). Thousand Oaks, CA: Sage.

Nafila, I. (2009) Code switching in cultural adjustment processes among the Javanese. Research paper, Indonesia University of Education.

Poplack, S. (1980) Sometimes I'll start a sentence in English y termino en espanol: Towards a typology of code-switching. *Linguistics* 18, 581–616.

Safitri, I.D. (2011) Code switching in Indonesian pop songs. See http://library.um.ac.id/free-contents/index.php/pub/detail/code-switching-in-indonesia-pop-songs-ifa-dewi-safitri-35368.html (accessed August 2013).

Soars, L. and Soars, J. (2009) *New Headway* (4th edn). Oxford: Oxford University Press.

Susanti, E.O. (2010) Teachers' use of code switching in teaching English as a foreign language for young learners: A descriptive study at 'Speak Up' English course. Research paper, Indonesia University of Education.

Vygotsky, L.S. (1978) *Mind in Society: The Development of Higher Psychological Processes.* Cambridge, MA: Harvard University Press.

Yin, R. (2009) *Case Study Research: Design and Methods* (4th edn). Thousand Oaks, CA: Sage.

6 Codeswitching in Universities in Brunei Darussalam and Malaysia

Case Study: Noor Azam Haji-Othman,
Hajah Zurinah Haji Yaakub, Dayangku
Liyana Putri Pengiran Abdul Ghani,
Hajah Suciyati Haji Sulaiman and
Saidai Haji Hitam
Commentary: Ain Nadzimah Abdullah
and Chan Swee Heng

CASE STUDY

Introduction

This chapter looks at the case of three Bruneian teachers teaching various languages at a language centre. All of these tutors were English–Malay bilinguals: two were teaching English and one was teaching both English and an indigenous language, Tutong. The tutors' reflections and responses to a set of questions are analysed to gain insights into practices of codeswitching (CS) in their lessons, and their beliefs about these practices. Although there are mixed feelings about CS during lessons, the reasons for their agreement and/or reticence much depend on factors of context, levels taught and the target language.

Context for the Case Study

Universiti Brunei Darussalam (UBD) is Brunei's oldest university, and remains the premier comprehensive university in Negara Brunei Darussalam since it opened in 1985. The Language Centre (henceforth LC) was established only in 2001, taking over the responsibilities of teaching compulsory English language skills courses, and offering a range of national and international languages, including Malay, Korean, Japanese and Arabic. In 2009, the LC began offering formal instruction in Tutong, Dusun and Iban, three largely unwritten indigenous languages of Brunei and Borneo.

The teaching staff at LC comprise 23 Bruneian and expatriate staff from the UK, Australia, Japan, Korea, the Philippines, Malaysia, Indonesia and Egypt. The students taking LC language classes generally are mostly Bruneians, with some international students. English Language and Communication Skills (Academic English) modules are compulsory for all UBD students, despite their having passed the prerequisite GCE Ordinary Level English language examination at secondary school. All the other languages on offer are elective courses, which the students are free to choose and for which they obtain credits towards their degree.

CS is a common phenomenon in all language classrooms around the world (Macaro, 2009), Brunei included. Brunei is a multilingual and multi-ethnic country; the official language is Malay but English is also widely used, and the two languages are the mediums of instruction in the education system. Many Bruneians do not have Malay as their L1, but rather one of the indigenous languages or a Chinese dialect. This fact is important to bear in mind in this study, as the focus is on Bruneian tutors who are teaching their fellow Bruneians. This provides a unique case study on the basis of the shared languages and cultural background between the tutor and the students (Malay and English), with the target language being the most salient variable (Martin, 1999, 2003; Saxena, 2009).

The cases that we present below will indicate the tutors' belief in the 'optimal' position that Macaro (1997, 2001; and in the Overview to the present volume) suggests with regard to CS. They believe that some L1 insertion should be allowed, as it facilitates communication and learning, but it must be controlled in some way so as not to encourage students to constantly resort to their L1 or to the language they share with their teacher. This does create some degree of conflict in the classroom, but it becomes apparent from this case study that students subscribe to the same conceptualisation of CS (that it should be allowed but not encouraged) as that of the tutors, in relation to the same intended educational outcomes: improved language and communication skills.

As educated Bruneians, the tutors at the LC all speak at least Malay and English. The profiles of the three tutors involved in the present case study are summarised in Table 6.1. One of them was trilingual. These three tutors were asked several set questions about their practices of CS in the context

Table 6.1 Tutors' profiles

	L1	L2	L3	Languages	Qualifications	Teaching experience
T1	Malay	English	–	English	MA (Australia)	5 years
T2	Malay	English	–	English	MA (Australia)	5 years
T3	Tutong	Malay	English	Tuton and English	PhD (UK)	16 years

of their typical lessons. Their responses analysed below provide a reflection of the practices at the university's LC.

Findings

Tutors' responses to the set of study questions

Both T1 and T2 indicated that they did not codeswitch in their English lessons, whereas T3 reported that he did codeswitch in class. T1 believed that maximum exposure, or in fact absolute exposure, to the target language (TL) is the only way to improve the students' linguistic performance:

> **T1:** I believe that for students to learn the English language effectively they need to be well exposed to the language and be given ample practice and opportunity to experiment [with] the language use.

Another reason shared by T1 and T2 was their personal linguistic background, each professing to being more comfortable speaking English on most occasions, although they both spoke Malay as well.

> **T2:** I was brought up with English; therefore I have never formally studied the Malay language. The Malay language that I speak at home is very basic, solely for the purpose of communicating with my parents and other relatives.... It is easier and faster for me to communicate in English rather than in Malay. Faster in the sense that when I want to convey my message my thoughts are in English; if I were to speak Malay, I would have to 'think about' and 'translate' my thoughts into Malay.

T3 provided an interesting insight into this discussion, stating that if he were teaching English, he would not codeswitch, but he would do so in his other language lessons:

T3: I teach two languages, English and Tutong. I find that with my English students, I'm unlikely to use codeswitching, but with Tutong, I am more willing to use it. This is probably because I think the students should already know English after 12 years of schooling before coming to UBD, whereas with Tutong, despite it being a native language in Brunei, to many of the students it is foreign because it is only spoken by a relatively small group of an indigenous ethnic group, and is dying as a language.

Although not explicitly stated, this factor might also contribute to T1 and T2's reluctance to codeswitch when they taught English. There appears to be a higher expectation when it comes to English because Bruneian students will have learned and used the language for at least 12 years, following the National Curriculum. In fact, a typical Bruneian student is introduced and exposed to English for two years in pre-school, six years in primary school, five years in secondary school, and two years in pre-university: at least 15 years altogether by the time they arrive at university.

Two more factors are of significance here: certainly the linguistic background of the students is a determinant in whether or not CS is necessary, but so is the status of the TL in relation to the students. So the degree to which the students are perceived to be familiar with the TL appears to be a main factor in the tutors' consideration of whether or not to switch between languages to enhance learning.

Codeswitching among students

All three tutors reported that their students did codeswitch in class, either when speaking to the tutors themselves, or when speaking with their classmates. T1 observed that CS was likely to happen (voluntarily) when the students were responding orally at length or when they had to provide complicated explanations.

T1: Students generally respond in English when short, simple answers are sufficient but it appears that the longer time they spend talking, the greater the likelihood is for them to codeswitch.

T1 suggested that this may be due to the students finding it difficult to grasp the right English words to explain or convey a particular concept, and that the students just find it more comfortable to express themselves in Malay in extended exchanges. T2 supported this suggestion:

T2: I believe they do so because, similar to me, they feel more comfortable speaking in Malay and they are able to convey their message/question accurately when Malay is spoken. If they were to convey their message in English, it probably requires them to 'think' and 'translate' their thoughts into English before speaking out. Moreover, when they attempt to 'think' and 'translate' into English, it will most likely be not as accurate as they would want it to be.

This perceived shortcut in the whole mental processing of a message could in fact be an 'act of desperation' on the part of the students, as T2 stated:

T2: I also notice that my students who codeswitch express their frustration in not being able to convey their question in English. When it comes to students' codeswitching, I do allow it in class because I do not want to scare and/or stop them from asking vital questions regarding their studies, but my response to them still remains in the English language.

It is interesting that all three tutors reacted in the same manner when students in their English lessons used Malay with them: they responded in English. This is illustrated below:

Extract 1

01 T3   So what do you think the article is about?
02 Ss   About the media.
03 T3   What about the media? What does it actually say?
04 S1   It talks about // apa ni, Sir // censorship kah Sir? *It talks about // what's it, Sir // is it censorship, Sir?*
05 T3   Yes, you're on the right track. But what about censorship?

In this example of a typically codeswitched exchange, the students produce a general response chorally but, when pressed, S1 volunteers a more specific answer, albeit without much conviction. The student responds and checks with the tutor using the Malay question-marker 'kah', to which the tutor replies in English. S1 appears hesitant about the switch into Malay. She is requesting confirmation of the meaning of the word 'censorship', which for her represents the answer to the teacher's initiation in turn 01. In turn 05, the tutor does not criticise the student's switch to Malay, nor does he respond to the student's request to clarify the meaning of 'censorship'.

Instead, his feedback is at first affective and positive ('Yes, you're on the right track') and then he tries to elicit more from S1 about what the article says about the topic of censorship.

The following example, supplied by T2, resulted from the tutor's explanation of an assignment for the students:

Extract 2

01 T2 Any questions, queries, comments or uncertainty regarding the assignment⸮

02 S2 Miss, for my assignment, can I choose 'belia masjid', boleh kah tu Miss⸮ *'youth of the mosque'⸮ Can I do that, Miss⸮*

03 T2 You need to tell me what aspect of the mosque youth group will you be choosing.

04 S2 I choose them because of their kebajikan *charity*.

05 T2 Okay. For your assignment you need to give me two examples of the sort of charitable activities they have done.

06 S2 You mean example like, they help rebuild a family's house from kebakaran, Miss⸮ Example macam atu⸮ *after a fire, Miss⸮ Examples like that⸮*

07 T2 Yes. Helping to rebuild a family's house that was caught on fire or affected by the recent floods⸮

08 S2 Oh, okay. Thank you, Miss.

In Extract 2, the tutor insists on speaking and responding to the student's questions in English. Each time, the student starts off in English (the TL) but finishes off her sentences in Malay. This could also be taken to mean that the student is wary of the tutor's disapproval of her using Malay, so she buffers her sentences using English first.

T3 taught Tutong, an endangered Bruneian language, to students who mainly spoke Malay as their first language and English as their second. Tutong was essentially a foreign language to the students and, predictably, the Tutong language classes featured a lot of CS in English and Malay. A vital factor is that the students and the tutors themselves shared a common language, that is Malay, to which they readily resorted when the need arose. This shared language between the students and the tutors appeared to be more readily employed by the students as a safety net when they felt that communication in the TL (be it English or Tutong) was not possible.

Types and percentages of classroom codeswitching

The tutors were asked to provide an estimation of the percentage of CS that occurs in their typical lessons. Whereas T1 and T2 indicated zero occurrence of CS in their English lessons, T3 admitted to using 99% English and 1% Malay in his English classes. T3, however, codeswitched between Tutong (50%), Malay (20%) and English (30%) in his Tutong language classes. While this means that the TL was still being prioritised, half of the time the lessons were being conducted in English and Malay, as demonstrated below (Tutong words and phrases are underlined in the extract; otherwise Malay and English are used, and presented in line with the transcription conventions used throughout the volume):

Extract 3: Lesson on prepositions and locatives in the Tutong language

01 T3   Lamin Zara ge dembo? *Zara's house is where?*
02 Ss   Ge … setepi' lamin Farah. *Next … to Farah's house.*
03 T3   Lurus, ge setepi' lamin Farah. Next to Farah's house. Correct, next to Farah's house. Rumah si Aziz dimana? Dembo lamin Aziz? Cuba' ti'an ge peta'. *Where is Aziz's house? Where is Aziz's house? Try to find it on the map.*
04 S1   Lamin Aziz inda jauh… *Aziz's house is not far…*
05 T3   … endo jawu' … *not far from …*
06 S1   Lamin Aziz endo jawu' kod bank. *Aziz's house is not far from the bank.*
07 S2   Sir, it's not near the mosque, kan, Sir? *Sir, it's not near the mosque, is it, Sir?*
08 T3   No, it's not. Look at the map carefully. Cuba' ti'an benor-benor atin. *Try looking closely again.*

T3 justified this trilingual CS by stating that 'English is used 30% of the time owing mainly to the tutor's linguistic repertoire, it being his main working language, while Malay is used less frequently (20%)'. That S2 requested confirmation from the tutor in English (turn 07) reflects the prominence of English in the linguistic repertoire of the Bruneian students and teachers. But what is most significant in this episode is S2's decision to ask the question in English rather than Malay. It could of course be a reaction to the tutor's use of English as his working language, yet this turn by S2 was not in response to any elicitation by the tutor. It seems ironic that English, essentially a foreign language, rather than Malay, should be used in teaching a Bruneian indigenous language (Tutong) to Bruneians who speak other languages, including Malay. Again, this reinforces the idea of the important role of English in Bruneians' daily usage.

The views of the tutors above suggest that CS, to whatever degree it may occur, should not be seen as detrimental to the students' learning outcomes. If there is 100% instruction in the TL or only 60% or 50% in the TL while the remaining teacher input is in another or other languages, the objectives and aims of the courses remain unchanged, that is, to impart language skills in the TL.

Perceived benefits of codeswitching

Despite their unwillingness to codeswitch, T1 and T2 accepted that there were some benefits to the practice:

T1: The students don't feel as restricted as they are able to express themselves more freely and easily.

T2: In my view, codeswitching would benefit those who are studying a language that is foreign to them. They would learn and understand more if the foreign language was spoken followed by the language they are much more comfortable in, English or Malay.

The latter statement by T2 supports the earlier contention that English is not seen as a 'foreign' language by Bruneian students and teachers alike, as it has been generally claimed as Brunei's L2. However, T2 added:

T2: It's just that students are not properly exposed and given enough practice to use and speak English confidently. From my personal observation, students are more comfortable writing in English than speaking English. For this reason, then, I wouldn't think that code-switching would benefit them in improving their English language. Like I said earlier, it is better for them to practise and experiment with the language, to be able to be confident with the language.

T2's justification for not encouraging CS among her students when speaking to her does appears reasonable. If, indeed, the problem is in oral communication (or lack of it), then students should be encouraged to speak in English as much as possible, rather than readily resort to CS, which could be detrimental to their skills development. A proviso here is that the English taught to students at UBD is academic English, to support their university study, and it is taught with the aim of improving their general communication skills. Given this objective, the English language tutors' somewhat dismissive attitude to the practice of CS is understandable. Meanwhile, T3, who allowed and used CS during his lessons, stated his belief that 'it draws on the students' multilingual ability'. While this comment could be a generalisation of the students' linguistic ability and background, it is a significant recognition of the students' multilingualism as a resource to aid learning.

Perceived disadvantages of codeswitching

All the tutors agreed that unregulated CS can restrict learning. For example:

T1: Allowing frequent codeswitching deprives students of the practice they evidently need in speaking in English.

T3: They risk becoming over-dependent on Malay and English (or on codeswitching) and reduce practice or thinking in the target language.

T2 offered a case in point:

T2: I do not have anything against codeswitching but, in my opinion, codeswitching may disrupt the ability to be engrossed in the language itself. For example, I have an in-service student. She is a very good student who achieves good to excellent grades; however, her main concern is her English language. She is very good in writing and she has the capability to be a very good English speaker but because she is not confident and loves to codeswitch she is still unable to express any of her thoughts wholly in English. She has been codeswitching most of the time and even sometimes she doesn't realise it and, because of this, she is afraid to speak English or rather has no confidence – it has become a habit to her.

Clearly, all three tutors, whether they themselves codeswitched or not, were opposed to an over-reliance on the practice among students. The example provided by T2 of the case of a potentially able student who habitually resorted to CS is a clear illustration of such behaviour having potentially debilitative effects on students' language learning.

Codeswitching among tutors in general

The tutors had mixed feelings about any suggestion that language teachers or instructors should limit CS during lessons:

T1: I personally feel codeswitching should be generally discouraged, with some exceptions; inserting a Malay word into an English sentence, for instance, shouldn't be a big issue.

T2: Personally, I do not see it as an issue because it depends on the students of the class. In English classes, I do not think codeswitching among staff is necessary though, because all UBD students understand English; it's only the matter of ... whether their lecturers allow [their students] to speak in Malay. As for me, I do allow [my students to speak Malay], like I said earlier.

Both these teachers, who were not generally in favour of CS during their English language lessons, begrudgingly would allow it among students, but not among tutors. T3 stated his view as follows: 'Bearing in mind the risk of overdependency on codeswitching as a learning and teaching tool, codeswitching should only be used by teachers when necessary or appropriate, particularly with the lower levels of language learning'. His suggestion that tutors should practise some flexibility and caution, and his belief that CS is in fact a necessity in lower-level (beginners') classes, is significant in that he actually supports T1 and T2's contention that the English language students in UBD are, or should be, considered upper-level learners, and therefore should be immersed in the TL.

Codeswitching among students in general

All three tutors recognised the need for some students to codeswitch to get their messages across:

T1: Students seem to lack [confidence in] conversing in English due to most likely having [inadequate] opportunities to do so in their personal time. Thus I feel that using English during class time should be standard practice – but again with some exceptions.

T2: There are some students who need to mix their language to ensure that their question or message is conveyed accurately. The only reason I allow it is because I want to ensure that students maximise their learning by asking questions and if they are unable to ask question[s] wholly in English then I allow them to mix.

What is clear in these comments is that the learning process is given priority, regardless of the tutors' misgivings and concerns about CS. If the learning experience can be maximised or enhanced for the students, then various learning strategies should be allowed, including CS.

However, T1 observed that 'students seem to automatically know/ perceive that speaking in Malay during an English class is not "allowed", as each instance of their CS is almost always followed up with an apology'. This awareness and the apparent sense of contrition do not prevent them from continuing to codeswitch. According to T1, this can mean that 'they either truly are not able to clearly express themselves in English or they know that they can "get away with" CS'. This, it seems, is the main dilemma, in which the tutors just have to be judicious.

Reflection

This case study of three tutors and their respective language classes provides some insights into the practices of CS at Universiti Brunei Darussalam's Language Centre. In particular, we offer insights into the minds of the Bruneian tutors involved, who all spoke at least two languages, one of which they teach to their fellow Bruneians.

A few mitigating factors need to be highlighted here. The students or classes being compared are typical groups according to each tutor, but not necessarily of equal proficiency levels between the three tutorial groups. So, as mentioned above, while the tutors of 'foreign' languages are more receptive to CS, the tutors of English are not so receptive, because they believe English is beyond being a foreign language to the students, who can join UBD only after they have passed the GCE 'O'-level English language exam. UBD students on English language courses are therefore more proficient in their TL than are their peers learning a truly 'foreign' language. In other words, bar the case of foreign students learning Malay, English is the Bruneian students' and the Bruneian tutors' common L2, so their degree of familiarity with English is higher than their familiarity with, for instance, Arabic or Tutong.

It remains to be seen whether similar findings would be obtained if this study were extended to include teachers of other languages at the Language Centre. But if the shared-language assumption holds true, then it would likely show that, with Korean, Japanese, French and German lessons, for example, students will codeswitch to English, because that is the language that Bruneian students share with their foreign language tutor.

The examples and scenarios discussed above consider CS as practised and perceived by both teachers and students, providing what is hopefully a balanced account for the situation in the Language Centre at UBD. While it is true, as Macaro suggests in this volume (p. 16), that much of the students' use of CS arose in the context of 'unknown lexical items', there were equally as many examples of CS for 'communicative efficiency' on the part of the students. The students, it would seem, feel encouraged to CS because they share the same L1 as the teacher, and/or they are fully aware of the fact that they and their teachers are 'cultural natives' – with shared views of how and to what extent CS can be used in the Bruneian classroom.

COMMENTARY

Introduction

The case study addresses CS in the context of a university in Brunei. Brunei is a member state of the Association of Southeast Asian Nations (ASEAN), alongside Malaysia, Singapore, Cambodia, Indonesia, Laos, Myanmar, Philippines, Thailand and Vietnam. In these countries, CS is quite predominant, especially in Malaysia and Singapore, where the population is multilingual. Nevertheless, in most of these countries, there is a dominant L1 and English is an international language and a lingua franca. In Brunei, similar to Malaysia, the L1 is the Malay language. In addition, language planners and policymakers have sought to achieve bilingualism. In the case of Brunei, the dominant language is Malay but English is used for wider communication, especially in tertiary education.

In Malaysia, the situation is similar yet in some ways different. The Malay language is the national language for all official purposes, but the vernacular languages exert their presence in school as well as in communities with English as a widely used language, especially in the commercial domain. Language planning and policy in both countries have moulded the current linguistic scenario where CS is a definite observable phenomenon within and outside learning institutions. Learning English and Malay in the school and tertiary curriculum is entrenched in both Malaysia and Brunei, with perhaps a higher incidence of multilingualism in Malaysia as a result of the more heterogeneous population.

In the higher-education context in both countries, the English language is widely used. Another similar feature is the institutional support for the learning of L1 and L2, giving rise to the setting up of language departments or centres that provide support services in order to develop and maintain the use of these two main languages. The tutors or language teachers are mostly from the local population and have thus been influenced by their national school system. Thus, their use of the language(s) in the classroom will be influenced by their prior language experience.

In the teaching and learning of an L2, the teacher draws on many resources in order to achieve particular goals. Among them is the strategy of using the L1 to facilitate understanding of the points raised in the teaching. Many researchers have argued that CS is a useful strategy (Burden, 2001; Cole, 1998; Critchley, 1999; Greggio & Gill, 2007; Lai, 1996; Schweers, 1999; Skiba, 1997; Tang, 2002; Tien & Liu, 2006). Researchers have also argued that CS is beneficial for increasing and developing the L2 lexicon, for reducing any anxiety surrounding language learning and for giving explanations and clarifications so that learners are familiar with the tasks and the rubrics involved. CS is not to be frowned on in classroom use (Burden, 2001; Chick & McKay, 2001; Dash, 2002; Tang, 2002; Widdowson, 2003).

Research has identified a variety of functions of CS. Such research can focus on the nature of classroom interactions or strategies used by learners and teachers in the learning of an L2. CS can also be studied as a communicative device (Adendorff, 1996; Myers-Scotton, 1995; Tay, 1989) – as an instrument to enhance discourse, such as to emphasise a point (Gal, 1979), mitigate a message (Koziol, 2000) – and even as a distancing strategy (David, 1999) or compensatory strategy (Gysels, 1992).

In the Bruneian case study, CS as a classroom activity is investigated and details are provided about its practice from the perspectives of three language tutors. The aim of the case study is to stress that CS is not a sign of language incompetence, as has often been suggested but, on the contrary, that CS is a normal behaviour linked with bi- and multilingual environments. The case study discusses the purposes of CS as observed in lessons delivered by two bilingual tutors and a trilingual tutor. To illustrate CS, examples from real classroom situations are presented to provide evidence that tutors frequently codeswitch as a common strategy to achieve their communicative goals.

Respondents were interviewed in order to provide reflective insights into their own and their students' CS practices. A study of this nature is necessarily limited due to the number of respondents and lack of observational data. In addition, the interpretations of the nature and functions of CS appear to be meshed (Michael-Luna & Canagarajah, 2007). Thus, the results are situated in descriptions of the nature of CS and its functions, whereas these dimensions are actually inseparable. The case study gives the Bruneian perspective, which could well be complemented by other studies that may further throw light on the practice of CS, especially in countries where a linguistic environment is shared.

The Bruneian case highlights a bilingual situation which needs to be recognised and also to be considered in the overall language planning and policy for further development of the languages in a diverse linguistic environment. For Malaysia, Gill (2009) proposes a policy that needs to be open and dynamic in order to accommodate changes that are taking place, especially at tertiary level, which has implications for the workplace and for the development of human capital. A policy that encourages multilingualism is forward-looking, as linguistic dexterity can be promoted and enhanced.

Findings from Comparable Malaysian Studies

There are divided opinions about the role of CS in the language classroom. Two respondents out of the three at UBD reported that they did not codeswitch at all, expressing the view that the learning of the target language is best done when there is maximum or absolute exposure to that language. These respondents also claimed that they were more comfortable speaking in English and they perceived students as having had ample exposure to the target language through their time at school. These were reasons against the need to codeswitch in the classroom at UBD.

In Malaysia, Yunisrina (2009) conducted a pragmatics analysis of a teacher's CS in a bilingual classroom. Her findings were more specific, in that she found the instances of CS related to word borrowings that were used in speech and it was less used for the purpose of giving emphasis or getting students' attention. In a non-language classroom, it was also observed by Then and Ting (2011) that CS takes place when science was taught (in English at that time); the Malay language was then used to explain content.

A study was carried out by the authors of this commentary at Universiti Putra Malaysia (UPM) on 14 language teachers to investigate whether there are parallels to the Brunei situation. When asked how often they used CS in their classes, 43% responded 'seldom', 21% 'always' and 36% 'often'. None of them said that they never codeswitched. The reasons for the CS were mainly to facilitate explanation and understanding, especially when vocabulary was a problem. A few said that CS is motivating and encourages students to speak out. On another level, a few mentioned that they codeswitch when they want to tell a joke. The findings more or less confirm those of Ahmad and Jusoff (2009), who revealed that nearly three-quarters (74.7%) of their student respondents said that their teachers codeswitch for nearly the same purposes, that is, to explain vocabulary, make students comfortable and give support to language learning.

In the Bruneian study, it is noted that the second part focused on CS carried out by students. In this section, some classroom exchanges between student and teacher were reported and they were mainly analysed for the functions behind the CS through the use of narratives. These narratives traced the manner of the exchange through attitudinal comments about the emotions of the students as they responded to the teacher. Special mention is given to the use of Tutong, which is considered to be a foreign language, and in the teaching of the language CS involves three languages, which are Tutong, Malay and English. What is surprising is the higher incidence of the use of English and not Malay, the language which would have been more familiar to the students. It was postulated that what could have motivated this switch was the teacher's perceived language preference, or it could have been a case of placing a higher value on English as a language of communication. These perspectives on CS are not peculiar to the Bruneian case: commonalities are also shared by countries where CS is a frequent phenomenon.

Many of the studies on CS in this part of the world focus on its socio-psychological implications. This is in contrast to CS studies that are more oriented towards linguistic descriptions and explanations (Ahmad & Jusoff, 2009; David, 1999; Then & Ting, 2009). Both kinds of study are valuable and relevant in giving insights into CS practices which can be said to be highly prevalent, especially when the world is engaging with many communities and languages in multilingual environments.

Concluding Remarks

Studies of CS can clarify the misconceptions that teachers of English as a second language (ESL) may have about whether they should follow the credo of using the TL only in the classroom, or see the worth of allowing the use of other languages. The pros and cons of CS have been argued by linguists and by classroom practitioners, as discussed in Macaro's Overview in this volume. The pros anchor mostly on the facilitation value, while the cons appear to be the widening of the learning gap as a result of overuse of one language over the TL, leading to a lessening of concentration and practice in learning. There needs to be a balance between the facilitative and debilitative effects of CS, although it would be hard to draw fine lines between these. Nonetheless, there are implications that should be considered for the learning of languages.

One of them is the need to exercise caution when using CS, in that it may be important to decide consciously which code to use in which instance and with whom. Teacher intervention is necessary to guide and support students in the right direction. For example, the teacher would need to ensure that alternation is meaningful and that effective lexicalisation of the TL is not sacrificed due to indiscriminate CS, as highlighted by Macaro and other contributors to this volume.

It has been found that rigidly limiting the use of the native language does not lead to better acquisition of the TL (Harbord, 1992). What matters is to allow CS and to adopt an eclectic approach if the students are to benefit.

Along with the issue of CS is also the concern about bilingual dictionaries. Teachers are divided about their use, as bilingual dictionaries can be seen as detrimental to the learning of the TL. In instances where the teacher has to make a decision, the consideration could rest with the assessment of the language ability of students in the classroom. For beginner students, it may be wise to tap prior knowledge that is best expressed in the native language, and as such it would be most facilitative if a bilingual dictionary were available. Better students could be weaned away from reliance on such a dictionary and move to a monolingual one.

Within the classroom, the environment is constrained. Teachers are able to push the boundaries only to a certain extent. They have to realise that it is unrealistic and impractical to mandate learners to refrain from using their native language altogether. Instead, classroom conditions require that the teacher adapts and adopts best practices to enable students to move from one stage to another to the best of their ability. Teachers, at the same time, should work within the students' abilities so that they can shape, refine and exploit all resources for the purpose of learning.

References

Adendorff, R. (1996) The functions of code-switching among high school teachers and students in KwaZulu and implications for teacher education. In K. Bailey and D. Nunan (eds) *Voices from the Language Classroom: Qualitative Research in Second Language Education* (pp. 388–406). Cambridge: Cambridge University Press.

Ahmad, B.H. and Jusoff, K. (2009) Teachers' code-switching in classroom instructions for low English proficient learners. *English Language Teaching* 2 (2), 49–55.

Burden, P. (2001) When do native English speakers and Japanese college students disagree about the use of Japanese in the English conversation classroom? *Language Teacher* 4. See http://jalt-publications.org/old_tlt/articles/2001/04/burden (accessed December 2006).

Chick, J.K. and McKay, S. (2001) Teaching English in multiethnic schools in the Durban area: The promotion of multilingualism or monolingualism? *South African Linguistics and Applied Language Studies* 19 (3–4), 163–178.

Cole, S. (1998) The use of L1 in communicative English classrooms. See http://jalt-publications.org/old_tlt/files/98/dec/cole.html (accessed January 2007).

Critchley, M.P. (1999) Bilingual support in English classes in Japan: A survey of students' opinions in L1 use by foreign teachers. *Language Teacher* 23 (9), 10–13.

Dash, P.S. (2002) English only (EO) in the classroom: Time for a reality check? *Asian EFL Journal* 4 (4). See http://www.asian-efl-journal.com/decart2002b.pdf (accessed January 2007).

David, M.K. (1999) Trading in an intercultural context: The case of Malaysia. *International Scope Review* 1 (2), 1–15.

Gal, S. (1979) *Language Shift: Social Determinants of Linguistic Change in Bilingual Austria*. New York: Academic Press.

Gill, S.K. (2009) Language policy and planning in higher education in Malaysia: A nation in linguistic transition. Available at http://ccat.sas.upenn.edu/plc/clpp/proposal/SaranMalaysia.htm (accessed August 2013).

Greggio, S. and Gill, G. (2007) Teacher's and learner's use of code-switching in the English as foreign language classroom: A qualitative study. *Linguagem and Ensino* 10 (2), 371–393.

Gysels, M. (1992) French in urban Lubumbashi Swahili: Codeswitching, borrowing, or both. *Journal of Multilingual and Multicultural Development* 13 (1–2), 41–55.

Harbord, J. (1992) The use of mother tongue in the classroom. *ELT Journal* 46 (4), 350–355. See http://dx.doi.org/10.1093/elt/46.4.350 (accessed August 2013).

Koziol, J.M. (2000) Code-switching between Spanish and English in contemporary American society. Unpublished MA thesis, St Mary's College of Maryland.

Lai, M.L. (1996) Using the L1 sensibly in English language classrooms. *Journal of Primary Education* 6 (1–2), 91–99.

Macaro, E. (1997) *Target Language, Collaborative Learning and Autonomy*. Clevedon: Multilingual Matters.

Macaro, E. (2001) Analyzing students teachers' code-switching in foreign language classrooms: Theories and decision-making. *Modern Language Journal* 85 (4), 531–548.

Macaro, E. (2009) Teacher use of codeswitching in the second language classroom: Exploring 'optimal' use. In M. Turnbull, and J. Dailey O'Cain (eds) *First Language Use in Second and Foreign Language Learning* (pp. 35–49). Bristol: Multilingual Matters.

Martin, P. (1999) Close encounters of a bilingual kind: Interactional practices in the primary classroom in Brunei. *International Journal of Education Development* 19 (2), 127–140.

Martin, P. (2003) Bilingual encounters in the classroom. In J-M. Dewaele, A. Housen and Li Wei (eds) *Bilingualism: Beyond Basic Principles* (pp. 67–87). Clevedon: Multilingual Matters.

Michael-Luna, S. and Canagarajah, S. (2007) Multilingual academic literacies: Pedagogical foundations for code meshing in primary and higher education. *Journal of Applied Linguistics* 4 (1), 55–77.

Myers-Scotton, C. (1995) *Social Motivations for Code-Switching: Evidence from Africa*. Oxford: Clarendon Press.

Saxena, M. (2009) Construction and deconstruction of linguistic otherness: Conflict and cooperative code-switching in (English) bilingual classrooms. *English Teaching: Practice and Critique* 8 (2), 167–187. See http://edlinked.soe.waikato.ac.nz/research/files/etpc/files/2009v8n2art8.pdf (accessed August 2013).

Schweers, C.W. Jr (1999) Using L1 in the L2 classroom. *English Teaching Forum* 37 (2). See http://exchanges.state.gov.forum/vols/vol37/no2/p6.htm (accessed December 2006).

Skiba, R. (1997) Code switching as countenance of language interference. *Internet TESL Journal*. See http://iteslj.org/Articles/Skiba-CodeSwitching.html (accessed September 2005).

Tang, J. (2002) Using L1 in the English classroom. *English Teaching Forum* 40 (1), 36–43. See http://exchanges.state.gov.forum/vols/vol40/no1/p36.pdf.

Tay, M.W. (1989) Code switching and code-mixing as a communicative strategy in multilingual discourse. *World Englishes* 8 (3), 407–417.

Then, D.C. and Ting, S.H. (2011) Code-switching in English and science classrooms: More than translation. *International Journal of Multilingualism* 8 (3), 299–323.

Tien, C.Y. and Liu, K. (2006) Code-switching in two EFL classes in Taiwan. In A. Hashim and N. Hassan (eds) *English in Southeast Asia: Prospects, Perspectives and Possibilities* (pp. 215–241). Kuala Lumpur: Universiti Malaya Press.

Widdowson, H.G. (2003) *Defining Issues in English Language Teaching*. Oxford: Oxford University Press.

Yunisrina, Y. (1999) A pragmatics analysis of a teacher's code-switching in a bilingual classroom. *Linguistics Journal* 4 (2), 6–39. See http://www.linguistics-journal.com/ December-2009.pdf (accessed August 2013).

7 Codeswitching in Universities in Singapore and the Philippines

Case Study: Kenneth Keng Wee Ong and Lawrence Jun Zhang

Commentary: Isabel Pefianco Martin

CASE STUDY

Introduction

In ethnographic interviews, the explanation typically given by bilingual people for their spontaneous codeswitching (CS) habits is their perception that CS is an economical way in which to formulate their speech (Gardner-Chloros, 2009). However, it remains unclear whether, for bilinguals, CS is indeed the easier solution, psycholinguistically speaking, than thinking and speaking in one language. Inhibition and excitation of languages appear to be effortful but psycholinguistic studies have shown that the bilingual lexicon activates both languages concurrently during processing (e.g. La Heij, 2005).

The advantage of possessing a second language is that the bilingual has more stored lexical entries to select for the expression of underlying concepts than a monolingual. This view is valid in the CS behaviour of proficient bilinguals employing CS as a speech style. In the case of Singapore, the majority of young people are considered simultaneous and proficient bilinguals, as both languages are learnt early on, from before puberty. In a previous study (Ong & Zhang, 2010), we found that bilinguals in Singapore tend to prefer the semantico-syntactically simpler language, namely Chinese, in filling the functional category which accounts for the codeswitched functional morphemes. This linguistic economy parallels the bilinguals' perception that CS is the easy or 'lazy' option in formulating thought and speech.

In our present study, the prevalence of naturalistic CS patterns is shown in codeswitched classroom discourse data culled from Singaporean English–

163

Chinese bilingual students. The transcribed data show that versatile Mandarin lemmas fill the functional category in the determiner phrase. The data do not support CS models such as those postulated by Myers-Scotton (1993), Jake and Myers-Scotton (2009) and Petersen (1988). Rather, we tend to argue that CS is an economical way of mapping thought onto language and this subconscious preference translates to the perceived ease of alternating between languages.

Theoretical Framework and Previous Research

According to Gardner-Chloros (2009), attitudinal research has consistently found that bilinguals often attribute their CS behaviour to laziness or linguistic economy – mixing two languages in an utterance is deemed to be an easier or lazier way of talking than monolingual speech. However, the concurrent activation and alternating inhibition of two languages appears effortful. The parallel access hypothesis, which is supported by recent neuroimaging, priming and Stroop studies, states that bilingual speakers process stimuli or input with concurrent activation of two languages (e.g. La Heij, 2005; Marian & Spivey, 2003a, 2003b; Marian et al., 2003; Preston & Lambert, 1969). The implication is that parallel activation is unavoidable and advantageous for the bilingual in processing either language. Correspondingly, Green's (1986, 1998a) inhibitory control model proposes that there is parallel activity of the two languages during CS, such that the bilingual subconsciously manipulates two languages between two levels of activation, namely selected and active levels.

There is corroborating evidence that both non-cognates that share meanings and cognates are co-activated during lexical access and are CS triggers (e.g. de Bot et al., 2009). Semantic priming studies have shown that semantic and translation access can be found across markedly dissimilar orthographies (cf. Altarriba & Basnight-Brown, 2007). Jiang (2000, 2004) found that semantic/syntactic information is more susceptible to lexical transfer than morphological information, as the latter is language-specific. Semantic similarity between languages at the notional sub-semantic level – such as motion, possession, perception, desire, causality and modality – can facilitate L2 vocabulary acquisition even in languages that are typologically distant. Yu (1996a, 1996b) found that Chinese native speakers who were learning English as a second language (ESL) outperformed their Japanese ESL counterparts in using motion verbs. Although Chinese and English are typologically dissimilar, they share semantic meanings in motion verbs; Japanese counterparts are not semantically similar to English motion verbs. Hence, lexical transfer can be accomplished via highly dissimilar orthographies (such as English and Chinese) at the level of lexical concepts. In our present study, English and Chinese are the two languages used by Singaporean bilingual participants.

Gardner-Chloros (2009) pointed out a key gap in CS research: further research is required to investigate whether CS is indeed a product of least effort, as many bilinguals would report it. We addressed this research lacuna by postulating a psycholinguistic filter of economy within natural CS schema, based on a prevalent code-paired determiner phrase pattern, namely Mandarin Det + English N, found in our data (see Ong & Zhang, 2010, for details). This pattern persists in spontaneous CS data culled in various CS studies on Singaporean students (e.g. Lee, 2003). This is indicated in the following example from Lee (2005: 137):

Not just for the info *leh*. They issue nà gè blue label is it because of nà gè,
                          particle   that   that

hǎo xiàng	yǒu	biàn	huà	nà	yàng	*lor*
like	have	change	form	that	way	particle

'Not just for the information. They issue the blue labels perhaps to indicate certain changes.'

The code-paired pattern holds regardless of differing pragmatic motivations and contextual variables, which suggests that the pattern is a function of internal control within the bilingual lexico-semantic system. The pattern also prevails in both English-dominated utterances and Chinese-dominated utterances. Notably, we found that the Mandarin determiner is frequently preferred over the English counterpart in codeswitched determiner phrases. We argued that the lack of articles and gender/neuter differentiation in spoken Mandarin translates to a perceived speech economy – Chinese demonstratives/numerals and third-person pronouns multifunction to denote definiteness/indefiniteness and gender/neuter classes, respectively.

It may be noted that Mandarin has a smaller pool of determiners than does English and that some Mandarin determiners play multiple functional roles. For example, Mandarin lacks articles as found in English, such as 'the' and 'a' or 'an', to denote definiteness and indefiniteness, respectively (Robertson, 2000). However, numerals + classifiers and demonstrative + classifiers are used as indicators of indefiniteness and definiteness, respectively (Chu, 1983). For example, the numeral + classifier determiner, yī gè can be translated in English as the number 'one' or the indefinite article 'a'. Symbolically, there is greater representational economy in grammatically

Table 7.1 Grammatical versatility of Chinese determiners

Determiner			Number	Definiteness	Demonstrative
Dem +	(Num) +	CL	+	+	±
zhè / nà	(yī)	gè			
Dem +	Qu		+	+	±
zhè / nà	xiē				
Num + CL			+	–	±
yī	gè				

versatile determiners since the same representations are used for more than one grammatical function. The multifunctionality of Mandarin numerals, classifiers and demonstratives is detailed in Table 7.1.

Another group of versatile Mandarin determiners is the pronouns, such as tā, which is undifferentiated across natural gender 'he' and 'she', and the neuter categories animate 'it' or inanimate 'it' in spoken Mandarin (Chao, 1968). The Mandarin pronoun tā remains *in situ* when affixed with the plural suffix mén or possessive subordinate suffix de to denote group pronouns and possessive pronouns. Mandarin pronouns lack case-triggered declension, unlike English plural pronouns, which are separate functional lexemes. Summarily, the Mandarin pronominal system is comparatively less differentiated. The grammatical versatility of Mandarin pronouns relative to English pronouns is detailed in Table 7.2.

Table 7.2 Comparison between Mandarin and English pronouns/possessives

Mandarin pronouns	Equivalent English pronouns/possessives
wǒ [de]	I/me/my/mine
nǐ [de]	you/your/yours (singular)
tā [de]	he/she/it/him/her/his/hers/its
wǒ mén [de]	we/us/our/ours
nǐ mén [de]	you/yours (plural)
tā mén [de]	they/them/their/theirs

The Present Study

Context and background

Singapore is a small nation state of about 5 million people. It has implemented a unique bilingual education policy since the mid-1980s. This bilingual education policy was born out of a pragmatic need anticipated by the then Prime Minister, Lee Kuan Yew, that Singapore will have to seek further development in a global economy through the medium of English. English is offered in the national curriculum as a 'first language' subject and used as the medium of instruction in all the subjects except the mother tongues, which are offered as 'second language' subjects. These vernacular languages, namely Chinese, Tamil and Malay, for obvious reasons, particularly due to Singapore's colonial past, enjoy far less prestige in Singapore society. All Singaporean students are required to learn at least two languages (English and a mother tongue). The expectation is that they should be competent and confident in using standard English and one of the mother tongues offered in the national curriculum. The aim of the bilingual education policy is to ensure that Singaporeans need not lose their cultural values or identity, while remaining viable economically. The intention of such a bilingual policy was to maintain the three main Asian languages widely used in Singapore society and the values the Asian cultures inculcate (Lee, 2000). Against such a backdrop, in this case study we intend to extend Ong and Zhang's (2010) findings by reporting CS data culled from spontaneous speech among university students, with a focus on codeswitched determiner phrases. The reason for our resumed interest in this particular phenomenon is that CS in Singaporean student populations, including university students, is typically imbued with the choice of determiner phrases. We also expound on the pedagogical implications of the findings, particularly for teaching English grammar to Singaporean students.

Participants

While our earlier study (Ong & Zhang, 2010) examined data culled from polytechnic students, the focus of this study was on classroom discourse among 22 undergraduate students. Also, the student participants of this study were markedly more proficient in both languages compared with the polytechnic students studied by Ong and Zhang (2010). One of the Singapore university admission requirements is that applicants must satisfy certain language criteria, which are based on their Singapore–Cambridge GCE 'O'-level English and Mandarin Chinese grades. All participants have completed their GCE 'O'-level English and Mandarin Chinese examinations and met the standard set by the university in which they study. These participants reported using English and Mandarin Chinese in their daily activities on the university campus or while they interacted with their friends in other social domains. All participants were Chinese–English bilinguals who had learnt English as the first language according to the Singapore Ministry of Education curriculum requirement and Mandarin as their second language in English-medium schools since pre-school education (Ministry of Education, 1991, 2010).

Data processing

Our data consist of audio-recordings (totalling approximately 137 minutes) saved by student volunteers who were also participants of task-based group discussions for an academic writing course conducted at a university in Singapore. These Singaporean undergraduates were discussing issues related to their academic study at various stages of project completion, ranging from brainstorming for research topics to delegation of work to group members. They professed to be Mandarin–English codeswitchers, particularly in interactions with their Singapore Chinese peers. Subsequently, they were surveyed for their knowledge of English or Mandarin equivalents of their CS utterances.

Results

The audio-recordings show that 19 of the 22 participants codeswitched between the two languages. Fifteen participants produced 67 occurrences of codeswitched determiner phrases. These were consistently of the pattern Mandarin Det + English N, as shown in Table 7.3.

The Dem + Cl + N/Dem + Qu + N is the dominant determiner phrase type, followed by Pron + Poss + N. The results correspond with the postulation that these bilinguals unconsciously preferred the more economical determiners to fill the functional category. Speech economy could be seen as associative within a determiner phrase type, as can be seen in the use of the wǒ de pronoun, which does not have an economical advantage over its English counterpart but which is associated with the speech economy of other Mandarin pronouns. The results corroborate Ong and Zhang's (2010) findings, which also show a predominant preference for Mandarin determiners, particularly Mandarin demonstratives and pronouns over the English counterparts.

In accounting for specific psycholinguistic parameters of the preference for speech economy, we present two probability expressions to encapsulate

Table 7.3 Compilation of codeswitched determiner phrases

	Frequency
Dem + Cl + N / Dem + Qu + N	
zhè gè (this) article	7
zhè gè (this) project	6
nà gè (that) article	6
nèi gè (that) paper	4
zhèi gè (this) tutorial	3
zhè gè (this) quiz	2
zhè gè (this) idea	1
nà gè (this) experiment	1
nà gè (that) report	1
nà gè (that) stand	1
nà gè (that) prof	1
nà gè (that) box	1
nà gè (that) text	1
zhè gè (this) website	1
nà gè (this) point	1
nà gè (this) thumbdrive	1
zhè liǎng běn (these two) textbooks	1
zhè wèi (this) gentleman	1
zhè xiē (these) bottles	1
nà bēi (that) bubble tea	1
(Pron) + Poss + N	
tā de (his) girlfriend	2
wǒ de (my) notebook	1
tā de (his) job	1
wǒ mén de (our) circuit	1
wǒ de (my) draft	1
zuó tiān de (yesterday's) class	1
tā de (her) phone	1
Num + Cl + N / Num + Qu + N	
yī bēi (one) bubble tea	1
yī gè (one) quiz	1
gè (one) question	1
sān gè (three) questions	1
wǔ gè (five) As	1
Postdet + N	
lìng wài de (other) bottle	1

likely code-paired outcomes in the formula below. Taking into account that a major CS trigger is semantically overlapping words, speech economy is represented as a net resource $(e-i)$ responsible for exciting or inhibiting a lemma relative to its translation equivalent.

$$P(l_2 \mid L_x \cap L_y) + e \geq P(l_1 \mid L_x \cap L_y) - i$$

(Speech economy of lemma l_2 relative to its translation equivalent leads to excitatory resource e meeting or exceeding inhibitory resource i, resulting in a higher probability of selected activation.)

$$P(l_2 \mid L_x \cap L_y) + e \leq P(l_1 \mid L_x \cap L_y) - i$$

(The lack of speech economy of lemma l_2 relative to its translation equivalent leads to excitatory resource e meeting or falling behind inhibitory resource i, resulting in a higher probability of selected activation.)

where $l_1 \in Lex\ (L_x),\ l_2 \in Lex\ (L_y)$

(Lemma l_1 is a subset of lexicon or language L_x while lemma l_2 is a subset of lexicon or language L_y.)

Discussion

The argument challenges the matrix language framework model (MLFM) first postulated by Myers-Scotton (1993). Definitions of 'matrix language' (ML) and 'embedded language' (EL) as posited by Jake and Myers-Scotton (2009) are problematic if they are examined in the light of the study's findings. As system morphemes or functional morphemes are predominant in Mandarin, MLFM determines that Mandarin is the ML, which provides the abstract morphosyntactic frame of the determiner phrases, such that content morphemes or lexical morphemes in English are predicted to be governed by the grammar of Mandarin. However, there is no evidence of a matrix language, as inflected English nouns are paired with Mandarin determiners. Illustratively, codeswitched determiner phrases found in our data consist of English nouns that are inflected for number, which would be incongruent with the lack of noun declension for grammatical number. This is exemplified in the following CS utterances.

Wŏ men hái méi yŏu tackle sān ge questions *leh*.
We   still not have   three   particle
'We have not tackled three questions.'

We need to read zhè gè article xiān rán hòu discuss online.
        this   first then
'We need to read this article first before discussing it online.'

I email wǒ de draft last week but I didn't receive your edited one.
       my

The first sentence is predominantly in Mandarin; the second sentence is roughly balanced in English and Mandarin; the third sentence is mostly in English. All three sentences show the use of the Mandarin Det + English N pattern despite the varying balance between English and Mandarin in the utterances.

This was also similarly found by Ong and Zhang (2010), which effectively questions the universal CS constraint predicted by the MLFM. Notably, there are no English Det + Mandarin N phrases in the data. The failings of MLFM have been previously dealt with in detail by Chan (2003, 2009), who shows evidence from Cantonese–English CS that MLFM is restrictively weak (see also Li Wei, 2011). Codeswitched Cantonese Det + English N phrases show that English nouns are incongruent with ML as they are inflected for number, whereas in Cantonese nouns do not inflect for number, violating the morpheme order principle and ML blocking hypothesis. Furthermore, MacSwan (2005a, 2005b) argues that there is no matrix language and attests that nothing constrains CS apart from the requirements of the separate grammars, mixed during CS.

The study's findings also show that the CS constraint predicted by Petersen's (1988) dominant language hypothesis (DLH) is not present. DLH claims that the dominant language supplies the functional morphemes within a functional-lexical code mixing, while the other language supplies the lexical category (Petersen, 1988). The DLH differs from the MLFM as the former accounts for early child mixing of two languages. However, Ong and Zhang (2010) found that students whose Mandarin was shown to be weaker than their English preferred to use Mandarin functional morphemes. In this study, 15 student participants who had GCE 'O'-level English grades higher than their GCE 'O'-level Mandarin grades and who indicated English as their dominant language used Mandarin Det + English N phrases. Thus, the claim that the language used for the functional category is the dominant language of the bilingual speaker does not hold. As the DLH is based only on child CS data, it can be concluded that the DLH does not extend to adult CS production, as is the case in our study.

Similar to the MLFM/DLH in the proposal of a unified syntactic system is Libben's (2002) homogeneity hypothesis (HH), which recognises that although bilinguals have differentiated lexical and phonological systems, the functional system is homogeneous, such that the grammar of one language governs the other language as well. It is noted that the HH does not assign matrix and embedded language statuses, as MLFM does. However, the findings of the present study show that the syntactic systems of Mandarin–English bilinguals are differentiated within functional-lexical phrases and that there is no evidence of a unified functional system. The presence of English noun declension, particularly the agreement relation between Chinese determiners (classifiers, numerals and demonstratives) and English inflected nouns, such as 'zhè liǎng běn textbooks', substantiates this view. This supports MacSwan's (1999) postulation of bilingual differentiation.

An adult experimental study carried out by Liceras *et al.* (2006) showed that there is a preference among Spanish L1 speakers to match the Spanish DET with the gender of the displaced Spanish N to the English N. This matching requirement is called the 'analogical criterion'. As Spanish L1 speakers were found to attribute lexical gender to English N, this implies that bilinguals have one unified syntactic system, as predicted by the HH. Nevertheless, the study participants were Spanish L1 speakers, that is, whose dominant language is clearly Spanish. It can be speculated that simultaneous bilinguals, such as the participants in the present study, differentiate the two syntactic lexicons better than sequential bilinguals. It can be further postulated that some L1 speakers have homogeneous syntactic systems, as shown in Liceras *et al.*'s (2006) study, as their L1 dominates and subsumes the other language syntactically, just as the matrix language does, as predicted by the MLFM. As competencies increase, bilinguals may be able to differentiate their syntactic systems better. It is noted that the positive relationship between competencies and bilingual differentiation is markedly different between simultaneous and sequential bilingualism. For example, Spanish–English simultaneous bilingual adults are shown to differentiate their syntactic systems, but not Spanish L1 speakers, who prefer to use the analogical criterion (Liceras *et al.*, 2006). Language dominance in L1 speakers may result in the dominant language interfering in the other language syntactically. For example, Liu *et al.* (2006) found that EFL learners tend to omit English bound morphemes '-s/es'. This finding implies that the EFL learners' L1, which is Mandarin, dominates the English morphosyntactically, as there is no plural inflection in Mandarin grammar. In the present study, there is an agreement relation between the Mandarin DET and the English noun similarly found by Ong and Zhang (2010). Also, the present data show that English noun declension is maintained. Macaro (2005: 64) points out that 'bilinguals codeswitch because they find it easier or more appropriate for the purposes of communication', and our data support this view.

Conclusion and Implications

The study was conducted with the intention of examining the patterns of CS in classroom discourse among English–Chinese bilinguals who were university undergraduates. We focused on their choice of determiners in using the two languages (English and Chinese) when engaged in task-based academic discussions. Our analysis of the data suggests that these bilinguals had a preference for Mandarin determiners over their English counterparts. We tend to assume that these bilingual students used fewer English determiners, including articles. This is compounded by the noticeable deficiency in the use of indefinite articles in Singapore English (see Wee & Ansaldo, 2004), similar to the non-native variation in the use of English articles by Chinese EFL learners (Robertson, 2000). As there are no societies that are efficient in requiring their members to use two languages with equal proficiency in all areas of life (Baetens Beardsmore, 1998), such linguistic defaults that prioritise Mandarin determiners over English determiners may underscore their possible lack of grammatical knowledge of English articles. Pedagogically, CS patterns or linguistic defaults can be exploited to predict hotspots of linguistic shortcomings, especially for less proficient L2 learners. Research on spontaneous student CS could be a valuable guide for language teachers to fine tune or calibrate their remediation efforts effectively. Of course, we recognise that competent bilinguals use CS as an affective or pragmatic resource. We argue that CS is the economical way of mapping thought onto language and this subconscious preference translates to the perceived ease of alternating between languages for both competent and less competent speakers.

Given such findings, we recommend that English language educators, including university lecturers and teachers in the classroom in schools, reinforce teaching English determiners to students, particularly those whose dominant language is Mandarin. These students may not have a thorough understanding of the grammatical roles of the indefinite and the definite articles in English. Through systematic teaching in task-based learning environments, teachers can scaffold their students in this process of fully understanding how determiners work for effective communication. This is because, in the past, pedagogical issues pertaining to the contrastive values of the two languages were always based on hearsay instead of empirical evidence. Worse still, some teachers simply brush aside the value of students' mother tongues in teaching the target language. In addressing CS in the classroom as a contentious issue, Macaro (2005: 67) presents all possible cases. We think that his point that 'teachers often complain that their students switch to their L1 in collaborative activities and particularly decry codeswitching in task-based oral activities such as pair work' is a point worthy of much thought. This is because usually in typical educational settings, teachers in Singapore discourage student CS for fear that their students' English may be contaminated, and their performance on the various tests and examinations consequently suffer. However, recent studies (e.g. Tian & Macaro, 2012) have found that selective and principled use of L1 constrained to short intra-sentential switches while maintaining L2 as the predominant medium and adhering to the grammars of both languages can aid L2 vocabulary learning. Consonant with this growing acceptance of CS in language learning, our view is that naturalistic CS among students can reveal linguistic hotspots which can aid teachers in identifying aspects of L2 for remedial action.

COMMENTARY

Introduction

The Philippines is a country with more than 170 different languages (Nolasco, 2008). Such a linguistic landscape is certainly conducive to bilingualism, and most Filipinos are believed to speak two or more languages equally well. I use the term 'bilingualism' here in the same sense as Li Wei; this goes beyond the traditional notion of possession of two languages. Bilingualism can 'also be taken to include the many people in the world who have varying degrees of proficiency in and interchangeably use three, four or even more languages' (Li Wei, 2000: 6).

Among the languages that dominate Philippine society is English, which for the educated class may be considered as functionally native (Kachru, 2005). However, it has also been observed that among those who speak English in the Philippines, CS is common. This was noted by Thompson (2003) when he described the frequent use of Tagalog and English CS, also known as Taglish, in basketball commentaries, television advertisements, interviews of public figures, radio shows, newspapers and other media sites. Bolton likewise argues that this preponderance of Taglish in Manila makes the CS 'the unmarked code of choice' (Bolton, 2003: 201).

Several studies on CS in the Philippines have pointed to the reality that CS is practised in various domains, by different groups, for different reasons. As early as the 1960s, CS had already been investigated by Filipino linguists. Azores (1967) listed English and Tagalog elements in a corpus from the biweekly newspaper *The Sun*. Bautista wrote several research articles about CS in the Philippines in a variety of domains such as radio drama (1979), radio broadcast interviews (1980) and email messages (1998). CS was also found to be used widely in the business domain, as revealed by Pascasio (1978). Chanco *et al.* (1998) investigated the widespread use of CS by television hosts. Dayag (2002) analysed CS in Philippine print advertisements. CS is certainly being used in various domains of Philippine society.

Codeswitching in Philippine Classroom Discourse

But what about classroom discourse? In the Philippines, CS in the classroom has become a tricky issue because Filipino teachers are expected to use only English in teaching content courses such as science and mathematics, in addition to the English subject. This is the practice prescribed by the Bilingual Education Policy (BEP) of the country. Still, researchers have documented the widespread practice of CS in the education domain, with positive contributions to learning outcomes. Borlongan found that most of the English language teachers in his study codeswitched frequently, in 'violation [of] the implementing policy of teaching English in English only' (Borlongan, 2009: 40). Asuncion (2010), in a study of oral compensatory strategies of university freshmen, found that switching to the mother tongue was the most frequently used strategy. Asuncion argues that CS 'should not be considered as wrong or illegitimate because it somehow helps the learners become communicatively competent bilingual members in the society' (Asuncion, 2010: 17). Nivera's research into spoken discourse in the tertiary-level mathematics classroom found that both teachers and students preferred to codeswitch (Nivera, 2003).

CS is not only a preferred mode of teaching in Philippine classrooms; it has been also found to have functional dimensions.

Limoso's research on CS in tertiary-level literature courses reveals that the practice 'serves a number of educational objectives in a literature classroom' and that CS 'facilitates cooperation and understanding' (Limoso, 2002: 84). My own study of CS in the science courses of two universities in Manila (Martin, 2006) also supports the claim that CS does in fact promote the educational goals of delivering content knowledge.

An Observational Study

In my study of classroom interaction between teachers and students, CS was found to be a pedagogical tool for motivating student response and action, ensuring rapport and solidarity, promoting shared meaning, checking student understanding, and maintaining the teaching narrative. These functions of CS in university-level science courses are illustrated in the following extract. Here, the teacher's switching to Tagalog prods students to respond or react to a question. Thus, CS functions as a strategy to ensure student participation in class discussion.

Extract 1

01 T   What's the main purpose of a valve? What? Dali! / Para hindi ano // *Hurry! / So as not to //*

02 S   Para hindi bumalik yung // *So that it will not go back //*

03 T   Para hindi bumalik yung ano? *So that what will not go back?* So as to prevent what?

04 S   xx <in Tagalog>

In turn 1 above, the teacher asks the student to hurry with the answer. But the manner and tone by which the teacher makes the request does not indicate impatience. It was instead a gentle prodding in the mother tongue to encourage participation in the class discussion.

It can also be observed from the extract above, as well as Extract 2, that the teachers tend to reply in Tagalog to student utterances in that language, despite the teachers' awareness that only English should be used in science classes. By doing this, the teachers make a conscious effort to connect to their students using the language the students are most comfortable with. A content course such as science, with many technical terms and scientific jargon, may be intimidating to students who are not very proficient in the English language. The teachers' use of CS in science classes may indicate their desire to reduce the distance between them and their students.

Extract 2

01 T   Identify first which are the ventricles / which is the left / which is the right. Identify first. Which is the left↗ Which is the left↗

    S   Yung may dalawang ano↗ *That which has two what↗*

    T   Yung may dalawang↗ May dalawang↗ *That which has two↗ Has two↗*

    S   Yung may dalawang hiwalay na // *That which has two separate //*

    T   May dalawang hiwalay na↗ *Has two separate↗*

06 S   Sanga. *Branches.*

In Manila, Tagalog is spoken by a majority of the residents, while English is used by the educated elite. The elevated status of the English language is known to intimidate Filipinos, especially students who are not yet confident about their proficiency in the language. Thus, by addressing their students in Tagalog, Filipino teachers may be exercising what Pakir, in her study of English in Singapore, describes as the 'rapport and solidarity factor', which unifies but also separates groups (Pakir, 1991). We see further evidence of this desire for rapport and solidarity in the following extract.

Extract 3

01 T   We go to the next topic. Look at your outline. Ah / hindi / babalik tayo sa page 1. *Ah / no / we will go back to page 1.* Page 1! Go back to page 1 / Okay↗ Fats and oils can be seen in general kinds of formula like this one. When will you consider a triglyceride fat and when will it be oil↗

02 S   Pano nga ba↗ *How can one tell the difference↗*

03 T   Pano nga ba? Hindi ba binasa nyo yung handout? *How can one tell the difference? Did you not read the handout?* Okay. What is number 1 difference?

04 Ss   Source.

05 T   Source! Where do you get fats?

06 Ss   Animals.

07 T   Tapos? *Then?*

08 Ss   Plants.

This desire for rapport and solidarity is also shared by the students when they codeswitch. In Extract 4, for example, one student speaks in Tagalog when he tries to connect a personal experience to the subject matter, which in this case is the flow of blood through the human body.

Extract 4

01 T   That is why there is what you call the blue baby // What happens? {S raises his hand} Yes.

02 S   Sir, yun ba yung sinasabi nila na, ano // Nagkakaroon po ng // *Sir, is that what they say that //Something is formed //*

03 T   Yes. Nagkakaroon ng ano? *What is formed?*

04 S   Nagkakaroon po ng butas? *A hole is formed?*

05 T   Bakit nagkakaroon? *Why does that happen?*

06 S   Hindi ko po alam // Kasi po yung kapatid ng tatay ko / ano po siya / blue baby / tapos ano / di po siya naoperahan tapos / kaya after 18 years / namatay po siya. *Because the sibling of my father / he is / blue baby / then / he wasn't operated on so / so that after 18 years / he died.*

Discussion

As illustrated in the extracts above, CS does have pragmatic functions in the education context. For example, in Extract 4 the desire to promote rapport and solidarity leads to the teacher (in turn 3) accepting and following the student-initiated switch into Tagalog. However, such revelations about CS in Philippine classrooms do not necessarily translate into acceptance of the practice among teachers, who remain constrained by government policy. Yet it is not only government policy that prohibits CS in the classroom; CS is also constrained by an unfounded sense of fear among school administrators that mixing two languages will result in the deterioration of one or the other. Elsewhere (Martin, 2010), I have examined language myths in the Philippines, one of which was the belief that English and Filipino are languages in opposition. The Bilingual Education Policy, by prescribing the use of one language for specific subject areas, is itself evidence of the prevalence of the myth that English and Filipino should not mix. The myth takes the 'perspective of language purity, or the notion that the two languages have mutually exclusive domains and should therefore be separated from each other' (Martin, 2010: 258).

From a linguistic standpoint, the extracts also point to CS in the Philippines as smooth and grammatical. The teachers and students who codeswitch are not imperfect bilinguals, as codeswitchers are traditionally believed to be. The utterances are characterised by what Poplack describes as a 'smooth transition between L1 and L2 elements, unmarked by false starts, hesitations or lengthy pauses' (Poplack, 2000: 241). This observation is consistent with the findings of Bautista (1998), who asserted in her analysis of CS in email exchanges between Filipinos that 'CS is a natural mode of discourse for the Manila speech community and ... therefore smooth CS is the norm' (Bautista, 1998: 137). In addition to identifying smooth switching in the extracts, I also found that all codeswitched utterances (the teachers' and the students') were grammatical. Thus, there is apparent ease in moving from one language to another. Such observation was also made by in the case study by Kenneth Keng Wee Ong and Lawrence Jun Zhang in the present chapter.

Codeswitching in Singaporean Classroom Discourse

There are parallels in the sociolinguistic profiles of Singapore and the Philippines. For one, both countries observe a bilingual education policy with English occupying a prestige position in the national curriculum. The policy in Singapore, which has been in effect since the 1980s, aims to ensure that the students are proficient in one of the mother tongues (Chinese, Tamil or Malay) but must first be confident and competent in using standard English. Thus, the policy puts a high premium on English, while downgrading the mother tongues to the status of second languages in the national curriculum.

There are important consequences of such a policy. Schneider (2007: 156) refers to 'decisive consequences', namely that English has become a language that is shared by all Singaporeans, and that children have become alienated from the language varieties spoken by their parents and grandparents. The latter consequence is attributed to the fact that the mother tongues promoted by the curriculum are the standard varieties, which are usually different from the varieties spoken at home. According to Schneider, 'Whether intended or not, this policy has effectively weakened the position and usefulness of the indigenous languages and, conversely, strengthened that of English' (Schneider, 2007: 156–157).

Against such a backdrop, Ong and Zhang's study focuses on university students who were believed to have high proficiency in two languages. The CS patterns in the task-based academic discussions of these English–Chinese bilinguals were examined specifically for their choice of determiners. Ong and Zhang found that the Singaporean students who codeswitched had a preference for Mandarin determiners over their English counterparts. This finding was consistent with the common assumption that bilingual students tend to use fewer English determiners. The authors argue that this preference for Mandarin determiners may be the result of a lack of knowledge about English articles. The phenomenon was also believed to be a 'subconscious preference [that] translates to the perceived ease of alternating between languages'.

The Singapore study suggests that the English–Chinese bilingual students, in their attempt to communicate with each other despite their limited knowledge of English determiners and articles, codeswitch to Mandarin to make communication easier and more effective. The researchers recommend that the teaching of these grammatical points, especially to students whose dominant language is Mandarin, be further reinforced. Specifically, the researchers push for a 'systematic teaching in task-based learning environments [where] teachers can scaffold their students in this process of fully understanding how determiners work for effective communication'. In the end, Ong and Zhang uphold the value of CS in achieving effective communication in classroom discourse.

Macaro, in his Overview chapter to this volume, asks whether naturalistic CS and classroom CS are irreconcileable. He asserts that classroom CS may be approached as having the features of naturalistic CS when all participants in the classroom discourse share the same learning goals and work together to achieve these goals. But he also argues that such a situation – arriving at a consensus about educational outcomes – is difficult to achieve. Despite the existence of empirical data about the value of classroom CS to learning goals, as well as the presence of policies that support education through the mother tongue in some countries, it is unfortunate that attitudes towards CS in the classroom remain ambivalent for many stakeholders. As in the case of the Philippines, myths about languages in education still exist and continue to hamper efforts to preserve the rich linguistic repertoires of multilingual communication.

Mother tongues do play an important role in teaching and learning. And in contexts such as the Phillines and Singapore, where English has an official status in the national curriculum, the mother tongues offer a wealth of linguistic resources which bilinguals draw from. CS, whether inside or outside the classroom, is the natural result of languages coming into contact with each other. CS is bilingual performance and does not necessarily result in the deterioration of one language. Thus, it must be viewed, in the words of cognitive psychologist Bernardo (2005: 161), 'not as a compromise or fallback option, but as a positive option for language in education'.

References

Altarriba, J. and Basnight-Brown, D. (2007) Methodological considerations in performing semantic and translation priming experiments across languages. *Behavior Research Methods, Instruments, and Computers* 39, 1–18.

Asuncion, Z.S. (2010) Filipino college freshman students' oral compensatory strategies. *Philippine ESL Journal* 5, 2–21.

Azores, F.M. (1967) A preliminary investigation of the phenomenon of language change in the Philippines. Unpublished masters thesis, Ateneo de Manila University.

Baetens Beardsmore, H. (1998) Language shift and cultural implications in Singapore. In S. Gopinathan, A. Pakir, W.K. Ho and V. Saravanan (eds) *Language, Society and Education in Singapore* (2nd edn) (pp. 85–98). Singapore: Eastern Universities Press.

Bautista, M.L.S. (1979) *Patterns of Speaking in Filipino Radio Dramas: A Sociolinguistic Analysis*. Tokyo: Institute for the Study of Languages and Cultures of Asia and Africa, Tokyo University for Foreign Studies.

Bautista, M.L.S. (1980) *The Filipino Bilingual's Linguistic Competence: A Model Based on an Analysis of Tagalog–English Code Switching*. Pacific Linguistics Series C-59. Canberra: Australian National University. (Published version of the dissertation submitted to the Ateneo de Manila University–Philippine Normal College Consortium for a PhD in linguistics, 1974.)

Bautista, M.L.S. (1998) Another look at Tagalog–English code-switching. In M.L.S. Bautista (ed.) *Pagtanaw: Essays on Language in Honor of Teodoro A. Llamzon* (pp. 128–146). Manila: Linguistic Society of the Philippines.

Bernardo, A.B.I. (2005) Bilingual code-switching as a resource for learning and teaching: Alternative reflections on the language and education issue in the Philippines. In D.T. Dayag and J.S. Quakenbush (eds) *Linguistics and Language Education in the Philippines and Beyond: A Festschrift in Honor of Ma. Lourdes S. Bautista* (pp. 151–163). Manila: Linguistic Society of the Philippines.

Bolton, K. (2003) *Chinese Englishes. A Sociolinguistic History*. Cambridge: Cambridge University Press.

Borlongan, A. (2009) Tagalog–English code-switching in English language classes: Frequency and forms. *TESOL Journal* 1, 28–41.

Chan, B. (2003) *Aspects of the Syntax, the Pragmatics and the Production of Code-Switching: Cantonese and English*. New York: Peter Lang.

Chan, B. (2009) Code-switching between typologically distinct languages. In B.E. Bullock and A.J. Toribio (eds) *The Cambridge Handbook of Linguistic Code-Switching* (pp. 182–198). Cambridge: Cambridge University Press.

Chanco, A., Francisco, E. and Talamisan, T. (1998) Code switching: A look into the language patterns of some television hosts in metro Manila. In M.L.S. Bautista and G.O. Tan (eds) *The Filipino Bilingual: A Multidisciplinary Perspective* (pp. 32–35). Manila: Linguistic Society of the Philippines.

Chu, C.C. (1983) *A Reference Grammar of Mandarin Chinese for English Speakers*. New York: Peter Lang.

Dayag, D.T. (2002) Code-switching in Philippine print ads: A syntactico-pragmatic description. *Philippine Journal of Linguistics* 3 (1), 33–52.

de Bot, K., Broersma, M. and Isurin, L. (2009) Sources of triggering in code switching. In L. Isurin, D. Winford and K. de Bot (eds) *Multidisciplinary Approaches to Code Switching* (pp. 85–102). Amsterdam: John Benjamins.

Gardner-Chloros, P. (2009) *Code-Switching*. Cambridge: Cambridge University Press.

Green, D.W. (1986) Control, activation, and resource: A framework and a model for the control of speech in bilinguals. *Brain and Language* 27, 210–223.

Green, D.W. (1998) Mental control of the bilingual lexico-semantic system. *Bilingualism: Language and Cognition* 1, 67–81.

Jake, J.L. and   Myers-Scotton, M. (2009) Which language? Participation potentials across lexical categories in codeswitching. In L. Isurin, D. Winford and K. De Bot (eds) *Multidisciplinary Approaches to Code Switching* (pp. 207–242). Amsterdam: John Benjamins.

Jiang, N. (2000) Lexical representation and development in a second language. *Applied Linguistics* 21 (1), 47–77.

Jiang, N. (2004) Morphological insensitivity in second language processing. *Applied Psycholinguistics* 25, 603–634.

Kachru, B. (2005) *Asian Englishes: Beyond the Canon*. Hong Kong: Hong Kong University Press.

La Heij, W. (2005) Selection processes in monolingual and bilingual lexical access. In J.F. Kroll and A.M.B. de Groot (eds) *Handbook of Bilingualism: Psycholinguistic Approaches* (pp. 289–307). New York: Oxford University Press.

Lee, C.C.P. (2005) The role of code-switching in a communications skills classroom. Unpublished MA (Applied Linguistics) thesis, Nanyang Technological University.

Lee, C.L. (2003) Motivations of code-switching in multilingual Singapore. *Journal of Chinese Linguistics* 31 (1), 145–176.

Lee, K.Y. (2000) *From Third World to First: The Singapore Story 1965–2000: Memoirs of Lee Kuan Yew*. Singapore: Straits Times Press.

Li Wei (ed.) (2000) *The Bilingualism Reader*. London: Routledge.

Li Wei (2011) Multilinguality, multimodality, and multicompetence: Code- and mode-switching by minority ethnic children in complementary schools. *Modern Language Journal* 95 (3), 370–384.

Libben, G. (2002) Representation and processing in the second language lexicon: The homogeneity hypothesis. In J. Archibald (ed.) *Second Language Acquisition and Linguistic Theory* (pp. 228–248). Oxford: Blackwell.

Liceras, J., Martinez, C., Perez-Tattam, R. and Perales, S. (2006) L2 acquisition as a process of creolization: Insights from child and adult code-mixing. In C. Lefebvre, L. White and C. Jourdan (eds) *L2 Acquisition and Creole Genesis: Dialogues* (pp. 113–144). Amsterdam: John Benjamins.

Limoso, R.J. (2002) Code switching among literature teachers of Miriam College: Patterns, functions, and implications. Unpublished masters thesis, Ateneo de Manila University.

Liu, J., Tindall, E. and Nisbet, D. (2006) Chinese learners and English plural forms. *Linguistics Journal* 1 (3), 127–147.

Macaro, E. (2005) Codeswitching in the L2 classroom: A communication and learning strategy. In E. Llurda (ed.) *Non-native Language Teachers: Perceptions, Challenges, and Contributions to the Profession* (pp. 63–84). New York: Springer.

MacSwan, J. (1999) *A Minimalist Approach to Intrasentential Code Switching*. New York: Garland Publishing.

MacSwan, J. (2005a) Codeswitching and generative grammar: A critique of the MLF model and some remarks on 'modified minimalism'. *Bilingualism: Language and Cognition* 8 (1), 1–22.

MacSwan, J. (2005b) Remarks on Jake, Myers-Scotton & Gross's response: There is no 'matrix language'. *Bilingualism: Language and Cognition* 8 (3), 277–284.

Marian, V. and Spivey, M. (2003a) Comparing bilingual and monolingual processing of competing lexical items. *Applied Psycholinguistics* 24, 173–193.

Marian, V. and Spivey, M. (2003b) Competing activation in bilingual language processing: Within- and between-language competition. *Bilingualism: Language and Cognition* 6 (2), 97–115.

Marian, V., Spivey, M. and Hirsch, J. (2003) Shared and separate systems in bilingual language processing: Converging evidence from eyetracking and brain imaging. *Brain and Language* 86, 70–82.

Martin, I.P. (2006) Language in Philippine classrooms: Enfeebling or enabling? *Asian Englishes Journal* 9 (2), 48–67.

Martin, I.P. (2010) Periphery ELT: The politics and practice of teaching English in the Philippines. In A. Kirkpatrick (ed.) *The Routledge Handbook of World Englishes* (pp. 247–264). London: Routledge.

Ministry of Education (1991) *The English Language Syllabus*. Singapore: Curriculum Development Institute of Singapore, Ministry of Education.

Ministry of Education (2010) *The English Language Syllabus for Schools*. Singapore: Curriculum Planning and Development Division, Ministry of Education.

Myers-Scotton, C. (1993) *Duelling Languages: Grammatical Structure in Codeswitching*. Oxford: Oxford University Press.

Nivera, G.C. (2003) Spoken discourse in the tertiary mathematics classroom. *Philippine Journal of Linguistics* 34 (2) and 35 (1), 7–13.

Nolasco, R.M. (2008) The prospects of multilingual education and literacy in the Philippines. In A. Bernardo (ed.) *The Paradox of Philippine Education and Education Reform: Social Science Perspectives* (pp. 133–145). Quezon City: Philippine Social Science Council.

Ong, K.K.W. and Zhang, J. (2010) Metalinguistic filters within the bilingual language faculty: A study of young English–Chinese bilinguals. *Journal of Psycholinguistic Research* 39 (3), 243–272.

Pakir, A. (1991) The status of English and the question of 'standard' in Singapore: A sociolinguistic perspective. In M.L. Tickoo (ed.) *Languages and Standards: Issues, Attitudes, Case Studies* (pp. 109–130). Singapore: SEAMEO Regional Language Centre.

Pascasio, E.M. (1978) Dynamics of code switching in the business domain. *Philippine Journal of Linguistics* 9 (1–2), 40–50.

Petersen, J. (1988) Word-internal code-switching constraints in a bilingual child's grammar. *Linguistics* 7, 479–493.

Poplack, S. (2000) Sometimes I'll start a sentence in Spanish y termino en español: Toward a typology of code-switching. In Li Wei (ed.) *The Bilingualism Reader* (pp. 221–256). London: Routledge.

Preston, M.S. and Lambert, W.E. (1969) Interlingual interference in a bilingual version of the Stroop color-word task. *Journal of Verbal Learning and Verbal Behavior* 8, 295–301.

Robertson, D. (2000) Variability in the use of the English article system by Chinese learners of English. *Second Language Research* 16 (2), 135–172.

Schneider, E.W. (2007) *Postcolonial English: Varieties Around the World*. Cambridge: Cambridge University Press.

Thompson, R.M. (2003) *Filipino English and Taglish: Language Switching from Multiple Perspectives*. Amsterdam: John Benjamins.

Tian, L. and Macaro, E. (2012) Comparing the effect of teacher codeswitching with English-only explanations on the vocabulary acquisition of Chinese university students: A lexical focus-on-form study. *Language Teaching Research* 16 (3), 361–385.

Wee, L. and Ansaldo, U. (2004) Nouns and noun phrases. In L. Lim (ed.) *Singapore English: A Grammatical Description* (pp. 57–74). Amsterdam: John Benjamins.

Yu, L. (1996a) The role of cross-linguistic lexical similarity in the use of motion verbs in English by Chinese and Japanese learners. Unpublished EdD thesis, University of Toronto, Canada.

Yu, L. (1996b) The role of L1 in the acquisition of motion verbs in English by Chinese and Japanese learners. *Canadian Modern Language Review* 53, 191–201.

8 Codeswitching by Korean Students in New Zealand and Lecturers in Korea

Case Study: Moyra Sweetnam Evans and Ha-Rim Lee

Commentary: Hyun-Ju Kim

CASE STUDY

Introduction

This case study reports on the recalls and comments on their reading of a group of Korean first-language undergraduates at the University of Otago. Their marked preferences for using Korean, along with their use of codeswitching (CS), suggest they used (and use) their first language in tandem with the second language to comprehend and interpret texts. Their responses indicate that they monitored their comprehension and engaged with textual content, producing both affective and aesthetic responses.

Unlike some of the other chapters in this book, our chapter does not report on students and teachers in a classroom environment. Nonetheless, our participants were bilingual students engaged in reading and writing tasks which could be (or could have been) carried out in second language classrooms. Our chapter thus has implications for classroom CS practices. It also has relevance to the beliefs about second language acquisition (SLA) which are held by students and teachers and to what Macaro (in the introductory Overview to this book) refers to as 'probably the most fundamental question facing ... SLA researchers, language teachers and policymakers in this second decade of the 21st century' – namely whether students and teachers should use the first language in the second language classroom.

Theoretical Framework: First and Second Language Reading

An essential principle in reading theory and research is that textual meaning is a feature of interaction between text and reader (see Kintsch, 2005). Skilled readers constantly monitor their reading comprehension, aiming for coherent meaning. As they construct and manage their mental representations of incoming texts, they re-read and question texts, and link textual features. They draw on higher-order cognitive strategies (Graesser *et al.*, 1997), including: activating and using background knowledge; constructing and revising inferences, hypotheses, expectations and predictions; elaborating on and attending selectively to textual detail; and suppressing irrelevant information (see Gernsbacher & Foertsch, 1999; Kolić-Vehovec & Bajšanski, 2007; Zwaan & Madden, 2004). When strategically and consciously applied, these procedures form part of overall comprehension monitoring.

Second language learners are sometimes characterised as inefficient readers, neither accessing their existing L1 strategies, nor constructing meaning by interaction with texts (Walter, 2007). They are said to focus on too many textual details as they decode words and sentences to establish literal meaning (Nassaji, 2002). However, L2 readers are also acknowledged as using higher-order comprehension monitoring strategies, but are sometimes considered to use them less effectively and/or less frequently than L1 readers do (Bensoussan, 1998; Bernhardt, 2005; Ruddell & Unrau, 1994).

Although the use of the L1 in L2 reading is still a relatively under-researched domain, it is becoming clear that the L1 is ever-present for bilingual individuals and that, while they are reading in the L2, bilinguals think about texts in their L1s (Macaro, 2005), and mentally translate and paraphrase texts into the L1 (Kern, 1994; Upton, 1997), effectively using their L1 to facilitate comprehension (Seng & Hashim, 2006).

Methodology

In this study, we wanted to determine whether L2 reading proceeded in the same way as L1 reading did, when readers were free to use their L1 to write about texts. The participants were Korean L1 undergraduates (seven women, seven men) in health sciences and humanities at the University of Otago, New Zealand, in their early 20s. All had completed their high-school education in Korea and, as international students, had fulfilled university English requirements, achieving scores in at least band 6 of the International English Language Testing System (IELTS).

Each participant was given five English texts to read, recall and comment on: a joke, two poems ('This Is Just To Say', about a bowl of plums, and 'Mirror', a riddle poem) and two short pieces of prose, one retelling Cinderella, the other giving instructions on cardiopulmonary resuscitation (CPR) (see Appendix A for references and information on the texts). The texts were chosen as samples of genres likely to elicit different reading responses (see Sweetnam Evans, 2011) and representing a spectrum of easy-to-process to more difficult texts. The joke was included as a special category of humour common in general text reception. No title was provided for 'Mirror' – a moderately complex literary text – making it harder to process (Collins & Levy, 2008).

The recalls and comments were essentially free – uninfluenced by questions or communication with researchers (Brantmeier, 2006). For each of these five texts, a cue page (single sheet) was provided in Korean (see Appendix B for a translated version), with the heading 'Text 1' or 'Text 2' and so on, and concise directions eliciting two sets of recalls and one set of comments for each text, the largest space being provided for the comments. Participants were told in Korean that they could provide their comments or recalls in a language of their own choosing. The stage was therefore set for CS and normal bilingual language use.

The researchers were deliberately absent when participants read and commented on the texts and it was partly for this reason that written rather than verbal recalls were used. While CS is probably less common in writing than in speech, and its forms and functions in speech have been researched more than their appearance in written language has (Gort, 2012), documented evidence nevertheless exists of written CS (Cummins, 2005) and it seemed reasonable to expect that this could take place.

To recreate leisure reading conditions, participants were asked to read the texts as though engaging in reading for relaxation and to read each text as many times as they liked. No time limits were imposed for reading. Participants were told that the researcher was interested in how they read rather than in how much they remembered about the texts. Participants were given no tasks to establish external reading goals or to influence the types of strategies they might use or inferences they might make (Horiba, 2000). No directives were given about discussing the texts with others, to avoid pre-empting such comprehension monitoring. No information was provided about the textual genres. The bilingual participants were consequently at liberty to construct their own meanings for each text.

Besides the cue sheets, participants were each given a reading strategy questionnaire, the responses to which are dealt with elsewhere (see Sweetnam Evans, 2011). The verbatim recalls of individual textual words (responses to the first item on the cue sheets) were not analysed for the purposes of this case study either. All recalls referred to here were cued by the instruction 'Please write what you remember about the text' (second item on the cue sheet).

Participants were requested not to look at the cue sheets or questionnaires before they had read all the texts and to complete the recalls and comments on the cue sheets before answering the questions. It was suggested that they wait a day or two once they had finished reading the texts before continuing with the project. They were asked not to refer to the texts once they had started filling in the cue sheets and questionnaires and were encouraged to undertake the tasks in a relaxed manner and to write as much as they wanted to. All their responses were collected a week after distribution.

The written comments and recalls were translated by the second author, a English/Korean bilingual. The first author transcribed the data and signalled all CS. The uses of English and Korean were quantified by counting words: Korean particles and English function words were not included in the word counts. Other aspects of the recalls and comments were calculated (discussed below) and the calculations were checked by an independent statistician.

Findings and Discussion: Language Choices for Recalls and Comments

For the recalls, most participants produced some type of paraphrase. For the comments, participants remarked on aspects such as the ease or difficulty of the text, indicated their affective responses and made comments on the structure and content of the texts. In the absence of instructions to use a specific language, the majority of participants showed a preference for Korean, as shown in Table 8.1. None of the participants used English

Table 8.1 Language use by the participants

	Korean only for all texts	Korean and English (CS)	No language chosen (no response)
% (number) of participants producing recalls	7% (1)	93% (13)	0% (no recalls)
% (number) of participants producing comments	14% (2)	71% (10)	14% (2) (no comments)

Table 8.2 Language use as a rounded percentage of overall responses

	Korean only	Names only in English - rest in Korean	English only	Korean and English (code-switching)	No responses given
% of total recalls	39%	0%	17%	39%	5%
% of total comments	41%	5%	8%	23%	23%

Table 8.3 Language use as shown by word counts

	Korean	English
% total words in recalls	75	25
% total words in comments	90	10

exclusively for all the recalls or for all the comments, although some did so for individual texts.

Korean was the preferred language for both recalls and comments, with more comments and responses in Korean than in English, as shown in Table 8.2. Not only were there more responses in Korean, but more Korean words than English words were used overall, as shown in Table 8.3. More use of English (L2) for the recalls than for the comments might suggest that participants were trying to remember textual details and hence used more text language than when they were giving their opinions of the texts.

Codeswitching in the recalls

A total of 115 codeswitches were used, of which 76% occurred in the recalls and 24% in the comments. CS seems to have a variety of functions in the recalls. Sometimes participants gave names of characters in English:

1.   **Sherlock Holmes** ey tayhan iyaki
     Story about **Sherlock Holmes**

At other times names were transliterated into Korean:

2.   Wassun.i hanulkamsanghanun pwupwun
     The part where Watson appreciates the sky

In the recalls, the CS also showed that specific words or phrases from the texts (or approximations of these) were remembered:

3. Sherlokhomculang takthe wassun.ilang **camping** kassta
    Sherlock Holmes and Dr Watson went **camping**

4. **stars** ey tayhan iyakilul hako iss.essta
    that was talking about **stars**

5. i **plum** un neuy **breakfast** yessta
    This **plum** *was your* **breakfast**

6. **CPR** hanun pangpep **for an adult & infant**
    Methods for **CPR for an adult & infant**

7. **nose** ta kalyeto toyntanun kes wa **mouth** aihantheynun
    That you can cover both **nose** *and* **mouth** *for a child*

Switches from Korean to complete sentences in English (when considered along with their accompanying comments in Korean) could be taken as indications that, while some textual elements were recalled, they were not totally comprehended and also not necessarily integrated into the mental texts constructed by the readers:

8. solcikhi kieknanunkey pyello epsta.
    Frankly, I don't remember much
    I am silver??? I am important to her. She comes and goes.

9. Sinteyleyllaka tangtanghi salamtul aph.eyse tanin kes at palace.
    How Cinderella proudly stood in front of people **at palace**
    Like a dog. Work harder than a dog?

There was no discernible pattern according to which specific words were recalled in English or translated into Korean. The same textual elements were recalled in both English and Korean and in different combinations.

10. nanun **lake** la hako yecaka **bends over me** lanun cangmyen.ul sangsanghay poassta
    I pictured the scenes where I say **lake** *and a woman* **bends over me**

11. kunyenun **young girl** iko **old woman** ita
    She is a **young girl** *and an* **old woman**

12. casin.ul hoswulako hako cichin halwulul ponay himtun nulk.un
    halmenilul kokiwa pikyohan kes
    *That it said I am a lake and made a comparison between the old lady who
    is tired at the end of the weary day and fish*

13. nanun **fish** ta
    I am a **fish**

Some words and phrases (such as terrible fish, icebox, first aid) were
possibly recalled in English because the participants experienced them as
unconventional or archaic:

14. macimak **'terrible fish'**
    The final **'terrible fish'**

15. **plum** ul mek.ko mianhatamye namkin meymo kath.un ke in **icebox**
    ey
    A sort of memo left there, saying sorry after eating the **plum** *in* **icebox**

16. kulim **first aid** ey kwanhanke
    Picture about **first aid**

Sometimes participants switched back and forth between Korean and
English, with Korean the obvious matrix language:

17. **Twist** lul. Wulika hunhi alko issnun tonghwa **Cinderella** ey. Chayk
    ceymok.i malhaycwutus **'politically correct'** kulayse yecatul.uy
    mommay, oymoey tayhan **obsession** tung cicekhako issta. Kuliko
    ippun yecalul chaci halyeko ssawunun namcatul.uy mosupto
    po.yecwum. Thukhi **fairy godperson** i wase sinteyleyllaeykey
    hanun mal wuskyesssum. kekiey tto palo **yes!** la taytaphanun
    sinteyleyllato
    A twist *was given in the well known children's story* **Cinderella**. *As
    the title says* **'politically correct'** *so it points out women's* **obsession**
    *of body shape. Also shows men fighting to get a pretty woman. Especially
    what* **fairy godperson** *came and said to Cinderella was funny. And also
    Cinderella who answered* **yes!** *straight away*

A few participants produced their entire recalls in the form of a phrase
or a sentence or two in English (L2, the textual language), some using
quotation marks to indicate that these were the exact words they remembered from the texts:

18. You idiot! Someone has stolen our tent.

19. I'm silver & exact. I'm not cruel but truthful. Now I'm a lake. A woman bends over.

20. I have eaten plum which were saved for breakfast. They were sweet and cold.

21. Seal your lips to the person, and blow the air into the lung.

22. Cinderella – her father married a widow with two daughters. Prince open ball party. Fairy godperson make Cinderella to go ball. Cinderella lived happily ever after with step-mother and step-sisters.

Codeswitching in the comments

For the comments, some of the participants (29%) codeswitched to actual words from the texts, as in the recalls:

23. **plum**.ey tayhan nayyongita
   A story about a **plum**

English names of characters were sometimes used in Korean sentences but were also transliterated into Korean (see 24, 28 and 31):

24. syellokhomculang **Dr. Watson** ilanun ilun.ul sa.yonghayse, tangyenhi chwuliiyakiilkelanun sayngkak.ul hayssnuntey, mak syellokhomcuka iyakilul na.yelhamyense cilwuhay...
   I thought it was a detective story because it used names like Sherlock Holmes and **Dr Watson**. *But Sherlock Holmes listed things and I got bored because...*

The one- or two-word switches to English in the comments tended to refer to textual structure, feature or function. For example:

25. cheum ilk.ess.ul ttaynun i **text**.ihayka hanato antoyssciman
   When I first read it, the **text** *didn't make any sense*

26. **paragraph**lo toyiss.ese cenglika cal toynta
   Easy to organise because it is sectioned into **paragraphs**

27. **instruction** i chalyeytaylo toyiss.ese kiek.ey cal namnunta
   instruction *is written in steps so it is easy to remember*

28. cenhye wenlay nayyongkwa mac.ci anhnun **New Version** uy
   sinteyleylla.
   A **New Version** *of Cinderella that doesn't match at all with the original
   story.*

29. ilum(**khaylikthe**) oywuki cohta
   Names – **characters** *– are good to memorise*

In addition, one- or two-word switches to English sometimes reflected
participants' subjective responses or evaluations of the texts. For example:

30. sichikonun com **simple**
   It's a bit **simple** *for a poem*

31. **weird**han nayyonguy sinteyleylla yessta
   It was a **weird** *story of Cinderella*

32. sasil wuskyessko ku oyeynun **no comment**
   Actually it was funny. Apart from that **no comment**

Whole sentences in English were also used in infrequent English-only
comments, for affective responses and to comment on difficulty or ease of
comprehension:

33. Funny. Better not try too hard to be 'cool'.

34. It was a bit hard to understand. So I read quite a few times.

35. Where did you find that text 5? It was quite funny. =)

There were also a few instances where a whole sentence in English
appeared after a Korean sentence, to comment on ease or difficulty of comprehension:

36. It was a little bit tricky.

As indicated above, there was less CS to English and greater use of
Korean in general in the comments. The comments on ease and difficulty
were made primarily in Korean:

37. meliey tan.etul.i cal antteolunta
    The words would not pop in my head

38. nemwu nanhayhapnita
    It's too difficult/knotty

39. com heyskallikito hayssko
    A bit confusing

40. aphpotanun ihayhaki swiwessta
    It was easier to understand than the previous one

41. sayngkak.eps.i kunyang ilk.ul swu iss.essten cimwun
    A text [that I could] read without thinking

42. wenlaynayyongto alko iss.ese sayngkak.i calnassta
    Could recall better because I knew the original story

43. yocem.i mwues.inci phaakhaci mosha.yessta
    I don't get the point of this

Affective responses and comments about aesthetic characteristics were also primarily indicated in Korean:

44. macimak pancen.ey caymiiss.essko culkepkey ilk.essta
    It was funny in the end and I enjoyed reading

45. ilk.ko nase caymi iss.essta
    It was fun to read

46. kwiyepta
    Cute

47. sinteyleyllaka tokliphayse cohta
    I like the fact that Cinderella was independent

49. namcalang yeca kulim.i mwenya? Yasikkwulihata kk
    What is this picture of a man and a woman? It's kinky kk
    {Note: *kk* represents sound of tittering/giggling, designated by the Korean voiceless consonant}

50. silase hungmika kutaci epsta
    I am not that interested in it because it is a poem

The preponderance of Korean in both the recalls and the comments – and the fact that most of the matrix sentences were in Korean – suggests that the participants constructed their mental texts in Korean rather than in English (the text language).

Difficulty and ease of comprehension

Immediate written recalls are effective indications of comprehension (Bernhardt, 1983). While the recalls and comments in this study were not immediate, they illustrate whether or not the readers understood the texts (or even parts of the texts). Comprehension is apparent when readers are clearly able to recall the gist of a text, to summarise main points and to appreciate humour. The ability to differentiate different genres also suggests a certain amount of textual comprehension, and is arguably one of the first steps in comprehension, contributing as it does towards the construction of a comprehension framework (global schema) for text reception.

Some participants voluntarily reported difficulty and/or ease of comprehension. Not surprisingly (given its literary features and that no title had been supplied), 86% of the participants reported comprehension problems with the riddle poem ('Mirror'); a few other instances of ease and difficulty were reported too, but none so marked. Although some of the comments showed that participants liked and partially understood the poem 'This Is Just To Say', which some said was easy, other data suggest that it was only easier to process than the riddle poem ('Mirror') and not easier to comprehend and process than the other texts, suggesting that literary reading was somewhat problematic.

For those texts for which individuals reported neither ease nor difficulty in reading, comprehension can be assumed if participants expressed positive affective comments, if they could identify genres, could determine the gist of a text or summarise it, got the point of a text, found the joke funny, appreciated other textual humour and recognised intertextuality. Participants were able to recognise poetry and one of the poems as a riddle. They gave the gist of most of the texts, understood and responded appropriately to the humour in 'Cinderella' and accepted it as a parody. They appreciated the humour and intertextuality in the joke. They engaged affectively with textual characters in 'Cinderella' and the joke, thus displaying a significant aspect of narrative comprehension. Their comments on the usefulness of the information in the piece on CPR and their ability to summarise it also point towards comprehension and genre differentiation.

Producing comments might have been experienced as more cognitively demanding than producing recalls. While all the participants produced some

Table 8.4 Percentage of participants and number of texts responded to

	Percentage of participants (n = 14)
Recall all five texts	71%
Recall four texts	29%
Comments on all five texts	58%
Comments on four texts only	14%
Comments on three texts only	14%
No comments on any texts	14%

recalls, some participants produced no comments, as shown in Table 8.4. Another indication of this relative difficulty is that, of the total possible number of responses, more comments than recalls were omitted. Of the 70 potential recalls (5 by each of 14 participants), 94% were provided and 6% were omitted. Of the 70 potential comments, 77% were provided and 23% (16 individual) were omitted. Perceived difficulty may be why more participants used the L1 in their comments than in their recalls. For a more cognitively demanding activity (such as the comments), the use of the L1 can lower the cognitive load and the use of the L2 can raise it (see Scott & De La Fuente, 2008). The participants may have been attempting to reduce their cognitive loads by using their L1, possibly as a kind of self-scaffolding.

Comprehension monitoring

The participants monitored their comprehension while reading and were possibly continued to do so while producing their written responses. Writing about texts can facilitate comprehension (Delayney, 2008) and some of the comments indicated that comprehension monitoring was taking place as they wrote. Comprehension monitoring is itself an indicator not only of a degree of understanding (Kolić-Vehovec & Bajšanski, 2007) but also of a certain skill in reading, even when total comprehension is not present. The difficulties participants experienced in reading and processing 'Mirror', for example, did not deter them from monitoring their comprehension as they strove to understand it. Their voluntary reporting of the use of cognitive reading strategies shows a metacognitive awareness, which itself can be considered comprehension monitoring.

Examples of comprehension monitoring strategies in the written responses include: asking questions (51); pondering authorial intention (52); indicating that texts had been discussed with others (53); mentioning re-reading (54); and realising that a comprehension framework already in place has to be changed because of new incoming information (55).

51. almyense nappuncis han nom.ey tayhayse ssun nayyonginkenyam?
   Is it about someone who did bad thing knowingly?

52. i kul.ul ssun iyuka molkka kwungkum
   I wonder the purpose of writing this text

53. chinkwuka kewul.ilako hayss.ul ttay nayyongul cokum ihayhal swu iss.essta
   When my friend told me it was a mirror, I could understand better

54. cheum ilk.ess.ul ttaynun i **text**.ihayka hanato antoyssciman
   *When I first read it, the **text** didn't make any sense*

55. ceymok.i '**The kiss of life**'yese lomaynthikhan sutholilul kitayhayssnuntey inkonghohuphanun pangpep.ilase silmanghayssta (sacin.uy yenghyangin tus siphta).
   *I expected a romantic story because the title was '**The kiss of life**' but was disappointed that it was about CPR. (Maybe it's the impact of the picture)*

Participants' responses also indicate the use of comprehension strategies such as reading for overall coherence (56) and making connections between texts, pictures and titles, and within texts (57, 58):

56. **Paragraph**lo toyiss.ese cenglika cal toynta
   *Easy to organise because it is sectioned into **paragraphs***

57. kulim.i iss.ese ilkci anh.ato taychwung mwusun nayyonginci al.assta
   Because there was a picture I roughly knew what it was about without reading

58. ceymok.ul poko sangsanghayssten keskwa talli nayyongi talla
   it was different from what I expected by reading the title

Conclusion

In this limited study the bilingual participants generally preferred to use their first language (Korean) to write about the different texts they had read. A small percentage of participants provided some of their responses in English only, but none used English exclusively for all the recalls or all the comments. The participants codeswitched freely to the L2 at times, using one or two words in English before continuing their responses in Korean. Occasionally some participants used whole sentences in English. Codeswitches to English were frequently made in order to produce words or phrases that were being recalled directly from the texts. There were significantly more instances of CS in the recalls than in the comments, and there was less use of the L2 and fewer instances of CS when participants were commenting on textual structure, evaluating texts or providing their own affective responses to textual content.

The reading comprehension and comprehension monitoring of the participants does not appear to have been impaired by limitations of competence in their L2. This may be because they were not constrained to comment in their L2 (English) and were able to use their L1 (Korean) freely and also to codeswitch between their L1 and the L2. Our findings suggest that participants used their L1 in preference to the L2 in tasks they perceived as more difficult. The L1 as the preferred overall language of response (with and without CS) further suggests that participants may have constructed mental representations of the texts mainly in their L1, and that the participants used their L1 to facilitate and monitor their comprehension of texts read in the L2.

For our participants, CS was apparently a normal practice which they used out of preference and which seemed to assist them in comprehending and writing about texts. Our findings suggest that it might be worthwhile for teachers to provide second language (L2) students with opportunities to use their first languages and to codeswitch between their L1 and L2 in tasks involving discussing, responding to and recalling written, spoken and visual texts in the classroom. Such tasks provide opportunities for output and facilitate comprehension and intake.

As Macaro points out in the Overview to this volume, tasks themselves are considered to drive acquisition in task-based learning. Although this connection is not a direct one (Ellis, 2003; Long, 1996), SLA researchers claim that input (Krashen, 1987, 2008), intake (Gass *et al.*, 1998), communication and output (Swain, 2000) are involved in SLA. Tasks provide input, opportunities for communication, interaction and comprehension, resulting in intake. They also provide opportunities for output. Researchers and theorists have argued that comprehension is essential for learning (e.g. Kintsch, 1994), for noticing and for intake (e.g. Pulido, 2004) and a step towards SLA (Krashen, 2008). Our belief is that adequate comprehension of all texts (including instructions, the written and spoken texts used in tasks, student–student communication and teacher–student communication before and during tasks) is an essential precursor to SLA and can be facilitated by CS. We trust that further research will show that opportunities for CS in reception and production tasks serve to promote comprehension and thus indirectly to promote SLA.

COMMENTARY

Introduction

This commentary is intended to complement Moyra Sweetnam Evans and Ha Rim Lee's case study of Korean students' written CS in the context of a New Zealand university. It will do so in three ways. Firstly, it will consider the language-in-education policy and situation in Korean universities. I will then present and discuss data emerging from a small-scale survey of professors' attitudes towards CS recently conducted within a university context in Korea. Finally, I will discuss specific aspects of the New Zealand case study, and relate them to my own findings.

Contextual Background

English was first introduced in Korea in 1883, when the Joseon dynasty opened an English institute to train interpreters. At that time English pedagogy mainly focused on grammar and translation, in the same way that European students learned Latin and Greek. English education was subsequently expanded and developed by the Korean government during and after the Korean War (1950–53). More recently, it has been widely recognised in Korea that English is the most powerful tool to advance social mobility and the nation's economic development. It is believed that English is so vital in the Korean employment market that, in order to get a job, many people are required to prove their competence in English by achieving high scores in tests such as the Test of English as a Foreign Language (TOEFL), the Test of English for International Communication (TOEIC) and the ACTFL Oral Proficiency Interview by Computer (OPIc).

Following a restructuring of the nationwide system of English education in 2009, teaching in the public sector now heavily emphasises spoken as well as written language, leading to some stress among English language teachers in schools, many of whom feel that they are not ready for teaching oral communication since they have not been adequately trained to do so (Kim & Petraki, 2009). As English has become more important in Korea, the number of private, as well as public, institutions providing English instruction has grown rapidly. Now most children in Korea are exposed to learning English from kindergarten and this is followed by more than 10 years of learning English at school, as well as in *Hagwon* (after-school classes). Many Koreans strongly believe that the best way to learn English is by the exclusive use of the target language (C-S. Park, 2007; J.K. Park, 2009).

The importance attached to the learning of English by the Korean government (reinforced by strident opinions frequently expressed in the mass media) has led policymakers in higher education to focus more on English communication skills, and there also are strong demands to teach content subjects at universities through the medium of English. Thus, one of the most prestigious universities in Korea, the Korea Advanced Institute of Science and Technology (KAIST), initiated an institutional policy in 2007 that required the exclusive use of English as the medium of instruction across the entire curriculum. Similar policies have since been adopted by an increasing number of other universities, because English competence has now become the one of the most important evaluation criteria in colleges and universities in Korea. Apart from anything else, this affects their status in the decisive ranking system.

Many university instructors are proficient in English, but both they and their students often have a hard time communicating entirely in English about issues raised in content subjects, a common effect of which is the dilution of course content to what is comprehensible rather than what is essential. Eventually, strict adherence to an English-only policy can cause emotional and psychological stress to the instructors and the students (Hsieh & Kang, 2010). There are even reports (Choi, 2011; Jee, 2012; Kim, 2011) of suicides by several university students attributed to exclusive use of English as the medium of instruction. Therefore, there are increasing criticisms of such a policy (e.g. Kang, 2012) and more attention is now being paid to the positive functions of using the first language (Korean) rather than, or as well as, English in delivering content knowledge through English. Therefore, the question arises as to what the optimal balance is between L2 and the L1 in content classes taught at Korean universities.

A Small-Scale Project

In early 2012, I conducted a modest study at a university located in Yongin, near Seoul, in order to explore the perceptions of CS of some of the academic staff who taught majors in English. I circulated an anonymous questionnaire (see Appendix C) to 183 of the staff and, although the response rate was low (approximately 12%), the feedback from the 23 respondents gives a reasonably fair, if limited, picture of their perceptions. The survey comprised 13 closed and two open-ended questions.

Findings

The first five questions elicited information about the participants (see Tables 8.5 and 8.6) and their classes and their estimate of the extent of their own use of CS in their classes. The range of their reported use of CS varied considerably: some said that they used English almost exclusively, while others suggested that most of their classes were conducted in Korean (Table 8.7). With regard to item 7 on the questionnaire, there was great variability among instructors as regards their views about the optimal proportion of L1 and L2 use. However, generally speaking, they felt comfortable using L2 when explaining content rather than expressing opinions, but they also said that they needed to switch from English to Korean to help the

Table 8.5 Instructors' English-medium teaching experience

Years of Teaching majors in English	Frequency	Percentage (%)
1–2 years	6	26
2–3 years	8	35
3–4 years	8	35
More than 4 years	1	4
Total	23	100

Table 8.6 Instructors' self-evaluated English proficiency

Levels of English proficiency	Frequency	Percentage (%)
Superior	2	9
Advanced	11	48
Intermediate	6	26
Low intermediate	3	13
Low	0	0
Total (missing)	22 (1)	96 (4)

Table 8.7 Use of L1 and L2

Instructors' L1 and L2 reported use	Frequency	Percentage (%)
Totally L2	6	26
Over 70% of L2	5	22
Over 50% of L2	5	22
Less than 50% of L2	4	17
Less than 30% of L2	3	13
Total	23	100

students' understanding. They said that their use of CS was affected by factors such as their personal beliefs, the instructional materials they used and their students' proficiency levels.

Questions 8–14 sought their views on the effectiveness of CS in teaching, in terms of the effect on the students' learning of new skills in both content areas and language development. Almost

Table 8.8 Effectiveness of codeswitching on language skills

Effectiveness	Frequency (%)				
	General	Listening	Speaking	Reading	Writing
Negatively	3 (13%)	3 (13%)	4 (17%)	2 (9%)	3 (13%)
No effect at all	3 (13%)	2 (9%)	7 (30%)	3 (13%)	5 (22%)
Somewhat positively	12 (52%)	15 (65%)	10 (44%)	10 (44%)	10 (44%)
Very positively	5 (22%)	3 (13%)	2 (9%)	8 (35%)	5 (22%)
Total	23 (100%)				

Table 8.9 Effectiveness of codeswitching on affective factors

Effectiveness	Frequency (%)		
	Confidence	Interest	Anxiety
Negatively	2 (9%)	3 (13%)	2 (9%)
No effect at all	3 (13%)	3 (13%)	5 (22%)
Somewhat positively	9 (39%)	9 (39%)	8 (35%)
Very positively	9 (39%)	7 (30%)	7 (30%)
Total	23 (100%)		

half of the respondents (48%) believed that CS is beneficial when teaching difficult issues in content areas, but many (44%) also indicated that the first language should not be used too much in the classroom. While they considered that it might be helpful for students to understand concepts, they did not think it served to improve students' English in general. However, they felt CS would be helpful in improving English reading skills, since students could understand the meaning of L2 words and contents by referring to their equivalents in L1 (see Table 8.8).

With regard to affective aspects, 78% of the participants agreed that CS would help the development of students' confidence in English and 65% said that it would be beneficial to lower students' anxiety. Most of the respondents (69%) also considered that it would be good to raise students' interest in studying English (see Table 8.9).

The following are some of the responses to the final open-ended question:

It's sometimes really helpful especially when I'm explaining major concepts. If they couldn't understand those concepts I couldn't go further. So I often switch English to Korean when I see students do not follow my explanation.

I use it to arouse students' interest in my class. It's hard to make a joke in English and I want my students to like my class.

It helps students to reduce errors in using English and help understanding the meanings of the English words. Since I'm using English textbooks, they know the words in English and if I switch them to Korean they naturally get the meanings of the English words.

In summary, these instructors perceived that CS might help the students to understand the content of the classes, and might reduce anxiety and raise motivation, but would not be beneficial for their students' linguistic development, apart from reading skills.

Written Codeswitching by Korean Students: Implications

The data presented by Sweetnam Evans and Lee were well selected and clearly demonstrated the intended categories. Themes included language choice for comments and recalls, affective responses, difficulty and ease of comprehension, and comprehension monitoring. The data are presented in a clear and logical way and the reader is left with a good sense of how the participants used Korean and English and the patterns of use that the researchers felt were significant.

What was particularly interesting was the 'free choice' of language use by the participants, and the authors went to great lengths to ensure that all participants were free to select their L1 or L2 according to their own needs and desires. Too often, English language teachers in Korea, as elsewhere, feel obliged to insist upon the use of the target language both orally and in writing. In such cases, it is difficult to identify individual learner-readers' depth of comprehension and quality of response when they have to express these in the target language. The many extracts of these Korean students' written responses presented and discussed by the authors clearly show the students' firm preference for using their first language to indicate the extent of their comprehension. Significantly, there was little evidence of CS at the inter-sentential level, and the English tags that were introduced were mainly key words taken from the text, rather than embedded in the learners' own lexicon. This adds weight to the conclusion by Sweetnam Evans and Lee that the English texts were first mentally deconstructed and then reconstructed in Korean.

Two questions then arise: at what stage in education should a shift from the first language to the target language take place, and how it should be done? It takes a long time, in my experience, for most second language learners to begin to *think* in English, particularly if they are learning the language in a foreign language context such as Korea, rather than in contexts where English is a second language – and we do want learners to think about what they read. Therefore, I would suggest a phased approach, whereby, initially, students may be permitted to use Korean when dealing with target language texts. For example, in group discussions they can speak in Korean to negotiate the meaning of English texts and then subsequently write their responses also in Korean. Later, the use of a double-sided flag could be used to monitor this. When the teacher shows them the Korean side, they *may* speak/write Korean, but when the American (or British) flag is shown they *must* use the target language. The use of the flag could be adjusted according to their development both within tasks and as their proficiency increases. As an example of the former, after group discussions have been carried out in Korean the students could be asked to write summaries of their discussions in a few English sentences. Similarly, they could work together to co-construct short English summaries of their written responses. From such beginnings in lower-intermediate levels, with increased pro-ficiency – and confidence – the amount of time that the Korean flag is shown could be reduced, firstly for speaking and then for writing.

This is a practical suggestion for teachers to adapt in their own specific contexts, and it would be interesting to find out how receptive teachers in Korean schools or universities might be to this procedure. Thus, it would be useful for such an idea to be included in professional development programmes and for the implications to be systematically investigated through (collaborative) action research projects. There is also a need for other methods of research to investigate the beliefs of Korean teachers and learners of English.

Turning attention back to the New Zealand case study, as the authors have acknowledged, one potential limitation in their research is that the process of recall, making comments and reporting on reading was treated as a more or less transparent process. For the reasons they stated, the researchers were not present during the data collection and they abstained from introducing leading questions or influencing responses in a dialogic sense. In other words, while great attention was paid to the higher mental functions facilitated by the use of the L1, little attention was paid to the process of actually reporting this process.

To obtain a fuller picture, the CS patterns detected in such data need to be related not only to specific theories of cognition and language choice, but to important sociocultural factors that play a major role in language choice. The process of language selection is influenced by numerous social and contextual factors in very complex ways (Kinginger, 2004; Liebscher & Dailey-O'Cain, 2005). Especially, the pragmatic and symbolic status of the target language in a society influences the perceptions and beliefs of the target language and causes different patterns of CS. That said, these caveats might be understood as limitations of this whole genre of research, rather than a critique of this case study *per se*. Therefore, further explorations into the issue of language choice, whether in written or spoken production, might benefit from a more nuanced theoretical framework in order to make better connections between the various cognitive and sociocultural categories and how they address fundamental questions about CS. Factors might include the perceived status of certain language choices, an investigation into certain reader/writer identities, or more general socially relevant perceptions about the use of English and Korean. This implies investigations into the beliefs, values and practices of both language teachers and language learners, as suggested by Borg (2006) – and the case studies discussed in the present volume might stimulate broader, deeper and longitudinal investigations in a range of other contexts. Further research could add depth to current theoretical understandings of the benefits as well as potential difficulties of L1 use in language learning.

References

Bensoussan, M. (1998) Schema effects in EFL reading comprehension. *Journal of Research in Reading* 21 (3), 213–227.

Bernhardt, E.B. (1983) Testing foreign language reading comprehension: The immediate recall protocol. *Die Unterrichtspraxis/Teaching German* 16 (1), 27–33.

Bernhardt, E.B. (2005) Progress and procrastination in second language reading. *Annual Review of Applied Linguistics* 25, 133–150.

Borg, S. (2006) *Teacher Cognition and Language Education: Research and Practice*. London: Continuum.

Brantmeier, C. (2006) Toward a multicomponent model of interest and L2 reading: Sources of interest, perceived situational interest, and comprehension. *Reading in a Foreign Language* 18 (2), 89–115.

Choi, M. (2011) Feature: KAIST's student suicide crisis. *KAIST Herald*, 21 April, p. 8. See http://herald.kaist.ac.kr/news/articleView.html?idxno=156 (accessed August 2013).

Collins, W.M. & Levy, B.A. (2008) Developing fluent text processing with practice: Memorial influences on fluency and comprehension. *Canadian Psychology* 49 (2), 133–139.

Cummins, J. (2005) Teaching for cross-language transfer in dual language education: Possibilities and pitfalls. *TESOL Symposium on Dual Language Education: Teaching and Learning Two Languages in the EFL Setting*. Bogazici University, Istanbul, Turkey. See http://www.achievementseminars.com/seminar_series_2005_2006/readings/tesol.turkey.pdf (accessed May 2012).

Delaney, Y.A. (2008) Investigating the reading-to-write construct. *Journal of English for Academic Purposes* 7, 140–150.

Ellis, R. (2003) *Task-Based Language Learning and Teaching*. Oxford: Oxford University Press.

Gass, S.M., Mackey, A. and Pica, T. (1998) The role of input and interaction in second language acquisition. *Modern Language Journal* 82 (3), 299–307.

Gernsbacher, M.A. and Foertsch, J.A. (1999) Three models of discourse comprehension. In S. Garrod and M.J. Pickering (eds) *Human Language Processing* (pp. 283–299). Hove: Psychology Press.

Gort, M. (2012) Codeswitchinging patterns in the writing-related talk of young emergent bilinguals. *Journal of Literacy Research* 44 (1), 45–75.

Graesser, A.C., Millis, K.K. and Zwaan, R.A. (1997) Discourse comprehension. *Annual Review of Psychology* 48, 163–189.

Horiba, Y. (2000) Reader control in reading: Effects of language competence, text type, and task. *Discourse Processes* 29 (3), 223–267.

Hsieh, P. and Kang, H. (2010) Attribution and self-efficacy and their interrelationship in the Korean EFL context. *Language Learning* 60 (3), 606–627.

Jee, M. (2012) Another suicide hits Korea's top sci-tech university KAIST. *The Dong-A Ilbo*, 18 April. See http://english.donga.com/srv/service.php3?bicode=040000&biid=2012041849518 (accessed August 2013).

Kang, H-S. (2012) English-only instruction at Korean universities: Help or hindrance to higher learning? *English Today* 28 (1), 29–34.

Kern, R.G. (1994) The role of mental translation in second language reading. *Studies in Second Language Acquisition* 16, 441–461.

Kim, E-J. (2011) (News Focus). KAIST student suicides spark debate over lectures in English. Yonhap News Agency, 11 April. See http://english.yonhapnews.co.kr/national/2011/04/15/47/0302000000AEN20110415001900315F.HTML (accessed August 2013).

Kim, Y. and Petraki, E. (2009) Students' and teachers' use of and attitudes to L1 in the EFL classroom. *Asian EFL Journal* 11 (4), 58–89.

Kinginger, C. (2004) Alice doesn't live here anymore: Foreign language learning and identity reconstruction. In A. Pavlenko and A. Blackledge (eds) *Negotiation of Identities in Multilingual Contexts* (pp. 219–241). Clevedon: Multilingual Matters.

Kintsch, W. (1994) Text comprehension, memory, and learning. *American Psychologist* 49, 294–303.

Kintsch, W. (2005) An overview of top-down and bottom-up effects in comprehension: The CI perspective. *Discourse Processes* 39 (2,3), 125–128.

Kolić-Vehovec, S. and Bajšanski, I. (2007) Comprehension monitoring and reading comprehension in bilingual students. *Journal of Research in Reading* 30 (2), 198–211.

Krashen, S. (1987) *Principles and Practice in Second Language Acquisition*. New York: Prentice-Hall International.

Krashen, S. (2008) Language education: Past, present and future. *RELC Journal* 39 (2), 178–187.

Liebscher, G. and Dailey-O'Cain, J. (2005) Learner code-switching in the content-based foreign language classroom. *Modern Language Journal* 89 (2), 234–247.

Long, M. (1996) The role of the linguistic environment in second language acquisition. In W. Ritchie and T. Bhatia (eds) *Handbook of Second Language Acquisition* (pp. 413–468). San Diego, CA: Academic Press.

Macaro, E. (2005) Codeswitching in the L2 classroom: A communication and learning strategy. In E. Llurda (ed.) *Non-native Language Teachers: Perceptions, Challenges and Contributions to the Profession* (pp. 63–84). New York: Springer.

Nassaji, H. (2002) Schema theory and knowledge-based processes in second language reading comprehension: A need for alternative perspectives. *Language Learning* 52 (2), 439–481.

Park, C-S. (2007) Fast increasing cost in private education. *The Hankyoreh*, 5 February, p. A3.

Park, J.K. (2009) 'English fever' in South Korea: Its history and symptoms. *English Today* 25 (1), 50–57.

Pulido, D. (2004) The relationship between text comprehension and second language incidental vocabulary acquisition: A matter of topic familiarity? *Language Learning* 54 (3), 469–523.

Ruddell, R.B. and Unrau, N.J. (1994) Reading as a meaning-construction process: The reader, the text and the teacher. In R.B. Ruddell, M.R. Ruddell and H. Singer (eds) *Theoretical Models and Processes of Reading*. Newark, NJ: International Reading Association.

Scott, V.M. and De La Fuente, M.J. (2008) What's the problem? L2 learners' use of the L1 during consciousness-raising, form-focused tasks. *Modern Language Journal* 92 (1), 100–113.

Seng, G.H. and Hashim, F. (2006) Use of L1 in L2 reading comprehension among tertiary ESL learners. *Reading in a Foreign Language* 18 (1), 29–54.

Swain, M. (2000) The output hypothesis and beyond: Mediating acquisition through collaborative dialogue. In J.P. Lantoff (ed.) *Sociocultural theory and second language learning* (pp. 97–114). Oxford: Oxford University Press.

Sweetnam Evans, M.E. (2011) Reading bilinguals reading. *New Zealand Studies in Applied Linguistics* 17 (2), 53–69.

Upton, T.A. (1997) First and second language use in reading comprehension strategies of Japanese ESL students. *TESL–EJ: Assessing the Metacognitive Growth of ESL Student Writers* 3 (1), 22.

Walter, C. (2007) First- to second-language reading comprehension: Not transfer, but access. *International Journal of Applied Linguistics* 17 (1), 19–35.
Zwaan, R.A. and Madden, C.J. (2004) Commentary and reply: Updating situation models. *Journal of Experimental Psychology, Learning Memory and Cognition* 30 (1), 283–288.

Appendix A. Texts Used in the Case Study

The five texts used in the study were: a joke featuring Sherlock Holmes and Watson (anon., n.d.); a riddle poem by Sylvia Plath ('Mirror') (Plath, 1963); a short poem by William Carlos Williams ('This Is Just To Say') (Williams, 1972); instructions on how to perform the 'kiss of life' in first aid (cardiopulmonary resuscitation, CPR) (anon., 1979); and a politically correct spoof of the Cinderella fairytale (Garner, 1994).

Anon. (n.d.) World's no. 1 joke: Sherlock Homes and Dr Watson. See http://www.daum. net/ (accessed August 2006).
Anon. (1979) Kiss of life. In M. Swan (ed.) *Kaleidoscope: An Anthology of English Varieties for Upper-Intermediate and More Advanced Students* (p. 84). London: Cambridge University Press. Reprinted from *The Essentials of First Aid*, n.p. *The St. John Ambulance Society and Brigade*, n.d. The text is a set of instructions rather similar to what may be retrieved at http://www.health.harvard.edu/fhg/firstaid/mResusc.shtml (accessed August 2006).
Garner, J.F. (1994) Cinderella. In *Politically Correct Bedtime Stories* (pp. 31–37). London: Souvenir Press. See http://www.morim.org/getfile.aspx?id=2873 (accessed August 2006).
Plath, S. (1963) 'Mirror'. See http://www.sylviaplathforum.com/mirror.html (accessed August 2006).
Williams, W.C. (1972) 'This Is Just To Say'. In L. Simpson (ed.) *An Introduction to Poetry* (2nd edn). New York: St Martin's Press. See http://www.americanpoems.com/poets/ williams/1047 (accessed August 2006).

Appendix B. Cue Sheets Used in the Case Study

One cue sheet was provided for each text, with spaces for recording recalls and comments, in the following format:

TEXT 1 Please write…

(1) Up to 10 words you can recall from the text.

(2) What you remember about the text.

(3) Any other comments you have about the text

Appendix C. Codeswitching Questionnaire Discussed in the Commentary

Please put a checkmark (✓) in the box (❑) that applies to you or specify the information about yourself in the other category.

(1) Sex
   ❑ Male
   ❑ Female

(2) Age
   ❑ 21–30
   ❑ 31–40
   ❑ 41–50
   ❑ 51–60
   ❑ Over 60

(3) Years of teaching majors in English
   ❑ Less than 1 year
   ❑ 1–2 years
   ❑ 2–3 years
   ❑ 3–4 years
   ❑ More than 4 years

(4) Level of your English
   ❑ Superior
   ❑ Advanced
   ❑ Intermediate
   ❑ Low Intermediate
   ❑ Low

(5) How much do you use L1 and L2 in your class?
   ❑ Totally L2
   ❑ Over 70% L2
   ❑ Over 50% L2
   ❑ Less than 50% L2
   ❑ Less than 30% L2

(6) Describe (1) when you mostly use L2 and (2) when you mostly use L1.
  (1)
  (2)

(7) How do you think of your codeswitching for teaching content areas in general?
  ❏ Helpful and should be used a lot
  ❏ Helpful but shouldn't be used a lot
  ❏ Not very helpful and shouldn't be used a lot
  ❏ Not very helpful and shouldn't be used at all

(8) Do you think your codeswitching works for improving students' English listening skills?
  ❏ Negatively
  ❏ No effect at all
  ❏ Somewhat positively
  ❏ Very positively

(9) Do you think your codeswitching works for improving students' English speaking skills?
  ❏ Negatively
  ❏ No effect at all
  ❏ Somewhat positively
  ❏ Very positively

(10) Do you think your codeswitching works for improving students' English reading skills?
  ❏ Negatively
  ❏ No effect at all
  ❏ Somewhat positively
  ❏ Very positively

(11) Do you think your codeswitching works for improving students' English writing skills?
  ❏ Negatively
  ❏ No effect at all
  ❏ Somewhat positively
  ❏ Very positively

(12) Do you think your codeswitching works for developing students' confidence in English?
❑ Negatively
❑ No effect at all
❑ Somewhat positively
❑ Very positively

(13) Do you think your codeswitching works for developing students' interests in English?
❑ Negatively
❑ No effect at all
❑ Somewhat positively
❑ Very positively

(14) Do you think your codeswitching works for lowering students' anxiety in English?
❑ Negatively
❑ No effect at all
❑ Somewhat positively
❑ Very positively

(15) Any comments on codeswitching?

Thank you very much for your participation in this survey.

Afterword

Andy Kirkpatrick

A common theme which runs through the chapters in this book is the disconnection between an official policy (and indeed the beliefs many teachers have) that only one language should be used in the classroom and what actually happens in the classroom. The studies in this volume consistently describe teaching situations where teachers do use more than one language – typically the first language of their students (and their own) in addition to the L2 – yet report being uncomfortable about this, as they feel it either transgresses official policy or that it does not represent best practice. This is why this volume is so important. As Macaro notes in his inspiring Overview, 'Classroom codeswitching … is in desperate need of some theorising'. As Macaro also notes, whether and to what extent the L1 should be used in L2 classrooms 'is probably the most fundamental question facing second language acquisition (SLA) researchers'. David Li in the Chapter 1 Commentary notes the 'the bilingual teacher's dilemma regarding how to strike a balance between adhering to an English-only instruction policy from above, and the need to ensure … students' understanding'. The aims of this volume are to help the multilingual teacher solve that dilemma in his or her specific context and to help policymakers become better informed about the pedagogical and practical issues involved.

The need for theorising is made further evident when we note that many of the teachers in the case studies reported here use codeswitching (CS) for different purposes. For example, while in Thailand 'English only' in the English classroom is the standard mantra, this is evidently not followed (Chapter 4). But, of the two teachers surveyed, one used far less CS than the other: Elspeth's lessons revealed 'extensive use of Thai with little use of English', while Bessie used less CS. Bessie used it for affective purposes such as praising. Most interestingly, she also used Thai politeness markers when speaking English, presumably because she felt it was important to display Thai solidarity with her students.

Similarly, in the case study on China (Chapter 2), where official policy is for the use of English only, both teacher participants used the L1 but, again, for different reasons: Ring used it to exemplify and discuss grammar; Jeng to give information. Similar results were found in Taiwan (Chapter 1), where the policy is also strictly 'English only'. The author of the study recorded three of her own lessons and found that she used the L1 between 6% and 31% of the time. She used the L1 for a variety of functions, including explaining linguistic knowledge, confirmation, emphasis, dealing with unknown lexical items, building up classroom solidarity and demonstrating authority. Yet she did not use it to explain grammatical points. However, this could well be due to the nature of the course she was teaching, which was 'Introduction to Linguistics'. The topic or subject matter is significant. A class whose purpose is to teach English as a second or foreign language is very different from one whose purpose is to teach a content subject such as linguistics or mathematics through English to people whose first language is not English. I return to this important distinction below.

A further reported motivation for the teachers' use of CS was their belief that their own English proficiency was low, even though this was not necessarily the case. Fuad Abdul Hamied (Chapter 5 Commentary), when discussing the situation in Indonesia, calls this motivation 'linguistic fatigue', as it is so much easier to use the L1 than the L2. This, no doubt, leads to more L1 use, especially in schools, where the teachers are likely to have to teach several classes a day.

What the studies reported in this volume show is that the standard policy is to use only the foreign language in the classroom – and in these studies, that is English. At the same time, however, the teachers discussed in these studies all actually do use CS, although they do so for different reasons. Furthermore, most teachers who used CS felt uncomfortable or guilty about doing so. These studies support the findings of Macaro's (2009) study into teachers' attitudes to CS and the 'continuum of perspective' regarding their potential code choice in the L2 class. At one end of the continuum, there is the 'virtual position', where teachers favour the exclusive use of the L2. At the other end, there is the 'maximal position', in which teachers acknowledge that exclusive L2 use is not attainable and so are prepared to use some L1, albeit rather uncomfortably. In Macaro's words (this volume), 'They adopted a somewhat unhealthy deficit model'. Finally, there is the 'optimal position', in which teachers believe that a judicious use of multiple codes at particular times could enhance learning. As Macaro reports in his Overview, those who adopt the optimal position (in which a multilingual pedagogy is considered beneficial) are in a minority. So we have a situation in which the majority of multilingual language teachers feel guilty about using their linguistic resources – and those of their students – in the foreign language classroom.

This feeling of guilt over using the L1 extends beyond the foreign language classroom. In situations where English is the medium of instruction, for example, the policy is also commonly one of 'English only' (Wang & Kirkpatrick, 2013). This is despite several studies which show that cognitively complex subjects and tasks cannot be successfully understood or processed in a second or foreign language unless the learner has sufficient proficiency in the language, and that the L1 is a more appropriate medium for such learning, especially in the early years of study (e.g. Bernardo, 2005; Cummins, 2007; Haddad, 2008). But, as we learn from the Commentary on the case study of Korean students (Chapter 8), the wisdom of using English only to teach content subjects at the tertiary level, even in prestigious institutions, is being questioned. The English-only policy promulgated since 2007 at the Korean Advanced Institute of Science and Technology (KAIST) is under debate. As Hyun-Ju Kim points out (this volume, p. 202), 'more attention is now being paid to the positive functions of using the first language (Korean) rather than, or as well as, English in delivering content knowledge through English'. The question that now arises is what an appropriate balance is between the use of Korean and English in such teaching and learning.

The issues extend to other contexts. For example, the official policy in mainland China for the teaching of Chinese as a foreign language is that only Chinese should be used in the language classroom. A recent study of Chinese language teachers based in Beijing (Wang & Kirkpatrick, 2012) showed, however, that, despite the official policy, teachers adopted the full range of positions on Macaro's 'continuum of perspective'. What was new about this study was that the classrooms were multilingual, with speakers of Korean and Japanese dominant, and that the majority of the students felt that the use of a shared language, English, should be allowed to help in the teaching and learning of Chinese, especially for beginning and lower intermediate students. Once again we see actual classroom practice running counter to official policy and teachers reporting that they feel uncomfortable about transgressing this L2-only policy.

Can we really be surprised to learn that teachers feel guilty? Most have been led to believe that the use of the L1 (or of any language other than the target language or the official medium of instruction) is harmful to learning, yet the great majority of them use the L1 and for disparate reasons.

In an attempt to help assuage teachers' guilt, colleagues and I produced a handbook for English teachers and teachers who were required to teach content subjects through the medium of English in Hong Kong's schools. Entitled *How to Have a Guilt-Free Life Using Cantonese in the English Class*

(Swain *et al.*, 2011), the handbook summarised the assumptions behind the monolingual 'English only' policy and offered arguments for re-evaluating such a policy and suggestions for when the L1 – in this case Cantonese – might be used. Here I provide a brief summary of these. We argued that different languages are not stored in separate parts of the brain, rather that languages in a multilingual brain are in contact with each other and that trying to separate them in the language classroom is unnatural. A second assumption is that learners need as much exposure as possible to the L2 and thus this should be the only language of the L2 classroom. But we know that the L1 can be used to scaffold L2 learning (Benson, 2008; Garcia, 2009). And, while it may sound rather defeatist for a classroom language teacher to say so, a language is best learned outside the classroom, in natural environments. And these days, even where there is little exposure to English in the physical environment, a wealth of computer-mediated communication channels are freely accessible.

Language teachers need to understand how language works and that, in many cases, CS is natural. As we pointed out in the handbook, multilinguals naturally use their multilingual resources and make use of a mix of their languages to express ideas, emotions and identities. But how can these multilingual resources be exploited in the classroom? We suggest, again in the context of Hong Kong, that ideas and topics taught in the Chinese class provide material for the English class. For example, if the class is studying a piece of poetry or a historical figure in the Chinese class, that material can be used in the English class. All too often we seem to implicitly assume that language learners' proficiency is equivalent to their level of intelligence, and thus give learners dull and ultimately unchallenging exercises or tasks in the language classroom. So, a class may move from studying Chinese philosophy in the Chinese class to a lesson on 'giving directions' in the English class. But why not use material from the Chinese philosophy class in the English class, thus allowing the learners to build their knowledge by using material that will engage them? Another example would be to ask students to relate (either orally or in writing, or both) a personal story in their L1 and then ask them to retell the story orally in English, before then asking them to write it in English. This can even lead to the creation of dual-language books (e.g. http://www.thornwoodps.ca/dual/books/hindi/0hindi.htm). If, however, we insist on the students using only the L2 in relating personal stories, we are likely to be regaled with the utterly mundane – as students will be able to use only the L2 language that they can control – and we are very unlikely to get a true story, just one that is 'tellable' in the L2.

As we have seen from several of the case studies, the L1 can be used to provide the meanings of words and phrases. Macaro provides a nice example of this in the Overview, where Italian students who were struggling with the meaning of 'fussy' in 'fussy clothes' are given the Italian equivalent, *fronzolosi* (for further examples see Macaro, 2009: 44–47). This use of the L1 allows students 'to progress more quickly to the more important stage of active use and internalization' (Littlewood & Yu, 2009: 8). This technique can also be used to alert students to the existence of 'false friends', those words that look similar across languages but have distinct meanings, and to explain how their meanings and uses differ. English 'assist' and French *'assister'* are examples.

Multilingual resources can also be exploited to show how languages present information in different ways. An example of this is that, in certain contexts, Chinese prefers to move 'from big to small' and English 'from small to big'. Thus, for example, postal addresses in Chinese start with the largest component and proceed to the smallest, while an English address does the opposite. Asking learners to 'translate' a Chinese address into an English one can therefore help establish these differences in Chinese and English information sequence. A second example is that Chinese prefers a topic–comment sentence structure while English prefers a subject–predicate structure (although both languages allow both structures). Asking students to translate Chinese topic–comment sentences into English subject–predicate sentences (and vice versa, of course, for English-speaking learners of Chinese) can help learners develop a feel for 'natural' expression. An example may help make this clear. A common Chinese topic–comment construction would be rendered literally into English as 'That tree, leaves, very big'. A more natural English rendition of the sentence would be the subject–predicate construction, 'That tree has large leaves'. Accessing the multilingual resources of the teachers and learners in these ways can help L2 learning.

Allowing learners to use CS during the process of completing a task can be as useful as it is natural. Multilinguals routinely use their multilingual linguistic resources when working on tasks in the real world. Preventing learners from using their L1 in the process of working on tasks in the classroom may be counterproductive, for two reasons. First, the quality and cognitive complexity of the task they complete will be limited by their forced exclusive use of the L2. Second, they will covertly make use of the L1 in any event. As we point out in the handbook, 'Being able to use Cantonese initially, learners are able to know the full range of what they want to express in English' (Swain *et al.*, 2011: 13). If restricted to the sole use of the L2, however, the final product will represent only what is achievable using only the L2. Thus we propose that the final *product* of the task should be in the L2, but that the L1 can be allowed in the *process* of completing the task.

Below I quote at some length our summary of a study carried out by a group of teachers of French as a second language (FSL) (Swain *et al.*, 2011: 18–19). This was originally reported by Behan *et al.* (1997).

Laurie, the FSL teacher, was quite concerned that the level of her students' French was not up to the rather difficult and complex task she was expected to teach although she knew the students would have no difficulty carrying out the activities in English. Up until that point, Laurie has meticulously followed the classroom monolingual rule: 'we only speak French in this class'. But she decided that for one activity, she would try something different.

Laurie's students had been seeking out information about the lifestyle of First Nations people in Canada. In small groups they were to work collaboratively to combine the information they had in order to understand the relationships between the climate, the food they ate, the clothes they wore, etc. As well as work out the relationships, they had to prepare for an oral presentation they would make the next day to the whole class on their discoveries. It was made clear to the students that, as always, they must use French in their groups.

Two groups were sent off to the cafeteria to do their work, and two groups stayed in the classroom. The groups in the classroom were closely monitored by Laurie who reminded the students to use French whenever they slipped into English. Both the talk of the students as they collaborated on this task, and their oral presentations the next day, were tape-recorded. Not surprisingly, the groups of students in the cafeteria, who were not monitored for their use of French, used English more than the monitored group. Interestingly, and seemingly paradoxically, the oral presentations given the next day in French by the groups who spoke more English were judged to be better than those who spoke French during the preparation time.

In discussing why this should be so, Laurie and her colleagues felt that it was because the unmonitored students had used English to mediate their task understanding so that they could work with their ideas in French. And, in fact, by examining the tape-recorded talk amongst the students, the teachers were able to hear that the unmonitored groups got busy right away figuring out how to say what they now knew what they wanted to say in French…. The oral presentations of the groups who used some English in preparing for their presentation were more coherent, more complex in the expression of the relationships between climate and food, and clothes worn, and their vocabulary was richer and more sophisticated. Behan, Turnbull and Spek concluded that 'L1 use can both support and enhance L2 development' (1997: 41).

This piece of action research should motivate teachers to conduct similar studies with their own students, ensuring one group uses only the L2, but allowing the other to use CS in the *process* of completing the task and then comparing the *products* – which must be in the L2 – of the groups. This would help provide contextually relevant empirical evidence – one way or the other – of the benefits of allowing the use of CS in the classroom.

Many of the studies reported in the present volume show that some teachers use the L1 for classroom management and to establish rapport and solidarity with the students, and this seems a natural use of CS. We suggest, however, that, generally speaking, teachers should use the L2 for classroom routines such as giving instructions and maintaining discipline, as such interactions are genuinely communicative. Using the L2 for affective purposes also allows its use in genuinely communicative situations, but there are times when the teachers and/or students want to establish a shared identity and the use of CS is the most natural way of doing this.

In conclusion, we need to remind ourselves how complex the issues surrounding the use of CS are. Not only are we dealing with the 'traditional' type of foreign language teaching where students who share the same L1 are learning an L2. We are also dealing with increasingly diverse and multilingual classrooms into which the students bring a vast range of language backgrounds. In such classes, where the language being taught is not English, we see English being used as a lingua franca in CS. At the same time, an increasing number of 'content' classes are being taught through English to learners for whom English is an additional language. This is a policy supported by advocates of content and language integrated learning (CLIL). Their view is that a language can best be taught through learning specialised content. But it is also important that the learners master the content (Kong & Hoare 2011) and there must also be a role for CS in such contexts. Encouraging learners to use their multilingual resources helps them understand cognitively complex concepts. This underlines the importance of this book. We need to be able to provide teachers and learners with empirically justified evidence of contexts and pedagogy in which and through which the use of CS is beneficial. In this Afterword I hope to have offered just a few examples of this, and feel confident that the publication of this volume will stimulate contextually relevant action research into the uses of CS in teaching and learning, the results of which will benefit all of us.

References

Behan, L., Turnbull, M. and Spek, J. (1997) The proficiency gap in late French immersion: Language use in collaborative tasks. *Le Journal de l'Immersion* 20, 41–44.
Benson, C. (2008) Summary overview. Mother tongue-based education in multilingual contexts. In C. Haddad (ed.) *Improving the Quality of Mother Tongue-Based Literacy and Learning: Case Studies from Asia, Africa and South America* (pp. 2–11). Bangkok: UNESCO.
Bernardo, A. (2005) Bilingual code-switching as a resource for learning and teaching. In D.T. Dayag and J.S. Quakenbush (eds) *Linguistics and Language Education in the Philippines and Beyond: A Festschrift for Ma. Lourdes Bautista* (pp. 151–170). Manila: Linguistic Society of the Philippines.
Cummins, J. (2007) Rethinking monolingual instructional strategies in multilingual classrooms. *Canadian Journal of Applied Linguistics* 10, 221–240.
Garcia, O. (2009) *Bilingual Education in the 21st Century: A Global Perspective*. Malden, MA: Wiley-Blackwell.
Haddad, C. (ed.) (2008) *Improving the Quality of Mother Tongue-Based Literacy and Learning: Case Studies from Asia, Africa and South America*. Bangkok: UNESCO.
Kong, S. and Hoare, P. (2011) Cognitive content engagement in content-based language teaching. *Language Teaching Research* 15 (3), 307–324.
Littlewood, W. and Yu, B. (2009) First language and target language in the foreign language classroom. *Language Teaching* 42, 1–14.
Macaro, E. (2009) Teacher use of codeswitching in the second language classroom. Exploring 'optimal' use. In M. Turnbull and J. Dailey-O'Cain (eds) *First Language Use in Second and Foreign Language Learning* (pp. 35–49). Bristol: Multilingual Matters.
Swain, M., Kirkpatrick, A. and Cummins, J. (2011) *How to Have a Guilt-Free Life Using Cantonese in the English Class*. Hong Kong: Research Centre into Language Education and Acquisition in Multilingual Societies, Hong Kong Institute of Education. See http://www.ied.edu.hk/rcleams/handbook/handbook.pdf (accessed August 2013).
Wang, D.P. and Kirkpatrick, A. (2012) Code choice in the Chinese as a foreign language classroom. *Journal of Multilingual Education* 2 (3), doi10.1186/2191-5059-2-3.
Wang, L.X. and Kirkpatrick, A. (2013) Trilingual education in Hong Kong primary schools: A case study. *International Journal of Bilingual Education and Bilingualism* 16 (1), 100–116.

Index